THE CONGRESSIONAL PROCESS
Strategies, Rules, and Procedures

The
Study of
Congress
Series

THE CONGRESSIONAL PROCESS

Strategies, Rules, and Procedures

LEWIS A. FROMAN, JR.

LITTLE, BROWN AND COMPANY · BOSTON

LIBRARY OF CONGRESS CATALOG CARD NO. 67-18261

FOURTH PRINTING

PUBLISHED SIMULTANEOUSLY IN CANADA
BY LITTLE, BROWN & COMPANY (CANADA) LIMITED

PRINTED IN THE UNITED STATES OF AMERICA

For Katie, Lizzie,
and Katrina

Foreword

The Study of Congress is sponsored by the American Political Science Association with the support of a generous grant from the Carnegie Corporation. The project was first conceived by a small group of scholars and congressmen (the latter led by Chet Holifield, D-Calif. and Thomas B. Curtis, R-Mo.) who held a series of discussion meetings on Congress with financial aid from the Philip Stern Family Fund. These discussions led to an agreement to seek support for a comprehensive study of Congress. A formal proposal was prepared by Evron M. Kirkpatrick, Executive Director of the American Political Science Association, and Donald G. Tacheron, Associate Director, which resulted in the grant by the Carnegie Corporation.

The Study of Congress gave political scientists an opportunity to cover ground in one concerted thrust which they might individually inch over in a decade. Such an opportunity was unprecedented, and it increased the urgency and importance of the basic questions: What should be the target of the study? Who should do it? How should it be done?

Reform of Congress is always in the air. Congress is criticized, even by its own members, because, as a representative body, it mirrors the weaknesses as well as the strengths of the represented. Moreover, it is powerful; almost alone among the national legislatures, it has withstood domination by the executive and has remained the coordinate branch the Founding Fathers meant it to be. What Congress does matters very much, here and abroad, and for that reason one is tempted to try to change it, to alter some procedure or structural arrangement in order to increase one's influence on the legislative product.

Nevertheless, reform is not the target of this research project. Congress does change, but slowly, adaptively in things that matter, and seldom according to blueprint. Structure and procedure are not neutral; they are used to work the will of those who control them. Moreover, alterations in them often have unforeseen consequences. This is more likely to be true when structure and rules, and to whose benefit they work, are imperfectly understood. The Study of Congress began, therefore, with a modest admission and an appropriate resolution: there are large gaps in what political scientists know about Congress and the Study would try to fill in as many as it could.

Each of the studies which make up the Study of Congress has been undertaken by a scholar already deeply immersed in the subject. The research in each case promises to produce a book, a monograph, or one or more scholarly articles. Each man is free to recommend changes in the organization and procedures of Congress, but there will be no "official" list of recommendations by the Study of Congress itself. The purpose of the Study is to produce original research studies of Congress. Like other research enterprises, the usefulness of this one will be determined by the people who use it.

The Study of Congress Series presents associated studies designed to tell interested people as much as possible about how Congress works. It provides analytical descriptions of Congress, its subsystems, and its relations with its environment. The series fills in research blanks and suggests relevant variables for future research. It provides some basis for stating the functions performed by Congress for the political system, evaluating the performance, and pointing out alternative structural arrangements and modes of action which realistically seem to be open to Congress. Until these tasks are completed, our lists of congressional reforms are little more than statements of personal preference.

In this volume, Lewis A. Froman, Jr., examines the organization, rules and procedures of Congress and their effect on the formulation of public policy. His analysis begins with a discussion of basic similarities and major differences between the House of Representatives and the Senate. Given the decentralized decision-making structures of the two houses, Froman sees bargaining as the principal mechanism for coordination and coalition-building. The core of the book consists of a careful assessment of the rules and procedures of each house and their impact on legislative strategy and the substance of legislation.

The reader is taken step-by-step from committee activity, through floor deliberation and on to the adjustment of differences between the Senate and the House. The concluding chapters discuss congressional reform and the consequences which modifications in rules and changes in party structure might have for democratic majority rule.

Ralph K. Huitt
Robert L. Peabody

Preface

This book is meant to provide interested observers of Congress with a description and an analysis of the rules and procedures in the House of Representatives and the Senate of the United States.

It is clear that *how* things are done in an organization or an institution may affect *what* is done. Rules and procedures are not neutral in their effects on the distribution of advantages and disadvantages in any human endeavor.

Rules and procedures also have to be taken into account by the participants in devising strategies and tactics. If one knows the rules of the game he is in a much better position to manipulate the outcomes more to his liking and to counter the strategies and tactics of others. Poker players or chess players or participants in any game have a low probability of success if they do not know what alternatives are open to them and what their opponents might do.

Nor can people understand a game if they are not familiar with the rules. Not to know the rules will result not only in poor play, but also in poor, inaccurate, and incomplete observations.

Although it may be misleading to carry the game analogy too far, congressional rules and procedures do affect what is done in Congress by impeding or facilitating the preferences of the various "players." Congressmen also devise strategies and tactics of winning which make full use of the multiple rules and procedures which are available. The more knowledgeable one is about the rules, the better able he is to play the game.

Knowledge of the rules also aids in understanding the Congressional process. Observers of Congress will simply miss certain important "plays" and will not understand the significance of moves and countermoves unless they are aware of the alternatives which may be used by the participants to achieve legislative ends.

This study is meant to encourage a better understanding of the "Congress Game."

The design of this book is relatively straightforward. Chapter One describes what Congress is like generally, and shows how the House of Representatives and the Senate differ from each other sufficiently to warrant separate treatment in the remainder of the book. Chapter Two provides a theory that will help to explain how and why bargaining goes on in Congress, and especially how such bargaining is related to rules and procedures.

Chapters Three and Four describe and analyze the "normal" rules and procedures in the House of Representatives. Chapter Five describes and analyzes what are here called the "abnormal" rules. Chapters Six, Seven, and Eight, do the same, respectively, for the Senate.

Chapter Nine describes and analyzes the procedures involved when the House and the Senate come to differing conclusions about matters of public policy. Chapter Ten analyzes Congress as an organization and begins to relate its decision-making structure to the problem of majority rule. Chapter Eleven returns to the question of majority rule and discusses problems dealing with congressional reform.

Several central questions pervade the entire book. They include: What are the rules and procedures of Congress? How are they used? Why are they used that way? What are the consequences for using some rules rather than others? How do rules and procedures fit into general strategies and tactics? Are there alternative routes which bills may take? If so, under what conditions will certain routes be taken? What are the costs for going one route rather than another? Do some rules favor certain kinds of groups and other rules favor other groups? How do all of these questions relate to the problem of majority rule? And how are these questions related to proposals for the reform of Congress?

I am deeply indebted to a number of people who helped at every stage in the development and writing of *The Congressional Process*. First, my family and I owe a good deal to the Congressional Fellowship Program of the American Political Science Association for making possible a year in Washington, D. C. To the Executive Director of the Association, Evron M. Kirkpatrick, and to the Associate Director, Don Tacheron, go special thanks for supporting and facilitating a genuine learning experience during 1963-64.

Second, I wish to thank the Graduate Research Committee of the University of Wisconsin for funds made available to me for this study.

Third, I would like to thank The Brookings Institution for office space during the Fall of 1963 and Summer of 1965.

Fourth, The American Political Science Association and the Study of Congress, under the direction of Professor Ralph K. Huitt, provided support at several crucial stages as this book was being written and re-written. That support is gratefully acknowledged.

Fifth, I would like to thank Senator Paul H. Douglas, a man of rare qualities, and his staff, especially Howard Shuman, Administrative Assistant, Kenneth Gray, Legislative Assistant, and John Linley, Banking and Currency Committee staff member, for their help and counsel. To Congressman Hale Boggs, his staff, and especially D. B. Hardeman, formerly right-hand man in the Democratic Whip Office and an especially sharing friend and colleague, and Argyll Campbell, my thanks for their immense help and support. My year in Washington was in no small measure made significant by my close association with these "Hill People."

Sixth, the Parliamentarians and Leadership Staffs, in both the House and Senate, were of enormous help.

Seventh, an extremely large number of colleagues have been helpful to me in the writing of this book. Herbert Jacob, Duncan Mac-Rae, Jr., John Manley, Robert L. Peabody, Nelson W. Polsby, Randall Ripley and Aaron Wildavsky read an earlier version of the entire manuscript and I benefited greatly from their comments. Ralph K. Huitt, Director of the Study of Congress, was greatly supportive of my work. Richard F. Fenno, Jr. and Theodore J. Lowi have always provided stimulation and ideas. Sheen T. Kassouf, James G. March, and Deane E. Neubauer commented on Chapter Two.

And last, I would like to thank my mother and father, who have left their mark on me in many ways, and my wife and daughters to whom this book is dedicated. One simply cannot write easily unless an environment is supportive. Mine, thankfully, has always been.

Lewis A. Froman, Jr.
NEWPORT BEACH, CALIFORNIA

Table of Contents

List of Tables

CHAPTER ONE

The Context of
Congressional
Decision-Making

The United States Congress is probably a unique institution among national, democratic, legislative bodies. This is not to say that the United States Congress has nothing in common with other legislative bodies, nor that the political processes of bargaining, coalition-building, and compromise at an abstract level differ fundamentally from some other democratic political institutions. It is to say, however, that there are many features of our national legislature which distinguish it from other national legislatures, and that knowledge of other systems will not necessarily aid in understanding the intricacies of Congress, nor will a knowledge of Congress necessarily aid in the understanding of other legislative bodies.

There are several reasons why this is the case. First, most national legislatures are framed within a parliamentary rather than a presidential system. Except for Liberia, the Philippines, and the countries of Central and South America which have presidential systems, all other democratic countries have parliamentary forms of government. This list includes, of course, all of the nations in Western Europe which are most like the United States in customs, traditions, level of education, industrial success, and general standard of living.[1] France and Switzerland have "mixed" systems, but they, too, operate quite differently from the presidential system in the United States.

[1] See Austin Ranney, *The Governing of Men* (New York: Holt, Rinehart, and Winston, 1958), pp. 62–66.

Thus, among those western democracies that because of other similar characteristics which they share are most easily compared, the United States stands alone in having a presidential form of government.

There are several characteristics of parliamentary systems which differ from presidential systems:

1. election of the *de facto* chief executive (usually called Prime Minister) from the legislature itself, in which the leader retains his membership (*"de facto"* because in many parliamentary systems there is a President or a reigning monarch who holds many formal powers but exercises few or none of them independently of the Prime Minister);
2. cabinet officials are also chosen from and remain in the legislature;
3. strong cabinet control over the members of the ruling party or coalition;
4. little division of labor within the legislature itself (such as well-developed committee systems).

For these reasons legislatures in parliamentary systems are usually dominated by the executive and are made to play a definitely subordinate role in policy-making. Their major function, often, is simply to accept and make legitimate the actions of the cabinet. If executive-sponsored proposals are rejected by the legislature, the government usually falls, Parliament is dissolved, and new elections take place.[2]

The United States Congress, of course, differs fundamentally from this model of parliamentary systems. The executive and legislative branches were designed to be, and after 175 years still are, independently elected, have a different set of leaders, and have different bases of support. Each is granted separate domains of power, although there is, and must be, considerable overlap and coordination.

A second feature of the United States Congress which distinguishes it from other legislative bodies is that most other legislatures, although formally bicameral, are unicameral in fact. That is, at some

[2] Probably the major exception to these generalizations is the French Fourth Republic.

time the lower house has taken powers away from the upper house to such an extent that the upper house has only the capacity to delay, not to prevent. The United States Congress, on the other hand, is bicameral in fact, a situation which creates a number of interesting problems.

The point to be made, however, is simply that the United States Congress is probably more powerful as a legislative body *vis-à-vis* ~~face to face~~ the executive than is any other legislative body in the world today. Although, as in other political systems, the executive is at least as powerful as Congress and, in balance, probably more powerful (depending upon who is President and how he exercises presidential power), it is also undoubtedly true that in no other country has the legislature so much capacity for acting independently and for thwarting the will of the executive as in the United States.

This unique arrangement of power between the executive and legislative branches in the United States focuses attention on the United States Congress. Because Congress is so powerful it means that supporters of the President are usually highly critical of Congress whenever the two come into conflict. And, under Democratic Presidents at least, since the Congress is then probably more "conservative" than is the President, Congress is often attacked whenever it refuses to pass, amends seriously, or even delays enactment of the President's program. Furthermore, if there are any features of the Congress which seem to be more conservatively oriented than others, these especially will come under strong criticism.

These criticisms could be avoided if the Congress of the United States represented basically the same interests as does the executive branch. But, for a number of reasons, this is not the case. First, because of the unit rule in the Electoral College which gives all of the state's electoral votes to the presidential candidate winning a plurality in that state, presidential candidates with any chance of winning must appeal to the interests in large states. For example, it is possible for a candidate to be elected President by winning pluralities in the 11 largest states, plus the District of Columbia, while losing all 39 other states. By and large the populous states are also two-party states with large urban populations. Metropolitan areas within these states have significantly large minority groups (such as Negroes, and various ethnic and religious minorities). For these reasons, winning presidential candidates tend to pay attention to relatively more "liberal" interests who favor and promote changes in the *status quo* in a direction benefiting them. Domestic presidential programs, therefore, usually emphasize these kinds of changes.[3] If a presidential candidate does not conform to this general strategy of election politics, as occurred in 1964, he is likely to be easily defeated.

Congressional interests, on the other hand, are relatively more "conservative" and *status quo* conscious. This is because there are two senators from each state, regardless of population, so that, for example, the 26 smallest states with 52 senators (a majority) represent only 17 percent of the population. The other 48 senators represent 83 percent of the population. In fact a majority of the population (over 51 percent) is represented by only 18 senators, far less than a majority of the Senate.

Malapportionment of legislative seats in the House of Representatives is another factor contributing to the conservative nature of Congress. But, perhaps more important, congressional districts over-represent conservative interests in any case, simply because they are composed of relatively small, homogeneous areas. In general the larger and more heterogeneous the areas represented, the more liberal will be that representation. Therefore, the Senate is often more liberal than the House of Representatives, and the Presidency more liberal than the Senate.[4]

An additional factor leading to over-representation of conservative interests in the legislature is the manner in which power within Congress is distributed. Generally, congressmen and senators must spend lengthy periods of time gaining positions of influence within their respective institutions. The ways of "getting ahead" in the House and Senate require that most members cooperate every bit as much with each other as with the Chief Executive.[5] Further, the operation of the seniority rule in distributing committee assignments and especially committee and subcommittee chairmanships favors those from one-party areas. When the Democrats are in control of

---

[3] For further discussion see Robert A. Dahl, *A Preface to Democratic Theory* (Chicago: University of Chicago Press, 1956), Chap. 5, and Lewis A. Froman, Jr., *People and Politics* (Englewood Cliffs: Prentice-Hall, 1962), Chap. 6.

[4] Lewis A. Froman, Jr., *Congressmen and Their Constituencies* (Chicago: Rand McNally, 1963), Chap. 6.

[5] Nelson W. Polsby, *Congress and the Presidency* (Englewood Cliffs: Prentice-Hall, 1964), pp. 102–103.

Congress, for example, over 50 percent of the committees in both Houses are chaired by Southerners.[6]

For these reasons (and others), Congress is a more conservative body, the Presidency a more liberal one. To illustrate the effects of this "built-in" conflict between the legislative and executive branches, Table I shows the percentage of presidential proposals approved by Congress over a thirteen-year period. Only once was the President successful more than two-thirds of the time (President Johnson in 1965), and on two occasions the percentage fell below one-third.

TABLE I

DISAGREEMENT BETWEEN PRESIDENT AND CONGRESS*

Year	Presidential Proposals Submitted	Approved By Congress	Approval Score
1954	232	150	64.7%
1955	207	96	46.3
1956	225	103	45.7
1957	206	76	36.9
1958	234	110	47.0
1959	228	93	40.8
1960	183	56	30.6
1961	355	172	48.4
1962	298	132	44.3
1963	401	109	27.2
1964	217	125	57.6
1965	469	321	68.4
1966	371	207	55.8

* Source: *Congressional Quarterly Weekly Report*, December 2, 1966, p. 2911.

DIFFERENCES BETWEEN THE HOUSE AND SENATE

There are two other general characteristics of Congress which will be helpful in our discussion of strategies, rules, and procedures within the institution. The first is that political power within Congress is highly decentralized. There are two reasons for this.

First, division of labor through the committee system grants to individual committees (20 in the House, 16 in the Senate), and

[6] For a detailed discussion of the effects of the seniority system see George Goodwin, Jr., "The Seniority System in Congress," *American Political Science Review*, vol. 53 (June, 1959), pp. 412–37, and Raymond C. Wolfinger and Joan Heifitz, "Safe Seats, Seniority, and Power in Congress," *American Political Science Review*, vol. 59 (June, 1965), pp. 337–349.

especially to committee chairmen, immense power over legislation which is referred to the committee. Committees may amend, add to, subtract from, report unaltered, or not report at all legislation which is referred to them. Although there are ways in which committees may be discharged of their responsibilities these procedures are cumbersome at best, seldom used, and when used, as often as not unsuccessful.

This decentralized institutional structure is combined with a weak political party structure. Although numerous studies have shown that the single most important factor explaining legislative outcomes (and especially roll-call voting) is political party, there are many deviations from party votes.[7] For example, during the Eighty-eighth Congress (1963–64) there were 337 roll-call votes in the House and the Senate on which a majority of Democrats opposed a majority of Republicans. On these roll calls the average Democrat voted against his party 31 percent of the time, the average Republican 29 percent. For the Eighty-seventh Congress (1961–62) the comparable figures were 30 percent for each party.[8] Variation in party support among the members of each party is, of course, considerable. By and large the major defectors within the Democratic party are Southern Democrats, and within the Republican party, urban Republicans.

This lack of strong party unity, then, further decentralizes power within Congress. A decentralized institutional structure through the committee system could be overcome if there were some other major organizing force. The most potent of such forces is political party; but, as the data indicate, the political party as an organizing structure is relatively weak. Because the United States is so large, political parties are coalitions of people representing, in many cases, quite diverse constituencies. Since election to Congress is primarily a state and local affair, congressmen and senators are to a considerable extent independent of the national party. Indeed, reelection to Congress may depend in some cases upon their voting against a stand taken by a majority of their party colleagues.

A second general characteristic of Congress is that the House and the Senate, while similar in some respects, are actually quite different

[7] Julius Turner, *Party and Constituency* (Baltimore: Johns Hopkins Press, 1951), Duncan MacRae, Jr., *Dimensions of Congressional Voting* (Berkeley: University of California Press, 1958), and Lewis A. Froman, Jr., *Congressmen and Their Constituencies* (Chicago: Rand McNally, 1963).

[8] *Congressional Quarterly Weekly Reports*, April 3, 1964, and October 30, 1964.

political bodies. The important similarities are two: First, both are relatively decentralized political institutions with a high degree of division of labor through the committee system. Second, both are equal in power. Except for the constitutional provisions which give to the Senate (but not to the House) the power to ratify treaties and advise and consent in political appointments, and which give to the House the privilege of originating all revenue bills (and, by practice, appropriation bills), actions of Congress require the consent of both houses. And, unlike many other legislative systems, neither house can legally force the other body to act, nor can bills become law without the concurrence of both houses.

It is the differences, however, between the House and the Senate (listed in Table II) which prove most interesting.

TABLE II

MAJOR DIFFERENCES BETWEEN HOUSE AND SENATE

House	Senate
Larger (435 members)	Smaller (100 members)
More formal	Less formal
More hierarchically organized	Less hierarchically organized
Acts more quickly	Acts more slowly
Rules more rigid	Rules more flexible
Power less evenly distributed	Power more evenly distributed
Longer apprentice period	Shorter apprentice period
More impersonal	More personal
Less "important" constituencies	More "important" constituencies
Less prestige	More prestige
More "conservative"	More "liberal"

Probably the two most important differences between the House and the Senate, and the two from which most of the others are derived, are that the House is more than four times as large as the Senate, and that senators represent sovereign states in a federal system whereas most congressmen represent smaller and sometimes shifting parts of states.

The fact that the House of Representatives is relatively large and the Senate relatively small affects the operation of the two houses in a number of ways. Perhaps the most striking difference noticed by most visitors to the Capitol is the apparent confusion and impersonality in the House chamber as contrasted with the relatively more informal and friendly atmosphere in the Senate. House members are less well known than Senate members. This is further accentuated by the fact that senators have fixed desks and visitors are allowed to take into the galleries a seating chart available at the office of the Sergeant-at-Arms which aids in identifying less well-known senators. There is more "electricity" in the galleries when Senator Dirksen or Senator Mansfield strides into the Senate chamber than when Carl Albert or Gerald Ford walks into the House chamber. Not only are the senators more visible (in a smaller chamber), they are also a good deal more "visible" in the sense that more people know approximately what they look like.

Furthermore, microphones are used in the House and not in the Senate. This adds to the impersonality and formality of the House proceedings as compared with the Senate.

The larger size of the House also requires a more hierarchical structure and organization if it is to work efficiently. Since it is unable to carry on elaborate clearing procedures as in the Senate because of the large number of people involved, the leadership in the House is more powerful *vis-à-vis* the members than is true in the Senate. The Speaker of the House, with the majority leader and whip, find it less practical to schedule legislation to the convenience of all the members. Only the principal parties are usually consulted (e.g., committee and subcommittee chairmen). It is not unusual in the Senate, on the other hand, to re-schedule a piece of legislation or even a vote to suit the convenience of any single member. Leadership activities in the House, then, are more isolated from the lives and activities of the average member.

Also because of size, House members are less likely to know, even by sight, all other House members, especially those on the other side of the aisle. The larger size of the House and the pursuant greater anonymity produce situations in which individual members violate the spirit of comity which is essential to the smooth functioning of any organization. Such situations undoubtedly occur in the Senate also, but probably with less frequency since it is smaller. After final passage of the Senate-amended 1964 Civil Rights Bill in the House, for example, Representative John Bell Williams from Mississippi tied up the House for an hour by objecting to routine unanimous consent requests before finally being persuaded to cooperate. The day following the passage of the Cotton-Wheat Bill in April, 1964, several Republicans monopolized the House with four hours of various procedural delays essentially in retribution for the Democrats having kept the House in session until nearly one A.M. the previous day. One can also find, in the House, a member's words being taken down because he has allegedly violated the rules by engaging in name-calling on the House floor.

This somewhat less frequent observance of comity in the House means that fewer things are accomplished in the House by unanimous consent. Action by unanimous consent is widely practiced in both houses, but in the House, relatively speaking, fewer unanimous consent motions are offered than in the Senate. When they are offered, and there is an objection, it causes more havoc in the House than in the Senate. The House can literally come to a standstill if all motions to proceed in order are forced to roll-call votes. It takes an average of twenty-five minutes to call the roll in the House, and five or six of these can take a goodly portion of the afternoon. Furthermore, some actions, like dispensing with the full reading of the *Journal* each day, require unanimous consent. Any member may object to this procedure with the consequence that further time is lost.

Another result of the larger size of the House and its concomitant greater formality and hierarchical organization, is that the House is able to dispense with its business more rapidly than the Senate. Procedural delays like those mentioned above are the exception rather than the rule, and the "normal" business of the House proceeds quickly. Table III shows the relative number of hours spent on the floor in the House and Senate during the Eighty-eighth Congress (1963–64).

TABLE III
DAYS AND HOURS IN SESSION, EIGHTY-EIGHTH CONGRESS*

	First Session Jan. 9–Dec. 30, 1963		*Second Session* Jan. 7–Oct. 3, 1964	
	Senate	*House*	*Senate*	*House*
Days in session	189	186	186	148
Time in session	1,044 hours 43 minutes	626 hours 14 minutes	1,350 hours 25 minutes	624 hours 33 minutes

* Source: *Congressional Record*, Daily Digest, D821, October 23, 1964.

It is rare, for example, for any but major bills in the House to take longer than one day for consideration. Time is strictly limited, usually by a rule from the Rules Committee (most rules provide for one or two hours of general debate[9]). Debate in Committee of the Whole (in which most important pieces of legislation are considered) may be limited by majority vote (usually by a motion to end discussion at a certain time). Only under unusual circumstances will debate extend longer than one day. The 1964 Civil Rights Bill was discussed for nine days; the President's 1964 anti-poverty program took three days. In both cases the leadership planned for such extensive debate, given the controversial nature of these bills.

The Senate, on the other hand, is a much more leisurely body. The Senate often finds itself juggling two, three, or even four bills at the same time, shifting from one to another as it suits the convenience of the members. It is literally unheard of for the House, however, to have more than one measure before it at any time (excluding Conference Reports, which are privileged, and may interrupt pending business). Consequently, action is more fluid and less predictable in the Senate. Debate on one measure can extend for days, weeks, and sometimes months, even without a filibuster.

This brings us to the differences in rules and procedures between the two bodies. It may simply be pointed out here that the informal and more congenial Senate is able to function with quite lax and flexible rules. The two rules which make it most difficult to foresee when action will end on a bill in the Senate are the rules which provide for unlimited debate (requiring two-thirds of those present and voting for cloture), and a very weakly enforced germaneness rule which, although requiring germane debate for three hours each day, is violated at will, either by asking unanimous consent to waive the rule (and the informal rules of comity honor such a request under normal circumstances) or simply by ignoring the rule. In addition, except for appropriation bills, the Senate has no rule of germaneness regarding amendments. Thus, any matter may be discussed on the floor simply by moving an amendment to the pending business.

The House would find it next to impossible to function under such procedures. The size of the membership and the difficulty of clearing with all interested parties would effectively preclude such seemingly cavalier and casual action. The smaller size and the greater im-

---

[9] James A. Robinson, *The House Rules Committee* (Indianapolis: Bobbs-Merrill, 1963), p. 54.

portance of comity in the Senate make such flexibility possible and in most cases workable.

Another consequence of the size difference between the House and Senate is the distribution of power within each body. Since the House, as previously mentioned, has only four more legislative committees than does the Senate (20 as compared with 16), but over four times as many members, each senator is appointed to more committees than each House member (usually three or four as compared with one or two in the House). Also, each senator is usually on at least one and more likely two of the more important committees. Each individual senator, then, can have influence over more issues, and over more important issues, than can each individual congressman.

Power is dispersed even further in the Senate in that a proportionately smaller number of House members usually assume positions of leadership than senators. There is a greater likelihood, for example, of a senator of the majority party assuming a committee or subcommittee chairmanship than for a congressman to do so. Table IV provides data to support this point.

TABLE IV

DISTRIBUTION OF COMMITTEE AND SUBCOMMITTEE
CHAIRMANSHIPS AMONG DEMOCRATS IN THE HOUSE AND SENATE,
EIGHTY-EIGHTH CONGRESS, SECOND SESSION (1964)

Number of Committees and Subcommittees chaired by each member	Senate	% of Democrats	House	% of Democrats
5	1	1.5	0	0
4	5	7.5	1	0
3	12	18.0	5	2.0
2	16	24.0	25	10.0
1	18	27.0	73	28.0
0	15	22.0	154	60.0

As Table IV shows, 78 percent of Senate Democrats have at least one committee or subcommittee chairmanship, while in the House the comparable figure is 40 percent. Also, in the Senate over 50 percent of the Democratic senators have two or more committee or subcommittee chairmanships, while again the comparable figure in the House is only 12 percent. To the extent that holding positions of importance is an index of power, these figures confirm the notion that power is more widely dispersed in the Senate than it is in the House.

It is also the case in the Senate as compared with the House that the time it takes to assume a position of leadership is shorter. This is true both for the party leadership positions and the committee and subcommittee chairmanships. For example, Speaker McCormack was in his thirty-third year as a member of the House before he assumed the office of Speaker. Carl Albert was in his fourteenth year before becoming majority leader. Mike Mansfield, on the other hand, was in office for eight years before receiving the Senate's major party position, although it took Hubert Humphrey twelve years to become assistant majority leader. Lyndon Johnson became Democratic leader after only four years in the Senate.

Senators may also attain committee chairmanships more quickly. House Chairmen in the Eighty-eighth Congress (1963–64) took an average of 16.35 years after entering the House to attain committee chairmanships and an average of 13.3 years after gaining a seat on the committee. The comparable figures for the Senate are 12.56 years after entering the Senate and 11.4 years after gaining a seat on the committee. It is even possible, in the Senate, for a member to become a subcommittee chairman in his first year, a happening unheard of in the House. Birch Bayh of Indiana, for example, became chairman of the Constitutional Amendments Subcommittee of the Judiciary Committee in the Senate in his freshman year.

The longer apprenticeship period in the House, plus the fact that serving a long period in the House is not as much of a guarantee, as it is in the Senate, of an eventual position of leadership, means that House members find it more difficult to develop a base of power from which they may operate. A senator will become more powerful earlier than will a House member. This is directly attributable to the fact that the Senate is a smaller body.

The second major factor which causes a number of differences between the House and the Senate is the kind of constituencies which senators and congressmen represent. Senators, of course, represent sovereign states in a political system which places some emphasis on a federal structure. Members of the House, on the other hand, normally represent only parts of states. This difference in base of support has a number of important consequences.

First, senators have more prestige than do House members. This is also a result of the fact that there are only two from each state. Senators get more press coverage and generally are more visible than members of the House.

More importantly, the fact that senators represent states rather than parts of states makes the Senate a more liberal body on most legislation. For example, it was the House of Representatives in the Eighty-eighth Congress (1963–64) that failed to pass an extension of the Area Redevelopment Administration, the Appalachia program, and Hospital Care for the Aged. The Senate passed all three of these top priority, liberal programs. Also, the Senate has often passed federal aid to primary and secondary schools education bills. Prior to 1965 the House passed the bill once (1960) only to have the Committee on Rules refuse to grant a rule to send the bill to conference with the more liberal Senate-passed version.

Findings also indicate that of 322 pieces of legislation which President Kennedy submitted to Congress in the First Session of the Eighty-seventh Congress (1961) they were, as a whole, more likely to get by Senate committees and the Senate floor than they were in the House of Representatives. Table V presents data on this point.

TABLE V

FAVORABLE AND UNFAVORABLE COMMITTEE AND FLOOR ACTIONS
IN THE HOUSE AND SENATE ON 322 PIECES OF LEGISLATION
SUBMITTED BY PRESIDENT KENNEDY,
87TH CONGRESS, 1ST SESSION (1961)*

ACTIONS ON KENNEDY LEGISLATION

House of Congress	Committee						Floor					
	Favorable		Unfavorable		No Action		Favorable		Unfavorable		No Action	
	N	%	N	%	N	%	N	%	N	%	N	%
House	192	(59.6)	56	(17.4)	74	(23.0)	166	(51.5)	66	(20.5)	90	(28.0)
Senate	207	(64.3)	44	(13.6)	71	(22.1)	185	(57.4)	51	(15.8)	86	(26.8)

* Data from the Congressional Quarterly Almanac (Washington, D.C.: Congressional Quarterly, Inc., 1951), Vol. XVII. Reprinted from Lewis A. Froman, Jr., *Congressmen and Their Constituencies* (Chicago: Rand McNally, 1963), p. 73.

The data in Table V confirm the generalization, at least for the First Session of the Eighty-seventh Congress (1961), that the Senate usually acts more favorably on the President's program than the House. The Senate also will act on more bills than the House, as indicated by the greater percentage of "no action" for the House at both the committee and floor stages.

It is also true that when the two bodies do pass different versions of the same legislation, the Senate version is often more liberal, the House version more conservative. Although this, of course, is not true for all bills (Civil Rights is probably the most notable exception), it is true in general. For example, again during the First Session of the Eighty-seventh Congress, it was found that on ten bills which were considered to be major parts of President Kennedy's domestic program, and which passed both Houses, of the 58 differing provisions which reached the conference committee, 33, or 57 percent, were liberalizing Senate amendments.[10] The Senate is also, for a number of reasons, likely to pass appropriation bills more nearly approximating what the administration requests than is the House.

The greater support for liberal legislation shown by the Senate is directly attributable to the differences in constituencies represented by senators and congressmen. Population characteristics of constituencies, for example, are associated with liberal-conservative voting. Members of Congress from urban districts with large numbers of voters who are blue-collar workers, who are economically less well-to-do, or who are first- or second-generation immigrants are more likely to support liberal legislation than are members of Congress representing districts with opposite population characteristics. But, voters with population characteristics associated with liberalism are not randomly distributed throughout the state. For example, large numbers of Negroes are often located in only a few congressional districts within a state. Hence most House members have few Negro constituents. Senate members, however, have all the Negroes in the state as constituents. The same is true for such factors as urbanism. There are more congressional districts below the state average on urbanism than above it. Since senators represent the state average, House members are by and large more conservative.[11]

The two factors of size and basis of representation, and the consequences of these factors, produce two quite different legislative

[10] See Froman, *Congressmen and Their Constituencies, op. cit.*, p. 79.
[11] *Ibid.*, Chap. 6.

bodies. Because the House and the Senate are so different from one another, they will be considered separately in this book. Each body has its own traditions, procedures, precedents, and rules, and it is more useful to keep each separate in an analysis of how the rules function.

CHAPTER TWO

Bargaining
in Congress

Congress is an intricate and complex institution. Each body has its own sets of leaders, its own complex division of labor (essentially through the committee system), its own set of formal rules and procedures which define the various ways in which the "game" may be played, and its own set of informal rules which help to set the conditions under which certain actions will take place, and will be considered legitimate and appropriate. As intricate and complex as congressional decision-making is, however, it is possible to make several generalizations about it.

First, as mentioned in Chapter One, it is widely accepted that each house of Congress is a highly decentralized political institution in which power is widely dispersed. Although political party affiliation is undoubtedly the most important organizing and coordinating force within the institution, other pressures (such as constituency, state party delegation, committee loyalty, personal stands on issues, interest group activity, and leadership rewards and punishments) are crucial in understanding how decision-making takes place within Congress. Committees in Congress, for example, are almost entirely autonomous. In addition, for many committees (Appropriations, Public Works, and Governmental Operations in the House, for example) subcommittees are also relatively autonomous. This dispersion of autonomous political power means that actions taken by the committees are usually the actions which are taken by the parent body.

A second point concerning decision-making in Congress is that a general method of coordination of these autonomous units is a system of reciprocity. Committees, and committee members, tend not to interfere with the work of other committees. The number of amendments which are offered on the floor and the number of successful changes in bills on the floor vary considerably from bill to bill and committee to committee. If the committee is cohesive in its recommendation (especially if it is bipartisanly cohesive), and if the bill does not involve conflicting ideologies, then few amendments will be offered and few will be successful. There is a strong tendency for members to accept the work and expertise of the other committees. In return, of course, they expect little interference in their own work.

Third, legislative decision-making is serial, involving a number of different approvals. It proceeds in stages, from the introduction of a bill, to committee, to subcommittee, back to committee, to the Rules Committee (if in the House), to the floor, to the Committee of the Whole (in the House), to final passage. Many things can happen to a bill along the way. A single negative action may be sufficient to defeat the bill. Bringing a bill to the floor to final passage requires the most skillful negotiation. Agreements reached must be cumulative.

Fourth, this legislative process is also lengthy and time-consuming with many opportunities for delay. A major reason is that the relatively autonomous committees often consist of members with different kinds of constituents. This usually produces built-in conflict in each unit. Reaching agreement among members with varying preferences (sometimes quite intense preferences) is no easy task, even in a relatively small unit like a committee or subcommittee. Since there is very little over-all coordination or control by the leadership over matters still within committees, the speed with which legislation passes the House or Senate is in large measure determined by the nature of the conflict and the ability of those opposed to use the rules and structure of this complex organization. Table VI shows the points at which delay and defeat may occur in the House of Representatives. A similar table, with some modifications, would illustrate the same points for the Senate.

Most criticisms of the House of Representatives center around these points of possible delay and defeat, especially those which can occur before the bill reaches the floor. Since the brunt of these arguments involves the idea that the majority should be able to work

Table VI
Points at Which Delay or Defeat May Occur in the House

Delay	Defeat
Committee inaction in referring to a subcommittee	Committee inaction
	Negative vote in committee
Subcommittee inaction (prolonged hearings; refusal to report)	Subcommittee inaction
Committee inaction (prolonged hearings; refusal to report)	Negative vote in subcommittee
	Rules Committee inaction
Rules Committee inaction (refusal to schedule hearings; prolonged hearings; refusal to report)	Negative vote in Rules Committee
	Defeat of rule on the floor
Slowness in scheduling the bill	Motion to strike enacting clause
Floor action (demanding full requirements of the rules)	Motion to recommit
reading of the journal	Final passage
repeated quorum calls	
refusing unanimous consent to dispense with further proceedings under the call of the roll	
prolonging debate	
various points of order	

its will, criticisms center on the places where less than a majority may delay or defeat legislation. In the House, legislative committees and the Rules Committee come under strongest attack; in the Senate, legislative committees and the loose rules of floor debate, especially filibusters, raise the strongest objections.

Although there are methods by which committees may be bypassed, members are reluctant to invoke these procedures. Committee chairmen are powerful individuals. They can be very helpful to younger congressmen wishing special favors (committee assignments, private and public bills, help "downtown," etc.); they can also take positive steps to damage the effectiveness of other members in hundreds of small ways. They are not, in short, persons to be trifled with. To oppose a committee chairman one pays a price, and often one is never sure what the price might be.

In addition, all bills come from committees. If one committee is bypassed what is to prevent a member's own committee from being by-passed in the future when something which he feels strongly about is being delayed? Lacking a strong, centralized leadership with weapons to force decentralized units to act, reciprocity becomes an operating rule of no small importance in coordinating the activities of the House and Senate.

Reciprocity and comity as informal norms of Congress, however, only partially explain how agreements are reached in the House and Senate. How, then, are winning coalitions formed? For many bills a winning coalition is a majority coalition, but in other cases much larger coalitions are required (for example, Consent Calendar, Private Calendar, Suspension of the Rules, Cloture). But even when "only" a majority is necessary, the problem of coalition-building is complicated by the existence of multiple decision-points. The problem of putting together a majority coalition is not simply a problem of one coalition. Under normal circumstances there must be a majority in the subcommittee, a majority in the committee, a majority in the Rules Committee (if in the House), a majority to defeat amendments on the floor, often a majority against a recommittal motion, and a majority on final passage. These "majorities" involve different people in different situations at different points in time. The problems which arise in building a coalition may vary considerably at each of these decision-points.

There is also a problem of "intensity" involved in coalition-building. How intense the opposition is in part determines how intense the proponents must be to succeed. That is, given apathetic minority opposition, not much more than apathetic majority support is probably required for passage. However, given intense opposition, at least some among the proponents must also be intense at each of the steps in the decision-making process. For various reasons intense majorities rarely appear. On most bills majorities are the *result* of the legislative process, not the pre-condition for it. It is during the legislative process that the wide variety of interests and personalities bargain and compromise on a bill, and its provisions, which make it acceptable to at least a majority of the members. It is seldom that a majority would support a *specific* bill before it reaches Congress. There may be general agreement that some kind of legislation is necessary, although even this may not happen very often, but the particular provisions of the bill need to be worked out to gain wide support for the specific legislation which will have to be passed.

There are many reasons for the general absence of intense majorities. The first is simply the diversity of interests being represented in the House. Northerners differ from southerners, Republicans differ from Democrats, representatives from rural areas differ from those from urban areas.[1] This, coupled with an absence of ways to enforce party discipline, means that there are often as many views on public policy questions as there are congressmen.

The second reason for the absence of intense majorities is that, even if there were not various combinations of constituency differences, individual members differ from each other on what they consider to be important legislation. For example, if we take constituencies which have elected more than one member from the same party during a ten-year period, and compare them with constituencies which have elected the same member over the same period of time, we find that variation in voting in Congress by the elected representatives is greater for those constituencies which elected more than one member. This illustrates that even with party and constituency held constant, some variation in congressional voting still exists which may be attributed to the values and attitudes of particular members.[2]

Third, many issues are salient to only a few members. That is, given any issue, it not only affects different congressmen differently (as the first two reasons suggest), but it also will affect some congressmen hardly at all. Many congressmen will have little personal stake in the outcome of many bills and will not be intense about the issues. Most congressmen are specialists in only a few areas and are intensely concerned with only a few issues.

Fourth, few bills embody only a single issue. Most bills have multiple provisions. Congressmen, therefore, will be selective in their attention and support for the bill. They may be quite intense about some provisions, mildly interested in others, and not concerned at all about still others. Their support, then, during the negotiating process may be quite erratic depending upon what is left in the bill, what is taken out, and what is added.

Given this lack of intensity and dispersion of issue concern, few bills are centrally important to a majority of congressmen. Other values come into play in a congressman's behavior. Congressmen, like other people, have multiple values and play many games, and it is rare that any single game or set of values will lead to the sac-

[1] Lewis A. Froman, Jr., *Congressmen and Their Constituencies* (Chicago: Rand McNally, 1963), Chap. 7.
[2] *Ibid.*, Chap. 8.

rifice of every other value. Other games include: running for higher office, hoping for an executive appointment, getting a job outside of Congress, trying to be influential in the House, wanting a committee appointment, and wanting a particular bill which directly affects his constituency. Hence, coalitions are formed and reformed on a number of criteria as the issues come up. These coalitions have in them some people who are very intense all the way down to some members who are not intense at all. A member who is not intense about an issue will not sacrifice other values (like the chance for an important committee assignment). Issues, after all, are not considered in a vacuum. Many things are at stake, including a congressman's or committee's prestige, his relationships with the leadership (and all this entails in terms of institutional rewards), and, of course, his constituency interests. Political actions have costs, and different issue-contexts will affect many congressmen quite differently in how far they are willing to pursue their interest in the issue to the exclusion of other important values they may have.

For these reasons, then, minorities, through the committee system, are able to exercise power over legislation. Since the major power structure of the House is the committee system, and since most institutional rewards and punishments are channeled through the committees, members are naturally reluctant to take actions which are adverse to their own potential interests.

To complicate this analysis even further, and to give some indication of the wide variety of variables which are involved, whether or not a bill passes Congress will depend upon:

1. what the bill is (that is, what the stakes of the game are);
2. how many members are intense in their support (the greater the number of intense members, the greater likelihood of passage);
3. the magnitude of intensity (the greater the intensity, the greater the likelihood of passage, assuming flexibility);
4. who the supporters are (leadership, committee chairmen, respected members, White House support);
5. where the supporters are located (on the committee to which the bill is assigned, on the subcommittee, on the Rules Committee);
6. and how many, how intense, who and where located is the opposition. These factors will also help to determine the kinds of procedures which will be employed to bring

the bill to a vote (for example "normal" rules and procedures such as the regular Calendars vs. "abnormal" ones
such as the discharge rule and Calendar Wednesday).

When certain combinations of these factors exist, one can predict
whether or not a bill is in trouble, and even say approximately how
much trouble. If it is known, for example, that those who favor
the bill constitute a majority, that some are relatively intense, that the
leadership favors passage, that neither the committee to which the
bill is to be referred nor the Rules Committee is hostile to the bill,
and that those who oppose the bill are few in number, not very intense, and not strategically located on the committee nor among
committee chairmen or others in positions of influence, then it can
be expected that the bill will not have much difficulty on its way to
final passage. If, however, just one or a few of these factors change,
an entirely different situation confronts the proponents of the bill.

With almost any controversial bill, there will be one or more
places along the decision-route which may be hostile. Given this
state of affairs for most bills, there must exist some mechanism or set
of mechanisms by which conflicts can be resolved or circumvented.
The alternative to such a mechanism would undoubtedly be stalemate, inability to operate, and, in the future, either a change in the
institution or a diminution of political power. The mechanism which
helps to coordinate decentralized decision-making within Congress
and which aids in coalition-building at the various decision-points is
bargaining.

BARGAINING AS A POLITICAL PROCESS

Bargaining as a mechanism of coordination and a device for building
coalitions is an incredibly complex phenomenon and it will be useful
at this point to make very clear just exactly how the term is being
used.

First, bargaining is not just one thing, but a number of things.
One very important distinction which separates two types of bargaining from the others is whether negotiation is involved. As Lindblom
has pointed out, there are methods of coordination in decision-
making which do not involve negotiation (defined as an actual interchange between two or more people).[3] Whether these forms of

---

[3] Charles E. Lindblom, *The Intelligence of Democracy* (New York: Free Press,
1965), esp. Chs. 1–5.

non-negotiated decision-making should even be called bargaining is a matter of definition. Our definition treats these as bargaining, but to distinguish them from bargaining in which negotiation is involved they will be called non-negotiated bargaining.

Second, bargains may vary as to whether they are implicit or explicit.[4] Bargains are implicit when the "counters" or "payoffs" being used are not known or are vague. Explicit bargaining involves known counters.

The following is a typology of bargaining with explanations of each type.[5]

NON-NEGOTIATED BARGAINING	NEGOTIATED BARGAINING
1. Unilateral action	3. Simple logrolling
2. Anticipated reaction	4. Time logrolling
	5. Compromise
	6. Side-payments

1. Unilateral Action. Unilateral action is a form of non-negotiated bargaining in which a decision-maker simply takes action without regard for its consequences or other decision-makers. There are many circumstances under which unilateral action may take place. Its most prevalent form probably occurs when a person issues an authoritative command or rule which he expects to be obeyed simply because he feels he is in a position of authority to issue the command. In some cases he may be quite correct. In other cases it may have been wise for him to negotiate with his subordinates and others who may be affected, or at least attempt to anticipate their reactions and take them into account.

Unilateral action may also occur out of naïveté or lack of knowledge. A decision-maker may simply not know that his decision will have certain effects on others, or he may not care.

Unilateral action is always an implicit bargain. There are no counters involved, or at least they are not considered by the decision-maker.

2. Anticipated Reaction. A second form of non-negotiated bargain-

---

[4] Lewis A. Froman, Jr., *People and Politics* (Englewood Cliffs: Prentice-Hall, 1962), Chap. 4.

[5] For two other typologies of bargaining see Lindblom, *op. cit.*, Chaps. 1–5, and William H. Riker, *The Theory of Political Coalitions* (New Haven: Yale University Press, 1962), Chap. 5.

ing will be called anticipated reaction. As in unilateral action this form of bargaining does not involve an actual interchange between two or more people, but unlike unilateral bargaining the possible reactions of other decision-makers are taken into account in the decision. Anticipated reactions may be used when it does not appear necessary to negotiate or it is not possible to negotiate. A move is made with the reactions of others in mind but actual negotiation is not present. A lot of bargaining, especially at early stages, is probably of this type; it is also quite prevalent when bargaining is adversary in nature.

Anticipated reaction may be either explicit or implicit, but the line between the two may be quite thin. Schelling has done some interesting work with this problem and the circumstances under which anticipated reactions may be shaped and, therefore, predictable.[6] In some cases the anticipated reactions may be clear to the original decision-maker but not to the person whose reactions he is attempting to anticipate. In other cases they may be clear to both parties.

3. *Simple Logrolling.* The next four categories of bargaining are more widely considered to be bargaining, that is, forms which involve direct negotiation between two or more people.

A simple logroll is a negotiated bargain which takes the form "You give me what I want and I'll give you what you want." Simple logrolling occurs when there are a number of smaller projects, issues, or programs which can be put into one bill. The process simply requires mutual support, or at least mutual non-interference. The most important point to be made with simple logrolling, however, as compared with the next category, time logrolling, is that in simple logrolling the payoffs to the partners to the bargain occur at the same time.

By its very nature, then, simple logrolling is explicit. To engage in this type of bargain each of the parties has to know what he wants and what he is willing to support in return for support from others.

In the omnibus Rivers and Harbors Bill (pork barrel), bargaining is likely to involve simple logrolling and anticipated reaction. The process of building a coalition with a policy involving smaller, separate projects simply involves putting into the same bill a large number of these separate and independent projects. The norm here is reciprocity. If a congressman or senator is going to get his project (a

---

[6] Thomas Schelling, *The Strategy of Conflict* (Cambridge, Mass.: Harvard University Press, 1960).

wider river, a new or deeper harbor, etc.) he must not interfere in other people's projects.

4. Time Logrolling. Time logrolling is a negotiated bargain of the form "You support me now, and I'll support you some time in the future." Time logrolling involves the same kind of process as simple logrolling except the support or non-interference promised is, for one of the parties, in the future. For example, there may be at least two separate bills involved in the bargain, rather than a number of projects in one bill.

Logrolling over time may be either implicit or explicit. That is, the promised future support may be on some definite issue or bill, or the second part of the bargain may be left indefinite.

A classic example of logrolling occurred in 1964 when two logrolls occurred on the same bill. First, a simple logroll took place in the Senate when a wheat section was attached to an already House-passed Cotton Bill. Then, when the bill was returned to the House a time logroll took place. Those who wanted the Cotton-Wheat Bill logrolled with those who wanted the Food-Stamp Bill. The price for support by the urban Democrats for the Cotton-Wheat Bill was support by the rural Democrats for the Food-Stamp Plan. As part of the bargain the liberals even demanded that the Food-Stamp Bill be reported to the floor of the House first. If successful, they would support the Cotton-Wheat Bill.

5. Compromise. Compromise is a form of negotiated bargain of the general form "You want x, I want z, let's settle on y." A compromise normally occurs when a bill specifies a certain thing or a certain amount of something, others want less (or none at all), and to gain sufficient support a policy or figure between the two positions is accepted and agreed upon. This is the "half a loaf is better than no loaf at all" bargain.

Compromise is not usually a form of bargaining in the early stages of negotiation. Rather, unilateral action or anticipated reaction will probably be tried first. In fact, anticipated reaction is often used in conjunction with compromise in the sense that decision-makers may anticipate opposition and ask for more than they really want with a view to later compromise. This is probably a major strategy in the budgetary process,[7] as well as in House-Senate bargaining. Alterna-

[7] Aaron Wildavsky, *The Politics of the Budgetary Process* (Boston: Little, Brown, 1964).

tively, decision-makers may perceive strong opposition and ask for less than they really want as a way of avoiding later compromise and especially to circumvent the possibility that later compromise will not occur because they asked, originally, for too much.

The original proponents of the 1964 Civil Rights Bill were forced to modify the provisions of the bill as the bill went from subcommittee to full committee to the floor in the House, and then more compromise was necessary to meet the extraordinary majority (two-thirds) needed to break a filibuster in the Senate. As the bill was exposed to larger and larger groups with diverse interests it required modification to win the support of a coalition large enough to pass the bill. The major portions of the bill which were changed involved sections regulating how the courts, businesses, and places of accommodation were to deal with Negroes.

If and when bargaining reaches the stage of compromise, however, such bargaining is explicit. That is, various middle-ground positions are tried (the most obvious one being the exact middle) to see whether a mutually satisfactory point can be reached. Compromise obviously cannot occur between inflexible bargainers, for example, idealogues. Compromise requires that both sides be flexible. In the absence of such flexibility bargaining of quite a different sort may appear (i.e., side-payments).

   6. *Side-payments.* A probably less often used, but highly publicized type of bargaining takes the form of "You support me and I will reward you," or, alternatively, "You support me or else I will punish you." Side-payments are non-policy rewards and punishments such as personnel positions (federal judgeships, postmasterships, patronage appointments in general), institutional positions (committee assignments, subcommittee chairmanships and assignments, party positions), and resources (campaign contributions and aid, additional staff members, money-producing speaking engagements, travel).

Side-payments can be either negative or positive. For example, a person can threaten to withhold aid, or can threaten to take some positive but detrimental step, or he can promise aid. Side-payments may also be for the particular individual, or they may be put at the disposal of the particular individual to give to someone else.

Side-payments may be either implicit or explicit. That is, what is promised in return for support (or opposition) may be made quite clear, or it may be left in doubt.

Certain highly controversial issues might involve, to the extent that bargaining is possible at all, the politics of side-payments. This will be especially true if these issues take something away from one group and give an approximately equivalent amount to another group. There will be strong pressure to replace what was taken away with something else. Side-payments are ideally suited for such replacement. There will also be strong pressure toward compromise, weakening the bill in a number of ways.

Bargaining on highly controversial issues might also involve bargaining by unilateral action. Decision-makers, because of the heated nature of these issues, find it difficult to negotiate, and in the absence of negotiation it is possible to find attempts to do by unilateral action that which cannot be done by forms of bargaining involving negotiation.

These forms of bargaining, unilateral action, anticipated reaction, simple and time logrolling, compromise, and side-payments, represent six ways in which coordination may be achieved in decision-making.

Conditions Under Which Various Types of Bargaining Take Place

The conditions under which the various types of bargaining referred to above take place are many. We will be concerned with six major types: (1) historical circumstances, (2) structure of the group in which the decision-making takes place, (3) position of people in the group, (4) personality of people making the decisions, (5) the time sequence of decision-making, and (6) the issues in the decision-making.

1. Historical Circumstances. Certain committees and subcommittees in Congress have developed relatively standard and routine ways of handling the issues which come before them. Similarly, people in positions of leadership, unless they are new to their job, may have developed ways of handling problems which repeatedly come across their desks.[8] Hence it would be important to determine whether

[8] For theories developed around this notion, see James G. March and Herbert A. Simon, *Organizations* (New York: Wiley, 1958), and David Braybrooke and Charles E. Lindblom, *A Strategy of Decision* (New York: Free Press of Glencoe, 1963). For an application see Wildavsky, *op. cit.*

certain committees or other sub-groups in Congress have any patterns of bargaining.

For example, Richard Fenno has suggested that the Appropriations Committee in the House of Representatives has developed relatively standard norms of bargaining within the Committee. Generally, bargaining in the Appropriations Committee may be described as logrolling, anticipated reaction (mutual non-interference among the subcommittees, reciprocity) and compromise.[9] Other committees may exhibit quite different forms of bargaining. The Education and Labor Committee in the House when chaired by Representative Graham Barden was one in which unilateral action was prevalent, given the circumstances which produced an inability to be flexible in negotiation.[10]

Actually, "historical circumstances" is probably a catch-all which hides to some extent other underlying variables (such as personalities, norms, or modes of operation) which would be very helpful to know.

2. *Structure of the Group.* It would be interesting to know if different kinds of group structures facilitate or impede various forms of bargaining. For example, highly decentralized decision-making units, like Congress, probably facilitate bargaining by logrolling. Decision-structures which are bi-polar in nature (House vs. Senate) probably facilitate compromise. Highly structured hierarchical decision-units probably facilitate bargaining by unilateral action. Loosely structured, less permanent decision-structures probably impede logrolling over time and encourage charismatic leadership.

3. *Position in the Group.* Obviously, the more resources one has at his disposal the better able he is to bargain. Although most everyone has some resources, leaders probably have more resources than anyone else. This would be especially true in the use of unilateral action and side-payments, and only slightly less true of compromise. Anyone

---

[9] Richard F. Fenno, Jr., "The House Appropriations Committee as a Political System: The Problem of Integration," *American Political Science Review*, vol. 56 (June, 1962), 310–24.

[10] Richard F. Fenno, Jr., "The House of Representatives and Federal Aid to Education," in Robert L. Peabody and Nelson W. Polsby, eds., *New Perspectives on the House of Representatives* (Chicago: Rand McNally, 1963), pp. 195–237.

with a vote can logroll, however, and this along with anticipated re-action, is likely to be the most prevalent form of bargaining among non-leaders.

4. Personality of Decision-makers. The personalities of the decision-makers are probably also very important in determining the extent and kinds of bargaining which go on. We are all familiar with this at a casual level. For example, ideologues find it very difficult to compromise but not at all difficult to logroll; statesmen find it very difficult to logroll (each proposal must be examined on its merits) but may not find it difficult to compromise (we must do what is right for the most number of people); leaders in positions of authority may find it difficult to issue commands (unilateral action); unintelligent people may find it difficult to anticipate others' reactions; highly moral people find it difficult to engage in side-payments. A proliferation of such personality types would be enormously useful in analyzing the use of bargaining.

5. Time Sequence in Decision-making. It may be that in many decision-making situations there is a sequence in which certain kinds of bargaining are tried before others. If the first types are unsuccessful, then others will be attempted. For example, in the preliminary stages of bargaining unilateral action and anticipated reactions may be employed. If these are unsuccessful, logrolling and compromise may be tried. If these in turn do not succeed then, and perhaps only then, will side-payments (probably the most costly of all bargains) be employed.

Another interesting time relationship is that of combinations of bargaining. For example, anticipated reaction may be employed purposely to set up a future bargaining situation of either compromise or logrolling. Leaders in the House may include a provision in a bill for trading purposes with the Senate. The leaders in the House will agree to delete its provision which is obnoxious to the Senate (and which the House leaders really did not want anyway) if the Senate leadership will, in turn, delete a provision which is unacceptable to the House. Or, the Senate may not include a provision in its bill because it is known that the House will not accept it. Other examples of combinations of bargaining will come readily to mind.

6. *Type of Issue.* There are a number of ways in which issues on types of policies may be distinguished.[11] The characteristic which will be of chief concern to us here is the extent of opposition which a bill generates in Congress. How divisive an issue is will structure, to a large extent, the way in which bargaining takes place.

How much opposition a bill will have is itself dependent upon several factors. We may say, for example, that the "newer" the program, the more "ideological" the program (especially in terms of a liberal-conservative dimension), the greater the probability that the program will touch on cleavages already existing in the society at large (such as race or religion), the less the acceptance of the bill by those who are to be directly affected by the program, and, the more the program deviates from past programs, the greater the opposition.

Rules, Issues, and Bargaining

The relationships among these many factors have a number of interesting consequences for the operation of decision-making in Congress. For example, we have already referred to the decentralized structure of Congress, the wide distribution of power within Congress, and the elaborate rules and procedures which require majorities at many points in the decision-making process. We have raised the question, given this decentralized system, how is coordination achieved? How are coalitions built? We have also suggested that the answer to this question is relatively complex. Generally speaking it is through bargaining that the many hurdles are overcome. But bargaining varies a good deal, and the difficulties in overcoming the hurdles also vary depending upon the kind of issue which is at stake, and the number, intensity, and location of the opposition.

On the basis of this discussion we can now draw some generalizations about the operation of Congress in a wider context. The kinds of issues which Congress is most admirably suited to handle are those which are relatively non-controversial. The fact that there are so many decision-points as a bill progresses through Congress, and the fact that most of these stages involve members with diverse interests, means that if a coalition is going to be put together it will probably be done, or it can best be done, by logrolling.

[11] Lewis A. Froman, Jr., "The Categorization of Policy Contents," paper delivered at the Social Science Research Council's Conference on Public Policy, 1966.

We also know that Congress is a relatively stable institution in which the membership remains relatively constant over a period of time (the evidence for this will be found in Chapter Ten). This is especially true for the leadership of Congress. Simple logrolling, involving as it does bargains within a single bill at a single point in time, does not require a stable institution. Time logrolling, on the other hand, does require that the participants remain over a period of time so that bargains can be fulfilled. Time logrolling, in a sense, requires that members expect other members to be around to fulfill their part of the bargain. Congress admirably guarantees that members, and again especially leaders who often tend to be recruited with safety of district in mind, will be in Congress from one session to the next.

On the other hand, Congress is less well equipped to handle issues which might raise strong opposition. We have suggested that such divisive issues are likely to have one or more of the following characteristics: new or ideological programs, or programs which bear on cleavages already existing in society, which are not acceptable to the groups directly affected, or which deviate markedly from past programs in the same area. Minorities are in positions, very often, to block such legislation. If they are in such a position, why should they bargain? If a group has a chance to win, there may be little incentive to take half a loaf when they can insure no loaf at all.

What has happened, then, on many controversial issues is that they have been delegated to some other agency of government. That is, because Congress itself finds it difficult to negotiate on these issues it will pass the buck to an administrative agency. Outside interests may themselves prefer the easier politics of administrative agencies rather than the labyrinthine and uncertain politics of Congress. Given a political system which allows relatively small minorities to prevail in situations in which they are intense (or at least to force a compromise) how much worse is this situation when relatively large numbers are intensely involved? The answer, very often, is stalemate.

Most issues which Congress handles are not likely to involve intense opposition. Pork barrel and subsidies are traditional rewards which congressmen and senators use to continue in office. Most congressmen and senators recognize this. Reciprocity through anticipated reactions is a prevalent form of bargaining on these kinds of issues. If intense opposition does arise, and if it is strategically located, it is usually possible to "overcome" the opposition through simple or time logrolling, compromise, or, if all else fails, side-payments. On very intense issues, given the nature of the decision-making apparatus in Congress, a majority coalition is difficult to put together — or, if not difficult to put together, difficult to exert against intense minorities strategically located. It forces congressmen and senators to employ rules and procedures which very often are not part of the "normal" decision-making process. This normal decision-making process is the very process which facilitates logrolling. What is required on very controversial issues is for congressmen and senators to be willing to by-pass the "normal" decision-making process and violate the norms which make that process operative.

These considerations, then, bring up the question of rules and procedures and the strategies involved in their use. Bargaining is the informal process by which issues brought before Congress are handled. What kinds of bargains will be used will depend upon the nature of the issue, which in turn affects the number of people engaged in the conflict and the level of intensity of the conflict. However, the "game" played on any given issue takes place within the framework of rules and procedures. Which rules and procedures will be used, whether stalling will take place, whether unusual rules and procedures will be invoked, will depend upon the same factors that determine the kinds of bargaining which take place.

For example, we would expect the rules and procedures defined as part of the normal legislative process to be employed on most non-controversial issues. In the House of Representatives, for example, Consent and Suspension Calendars are used primarily for issues of this kind. If there is an intense opposition, the bill will probably not be able to "skip" the Committee on Rules. On highly controversial issues, extraordinary procedures (such as discharge or threat of discharge, and Calendar Wednesday) may have to be resorted to. If the issue cannot be resolved through the normal channels, if the bargains cannot be struck, and the rules cannot be made to work, the bill will languish in committee, or will be defeated somewhere along the line.

The same considerations apply to both houses even though their specific rules and procedures are considerably different. The "normal" legislative channels will be employed when logrolling, compromise, and side-payments are able to settle the conflict within the normal rules. When, however, issues are presented which create situations that break down the normal channels, when policies are presented to Congress which cannot be negotiated within the system of rules and procedures by bargaining, then other routes and procedures, the "abnormal" rules of the system, will be employed.

Decision-making in Congress, then, is an extremely complicated process. The rules, procedures, and strategies employed using alternative routes, are closely linked with the type of issue which Congress has before it, and the ability of the normal rules and procedures to contain the conflict within the normal bargaining procedures. Abnormal rules and procedures are resorted to only when the normal legislative system is not able to handle the conflict through bargaining.

CHAPTER THREE

Pre-floor Rules and Procedures in the House of Representatives

In the first two chapters we have been concerned with placing a discussion of congressional rules and procedures in a context which, hopefully, will make the remainder of this book more relevant to citizens and students of the political process. We have suggested, for example, that rules and procedures loom large in the discussion of Congress because the United States legislature, unlike the legislatures of most nations, is a powerful and independent cog in the national policy-making machinery. Congress does help to determine public policy, not simply ratify it, and because this is true the rules and procedures involved in Congress undoubtedly have effects, as we will show, on the kinds of public policies which emerge.

In this and the following two chapters we will discuss the rules and procedures in the House of Representatives. At the same time that we discuss rules and procedures we will also be concerned with some of the same questions which have already been raised in the first two chapters. Foremost among these are the functions which rules perform in the legislative system, the purposes to which they are put, and, most importantly, their effects on such things as the distribution of power within the legislature. Rules, we will discover, are seldom neutral in their effects. When rules and procedures are invoked they are invoked for some purpose. This discussion will aid us in the concluding chapters in understanding the congressional system as a whole, the likelihood that rules changes will be successful, and the desirability of changes in the rules.

INTRODUCTION OF BILLS

The first step in the legislative process is the introduction of bills. Any member may introduce a bill in the House of Representatives simply by placing it in the hopper at the clerk's desk in the House chamber, giving it to the bill clerk or parliamentarian, or having someone do it for him. A member need not gain recognition on the floor for the purpose of introducing a bill. There is no limit on the number of bills which a member may introduce and, except for an unimportant restriction having to do with private bills (as provided for in the Legislative Reorganization Act of 1946 and Rule XXII, clause 2), there are no restrictions on this right of introduction. Members are not allowed, however, to co-sponsor other members' bills (as they are in the Senate), so that members wishing to introduce the same legislation must introduce separate bills.

The number of bills introduced in each session of Congress is enormous. In the House of Representatives, 11,296 bills and resolutions were introduced to the First Session of the Eighty-eighth Congress (1963), and 4,003 bills and resolutions were introduced in the Second Session (1964). Four to five times as many bills are introduced in the House as compared with the Senate, due primarily to the rule which prohibits multiple sponsorship of bills in the House.

Bills and resolutions may be categorized in many different ways (e.g., public bills, joint resolutions, concurrent resolutions, simple resolutions, private bills), but two major distinctions which are probably of most importance are: (1) is it a bill sent down by the Administration and essentially written in the executive branch? and (2) who is the member introducing the bill? The first point distinguishes important Administration bills from the thousands of private and public bills which individual members introduce at the request of and for the benefit of their own constituents. The second point distinguishes bills which are going to receive attention by committees from those which are probably not. If the bill is introduced by the leadership (party leaders or committee and subcommittee chairmen) it is much more likely to be considered by the committee to which the bill is referred than are bills introduced by "ordinary" members.

Members, of course, may have a number of reasons for introducing bills. Generally, important Administration bills are introduced by the committee or subcommittee chairman to which the bill will be referred, or, in the case of a hostile committee, by a party leader of the

President's party. These Administration bills take up the bulk of congressional time and energy. Other bills are introduced by members at the request of important individuals or groups within the members' districts. In some cases the members themselves who introduce the bills do not favor them. They simply introduce the bill as a favor or as a way of relieving pressure on themselves from the folks back home. Since introduction of bills is a relatively simple process, a member can do it and can then report what he has done, placing the blame for inaction on the committee to which the bill is referred. In other cases the members themselves do favor passage of the bills and work very hard to get the committee to which the bill is referred to hold hearings and to report the legislation out of the committee. Of the 15,299 bills and resolutions introduced in the House in the Eighty-eighth Congress (1963–64), 1,742 or a little over 11 percent were reported by committees. Most bills, then, which are introduced, are never reported from the committees to which they are referred.

REFERRAL TO COMMITTEES

The next step in the legislative process, and sometimes a very crucial step, is the referral of a bill to committee. The Speaker refers bills to committees; he is bound, however, by relatively strict jurisdictions of committees which are established by the rules of the House, and by the precedents of past Congresses. Occasionally there will be bills which could be referred to more than one committee. Some bills concerned with foreign affairs, for example, deal with agricultural matters (e.g., sale of surplus wheat to Russia), some refer to commerce (e.g., shipping involved in foreign aid). Whether a bill which seems to overlap the jurisdictions of several committees goes to one committee rather than another is at the discretion of the Speaker's referral power. In most cases he will refer bills to the committee which is given jurisdiction by Rule X of the Standing Rules of the House or which precedent has established as the committee to which the bill should be referred. Occasionally the Speaker will have some choice in which committee gets a bill. This is especially true of new programs and new legislation which has not yet developed a legislative history.

One interesting example of the discretion of the Chair in referring bills occurred in 1963 in regard to the Civil Rights Bill. Constitutional justification of the Civil Rights Bill rested, in part, on the commerce clause of the Constitution. In the Senate the bill was referred to the Commerce Committee, chaired by Warren Magnuson of Washington, rather than to the Judiciary Committee with James Eastland of Mississippi as Chairman. In the House the bill was referred to the Judiciary Committee, Emanuel Celler of New York, Chairman, rather than to the Interstate and Foreign Commerce Committee which was chaired by Oren Harris of Arkansas. The strategy in each instance was obvious.

Because the Speaker does have some discretion in referring bills, members may attempt to draft a bill which could go to one of several committees in such a way as to make it easier for the Speaker to send the bill to the desired committee. Since committees have different chairmen and different personnel, some committees are more favorable to a certain kind of legislation than other committees. The major area of discretion for the Speaker is with new programs, and especially new programs with several titles in the bill, some of which relate to one committee and some to other committees. Since bills may not be divided among two or more committees, one committee must be chosen.

COMMITTEES AND SUBCOMMITTEES

All bills which are introduced are referred to a committee. What happens after that depends upon what kind of bill it is, to which committee it is referred, and whether the committee has subcommittees. Whether a bill is reported out of a committee or not is entirely dependent upon the committee itself. As we will discuss in later chapters there are methods by which committees may be by-passed, but these are unusual procedures, not part of the normal legislative process to which these chapters are addressed.

As has been mentioned, in the Eighty-eighth Congress (1963–64) only 11 percent of the bills which were introduced were reported from committee. The other 89 percent were simply left to languish in committee. For the most part these were non-Administration bills, introduced by members for a number of different reasons. It is the bills sent to Congress by the Administration which probably will receive most attention by the Committees. In many cases, with major controversial bills, hearings will be held by the committee at which witnesses from executive agencies, members of Congress, representatives of interest groups, and private individuals will be allowed to testify for or against the legislation. These hearings can take place either in subcommittee, or full committee, or both. After public hearings, the subcommittee or full committee goes into executive (private) session to discuss the bill, redraft it if necessary, and vote on its various provisions. The bill as a whole is then voted on and if passed, reported and placed on a Calendar.

Seventeen of the twenty House Standing Committees have regular subcommittees (all except Rules, Un-American Activities, and Ways and Means). Table VII provides a list of committees, committee ratios, committee chairmen, and number of subcommittees in the House of Representatives for the Eighty-ninth Congress (1965–66).[1]

The existence of these 125 subcommittees adds to the specialization of the members and to the division of labor in the House. Most bills which are referred to committees are later referred by the chairman of the committee to a subcommittee. Subcommittee chairmen have the same power over bills referred to them as do full committee chairmen over bills in full committee subject, of course, to the wishes of the full committee chairman. Subcommittees develop expertise concerning certain kinds of legislation and in many cases are able to block, amend, add to, subtract from, or report to the full committee unaltered, legislation which is referred to them. In some cases, most notably in the Appropriations Committee, subcommittee decisions are simply ratified by the full committee before being reported to the Calendar.[2] In other cases, however, the full committee reviews carefully the actions of the subcommittee and may reverse any decision made in subcommittee.

The existence of subcommittees affects the power of full committee chairmen in various ways, depending upon how autonomous the subcommittees are. The chairman (working somewhat within the seniority system, but not strictly bound by it) decides whether there will be subcommittees, how many members on each, who the majority party members will be, and who will be chairmen. If the chairman is against a particular kind of legislation which is assigned to his committee, he can establish a subcommittee unfavorable to the legislation. Similarly, if he favors legislation of a particular kind he may help it along by creating and staffing a favorable subcommittee to

---

[1] *Congressional Quarterly Weekly Report*, #18 (April 30, 1965), Part I (Washington, D.C., Congressional Quarterly Service, 1965).

[2] See Richard F. Fenno, Jr., "The House Appropriations Committee as a Political System: The Problem of Integration," *American Political Science Review*, vol. 56 (June, 1962), pp. 310–24.

Table VII

HOUSE COMMITTEES — EIGHTY-NINTH CONGRESS

House Committees	Committee Ratios	Committee Chairmen	No. of Subcommittees
Agriculture	D 24–R 11	Harold Cooley (N.C.)	15
Appropriations	D 34–R 16	George Mahon (Tex.)	12
Armed Service	D 25–R 12	Mendel Rivers (S.C.)	7
Banking & Currency	D 22–R 11	Wright Patman (Tex.)	7
District of Columbia	D 17–R 8	John McMillan (S.C.)	5
Education & Labor	D 21–R 10	Adam Powell (N.Y.)	7
Foreign Affairs	D 24–R 12	Thomas Morgan (Pa.)	10
Government Operations	D 23–R 11	William Dawson (Ill.)	8
House Administration	D 17–R 8	Omar Burleson (Tex.)	7
Interior & Insular Affairs	D 22–R 11	Wayne Aspinall (Col.)	6
Interstate & Foreign Commerce	D 22–R 11	Harley Staggers (W.Va.)	5
Judiciary	D 24–R 11	Emanuel Celler (N.Y.)	7
Merchant Marine & Fisheries	D 21–R 10	Edward Garmatz (Md.)	5
Post Office & Civil Service	D 17–R 8	Tom Murray (Tenn.)	8
Public Works	D 23–R 11	George Fallon (Md.)	6
Rules	D 10–R 5	Howard Smith (Va.)	none
Science & Astronautics	D 21–R 10	George Miller (Cal.)	5
Un-American Activities	D 6–R 3	Edwin Willis (La.)	none
Veterans Affairs	D 17–R 8	Olin Teague (Tex.)	5
Ways & Means	D 17–R 8	Wilbur Mills (Ark.)	none

handle it. Also, the chairman may assign bills to subcommittees regardless of the intended scope of the subcommittee, he may keep the
bill in full committee and not refer it to a subcommittee, or he may
establish a special *ad hoc* subcommittee to handle a particular bill.
The discretion of the full committee chairman, in other words, is
absolute in the manner in which a bill will be handled. A few examples will illustrate this point.

The late Clarence Cannon, a powerful and irascible chairman of
the Appropriations Committee, selected Otto Passman of Louisiana
to head the Foreign Operations Subcommittee. This is the subcommittee to which the Foreign Aid Appropriation Bill is submitted
each year. Cannon also selected the Democratic members of the subcommittee to insure Passman's control of the subcommittee. During the period in which Passman was subcommittee chairman, the
Foreign Aid Bill was cut substantially each year.

In early 1964, Clarence Cannon died and George Mahon of Texas
became chairman of the full committee. Mahon, at least in 1964, decided to support President Johnson's foreign aid request. When hearings were held in the Foreign Operations Subcommittee on the
President's bill, Passman found that not only was the chairman going
to fight Passman's attempt to cut the bill, but Mahon himself had
decided to chair the subcommittee meetings. Several of the Democratic supporters of Passman (and Cannon) on the subcommittee,
when faced with a choice between their new full committee chairman and their subcommittee chairman, sided with Mahon against
Passman. Passman temporarily stepped down from his subcommittee
chairmanship and decided to fight the action of the committee on
the floor of the House. Mahon led the floor fight for the President's
bill, Passman led the fight against it. When the smoke had cleared
Otto Passman found himself on the losing side. Passman had been
the winner so often before that he did not realize that his power as
subcommittee chairman rested substantially on the will of the full
committee chairman. Passman's power under Cannon was quite different from his power under Mahon.

Another example of a strong chairman stacking the deck in favor
of a bill occurred in 1964 when Adam Clayton Powell, Chairman of
the Education and Labor Committee, decided to set up a special *ad
hoc* subcommittee to consider the President's Anti-Poverty Program.
Powell decided on this strategy rather than referring the bill to a
regular subcommittee or keeping the bill in full committee to insure

that the bill received a favorable hearing. In past years the Education and Labor Committee had been racked by ideological conflicts. Compromises in the committee had been difficult to negotiate. Very often Republicans and Southern Democrats were able to prevent bills being reported by the full committee.[3]

It had been decided, early in the consideration of the bill, to try to get the full program as requested by the President even if this meant solid opposition by the Republicans. It was reported that the Republicans were willing to cooperate, but only if they could have a strong hand in writing the bill. Administration supporters felt this to be too high a price to pay, and decided instead to court the support of Southern Democrats and make the bill a partisan bill. It was extremely important, then, that the members of the subcommittee which was to consider the bill be picked carefully and with a view to providing a solid front of Northern and Southern Democratic support against the expected strong Republican opposition.

Early in the stages of the subcommittee's deliberations the Republican members of the subcommittee were actually locked out of subcommittee meetings. The hand-picked Democrats on the subcommittee had decided to iron out their differences first, thereby preventing Republicans from splitting the Southern Democrats from the coalition. When the full subcommittee met, the vote was a straight partisan one to report the bill to the full committee. The full committee then voted, again along straight partisan lines, to report the bill to the floor. The method of an *ad hoc* subcommittee helped to insure the success of this strategy.

A third example of a chairman's discretion with respect to subcommittees occurred on the President's 1964 Appalachia Program. Referred to the Public Works Committee, its chairman, Charles Buckley of New York, sent the bill to the Flood Control Subcommittee, chaired by Clifford Davis of Tennessee, a proponent of the bill from an area which would be covered by the Appalachia Bill, rather than to the Roads Subcommittee headed by George Fallon of Maryland. The Roads Subcommittee would have been more appropriate since most of the program involves building roads in the economically depressed Appalachia region. The same bill was in fact referred

---

3 See Richard F. Fenno, Jr., "The House of Representatives and Federal Aid to Education," in Robert L. Peabody and Nelson W. Polsby, eds., *New Perspectives on the House of Representatives* (Chicago: Rand McNally, 1963), pp. 195–236.

to the Roads Subcommittee of the Public Works Committee in the Senate rather than to the Flood Control Subcommittee to allow Senator Randolph from West Virginia (a hard hit depressed area included in the Appalachia Program) to manage the bill. This move to send the bill to Davis's subcommittee was made to provide additional support for the program and to allow Davis, rather than Fallon, to manage the bill on the floor.

These three examples of Foreign Aid, Anti-Poverty, and Appalachia illustrate three different ways in which a committee chairman may act to provide support for a bill. In the case of Foreign Aid the chairman actually took over the subcommittee; on the Anti-Poverty Bill a special *ad hoc* subcommittee was established to handle the bill; and on the Appalachia Program a more favorable subcommittee was chosen over a less favorable one even though it was not the most appropriate subcommittee to consider the bill.

It is also possible for subcommittees to be "packed" by the committee chairman in favor of or against certain legislation. For example, at the beginning of the Eighty-ninth Congress (1965–66) George Mahon reduced the size of Passman's subcommittee, arranged two transfers of Passman's supporters, and at the same time filled vacancies with supporters of foreign aid. Similarly, Emanuel Celler of New York, Chairman of the House Judiciary Committee, increased the size of Michael Feighan's subcommittee, which considers immigration legislation, to provide an easier path for the President's immigration bill. Subcommittee packing such as this usually takes place at the beginning of a new Congress when vacancies often occur and when changing the size of subcommittees is easier to accomplish.

The usual procedure followed on bills which are sent to Congress by the President (and on some major bills which originate in Congress) is to have public hearings in which witnesses from the executive branch, Congress, interest groups, and private citizens are invited or invite themselves to testify. These hearings are normally held in subcommittee, but occasionally a full committee will hold hearings. The functions of these hearings are many, including attempts by the chairman to provide public support or opposition for the bill (depending upon his predilections), to stall the legislative process, to act as a check on the executive branch, to "test" the proposed law in terms of popular and interest group support, to provide citizens with an opportunity to make their views known, and to give a chairman an opportunity to become visible to the general public. The functions of hearings, then, vary tremendously depending upon the legislation being considered and the purposes of the chairman or other members.[4]

After public hearings the committee or subcommittee will go into executive session for "mark-up" of the bill. It is here that the legislative language is hammered out.[5] The bill is then reported to the full committee where additional hearings may be held, language changed, amendments added, provisions taken out, or possibly the legislation is shelved if support cannot be won.

GETTING A BILL TO THE FLOOR

Once a bill is reported from committee there are a number of alternative routes open to it, depending upon the kind of bill it is and the amount of opposition which it might have. The choice of the route which the bill will take is sometimes within the discretion of the leadership or the member sponsoring the bill. In other cases, if the bill fits into one of a number of specific categories, the route it will take is pre-determined by the rules and practices of the House. All of the routes which are available, however, have certain dangers, and most are relatively complicated. This is especially true of controversial legislation. We will be concerned in this section, as we are generally in this chapter, with the "normal" flow of legislation. Extraordinary procedures, by-passing certain steps or using rules designed to get around a strong minority, will be discussed in Chapter Five.

When a bill is reported from committee it is placed on one of three Calendars: the Union Calendar (bills raising revenue, general appropriation bills, and bills of a public character directly or indirectly appropriating money or property); the House Calendar (all bills of a public character not raising revenue nor directly or indirectly appropriating money or property); and the Private Calendar (bills which affect named individuals). General appropriation bills which are reported from the Appropriations Committee must lie over three days before consideration, and rules reported from the Rules Committee must lie over one day unless two-thirds of the House determine otherwise.

[4] See Ralph K. Huitt, "The Congressional Committee: A Case Study," *American Political Science Review*, vol. 48 (June, 1954), pp. 340–365.

[5] For a brief description by a former Congressman see Clem Miller, *Member of the House*, ed. John W. Baker (New York: Scribners, 1962) pp. 13–18.

The House has developed an elaborate set of rules governing how bills are to be taken from the Calendars for consideration by the House. Basically, the question of consideration involves special legislative days and special rules and procedures by which some bills become more privileged than others.

PRIVATE CALENDAR

Private bills are bills which compensate or benefit particular, named individuals. It is estimated that well over two thousand such bills are introduced in each session of Congress. Approximately 300 to 500 private bills are reported by committees each year (mainly the Judiciary Committee) and are placed on the Private Calendar. Of these, approximately one-third are finally enacted into law by both houses of Congress. For example, in the Eighty-eighth Congress (1963–64), excluding concurrent and simple resolutions, 1,026 bills were enacted into law. Of these, 360, or 35 percent, were private bills. But more than twice this number were reported and placed on the Private Calendar, and more than ten times this number were introduced in the House. As with public bills, there is sifting and winnowing of private legislation.[6]

Most private bills are of two kinds: (a) Bills which direct payments to individuals who have been affected adversely by actions of the federal government or businesses under contract to the federal government. These would include property damage and personal injury, and claims of non-payment of benefits under various governmental programs. (b) Immigration bills allowing for individual exceptions to the immigration laws, such as allowing certain people into the country who ordinarily would not be eligible because of quotas or certain restrictions, and bills having to do with aliens already in the country.

In handling this large quantity of private bills, Congress is acting as a "court of appeals" from administrative rulings adverse to certain people. When other remedies fail, a private bill is a last resort. Since

[6] See the *Congressional Record*, Oct. 23, 1964, p. D821, James A. Robinson, *The House Rules Committee* (Indianapolis: Bobbs-Merrill, 1963), p. 5; Floyd M. Riddick's annual articles on Congress in the *Western Political Quarterly*; and George B. Galloway, *The Legislative Process in Congress* (New York: Crowell, 1953), pp. 529–535.

most private bills concern claims against the government and immigration matters, they are referred to the Judiciary Committee. Two subcommittees of the Judiciary Committee handle the bulk of the private bills. If such bills are not able to clear the subcommittee they will not be reported to the floor. And even if they are reported by the subcommittee and then approved by the full committee, less than 50 percent will become law.

On the first Tuesday of each month bills on the Private Calendar are privileged and the Speaker is required by the rules to direct the Clerk to call the bills on the Private Calendar. No other business is in order on this day except by two-thirds vote of the House. On the third Tuesday of each month the Speaker may direct the Clerk to call the Private Calendar, but the Speaker is not required by the rules to do so.

The rules are quite strict during consideration of the Private Calendar. Consideration of bills on the Private Calendar is in the House as in the Committee of the Whole (with the advantage of a smaller quorum required to conduct business and other advantages which will be discussed later), and debate is limited to ten minutes for each bill (five minutes for proponents and five minutes for opponents). If two members object to a bill on the Private Calendar it is recommitted to the committee which reported it. Bills which are objected to are rarely reported a second time by the committee. The official objectors from both parties have, since 1958, agreed that a bill must be on the Private Calendar for seven days before it can be brought to the floor.

Both parties designate certain members to be official objectors during the call of the Private Calendar. Any member, of course, may object to consideration of a private bill, and if there are two objections the bill is stricken from the Calendar and recommitted to committee. If a member knows he will be absent or otherwise detained during the call of the Private Calendar, or if he does not want to make his opposition public, he may ask the official objectors to object for him.

The Private Calendar, then, is not a majority rule Calendar. Bills on the Private Calendar must, for all practical purposes, have the unanimous consent of the membership to pass. Even with this strict requirement, over a third of the bills enacted into law by the Eighty-eighth Congress (1963–64) were private bills.

House and Union Calendars: Consent Calendar

A second Calendar by which a good deal of legislation is handled relatively quickly is the Consent Calendar. Any member may ask that any bill on the Union or House Calendars be placed on the Consent Calendar. On the first and third Mondays of each month the call of the Consent Calendar is privileged business and takes precedence over other business. The Speaker must direct the Consent Calendar to be called.

Consideration of bills on the Consent Calendar is in the House as in the Committee of the Whole. The major effect of the rule for Consent Calendar is that the number of members constituting a quorum is reduced from 218 to 100. But very few members attend anyway while the Consent Calendar is being called. When a bill is called on the Consent Calendar, if any member objects the bill is passed over to the next call of the Calendar when, if objected to by three members it is stricken from the Calendar. In practice, members usually ask unanimous consent either that the bill be passed over without prejudice (meaning it still has two more chances) or that it be stricken from the Calendar. Bills which are objected to on the Consent Calendar may be brought up in the House through other procedures.

Because virtual unanimous consent is required to pass bills on the Consent Calendar, bills placed on this Calendar with any chance of passing must be non-controversial. Normally such bills involve relatively small requests for the benefit of particular constituencies, such as in the disposal of public lands, or requests by executive agencies for authorization to make small changes in existing laws. Consent Calendar business can come from any committee, but the majority of such bills are reported by the Committees on Interior and Insular Affairs, Veterans' Affairs, and Armed Services.

There are occasions when opposition to bills placed on the Consent Calendar comes unexpectedly. For example, on June 1, 1964, three bills from the Veterans' Affairs Committee were called on the Consent Calendar. Each of these bills was for authorization to name a Veterans' Administration Hospital after former congressmen. Such bills usually pass as a matter of course, leaving the naming of the hospital to the discretion of the people concerned where the hospital is located. One of the bills, however, was to designate the Veterans' Administration hospital at Jackson, Mississippi, as the

John Elliott Rankin Memorial Veterans Hospital. John Elliott Rankin was a former member of the Mississippi Congressional delegation who was noted for his strong anti-Negro, anti-Catholic and anti-Semitic sentiments. Objection was heard to this bill and promptly objection was heard to the other two bills naming hospitals after former congressmen (including one to be named after former Speaker Sam Rayburn).

To police the Consent Calendars, and to act for absent members, each party in the House, as with the Private Calendar, designates three members to act as official objectors. It is their job to attend each call of the Consent Calendar and to object to bills at the request of members of their party. During the Eighty-eighth Congress (1963–64) the official objectors for the Democrats were Aspinall of Colorado, Boland of Massachusetts, and McFall of California. For the Republicans the official objectors were Ford of Michigan, Pelly of Washington, and Conte of Massachusetts. In the Eighty-ninth Congress (1965–66), Aspinall, McFall, and Boland continued as the official objectors for the Democrats, with Pelly of Washington, Hall of Missouri, and Johnson of Pennsylvania acting for the Republicans. Any member, however, may object to a bill on the Consent Calendar and need not act through the official objectors.

As has been the practice in recent history, the majority and minority party objectors have agreed on several ground rules for bills to be included on the Consent Calendar. They have agreed that no bill should pass by unanimous consent if it:

1. involves an aggregate expenditure of more than one million dollars;
2. changes national or international policy;
3. applies to the districts of more than a majority of the members, unless the members are fully informed of its content and it is cleared by the leaders of both parties. With such a bill, it will be passed over without prejudice one or more times to give an opportunity to the members to become informed as to its contents;
4. has not been cleared by the Bureau of the Budget and the relevant executive agencies, or if it is not in accord with the President's program. If the bill is not approved, it is the responsibility of the chairman of the reporting committee or the sponsor of the bill to so report to the house;

5. has not been before the official objectors at least twenty-
   four hours before the Consent Calendar is called.

Essentially, then, the major function of the Consent Calendar is
to expedite the business of the House on bills which cause little or
no controversy. There is no harm in trying to have a bill passed on
the Consent Calendar since if it fails it may be brought up through
some other procedure. Next to the Private Calendar, the Consent
Calendar is responsible for the largest number of bills passed by the
House of Representatives.

SUSPENSION OF THE RULES

On the first and third Mondays of each month motions to suspend
the rules are in order in the House of Representatives. Recognition for such motions, however, is entirely within the discretion of
the Speaker. Any bill, whether reported from a committee or not,
or even whether introduced or not, may be considered under suspension of the rules. In practice, however, only bills which are on
a calendar are brought up in this fashion. Debate on the motion
to suspend the rules is limited to 40 minutes, 20 minutes to a side,
and passage requires the affirmative vote of two-thirds of the members. Most votes, however, are simply voice votes unless there is a
demand for a roll-call.

The use of the Suspension of the Rules procedure, because a two-
thirds vote is necessary, is useful only for relatively non-controversial
bills. Bills, for example, which cannot pass by unanimous consent
but are less controversial than other bills may be brought up on
suspension. It is simply another method of expediting the business
of the House on bills which involve little controversy. The Speaker
has absolute discretion to recognize members for the purpose of
suspending the rules and hence he may use this power, if he chooses,
as a way of granting favors to committee chairmen or others. The
suspension route may also be used by members of committees whose
chairmen do not want to report the bill for full-scale debate. The
chairman may allow the bill to be reported, but only if the member
discontinues his efforts if it does not pass either by unanimous consent or by suspension of the rules. This is the case, for example, with
a number of Ways and Means bills. The Chairman may allow a
bill to be reported out of his committee with the understanding that

if the bill cannot get on the suspension list, or fails in passage by suspension of the rules, that further action will not be taken.

District of Columbia Business

The Congress of the United States is the governing agent for the District of Columbia. Three Commissioners are appointed by the President and confirmed by the Senate, but these Commissioners have little power other than day-to-day administration. There have been demands for home rule for the District for a good many years, and such bills have actually passed the Senate, but in each case the House of Representatives has defeated such proposals.

In each house there is a District of Columbia Committee as well as an Appropriations subcommittee for the District of Columbia. The rejection of home rule for the District by the House can be explained by the almost total control of the District of Columbia Committee in the House by Southern Democrats. Southern Democrats are reluctant to grant home rule to the District primarily because over 50 percent of the population in the District is Negro. The extent to which Southerners dominate the District of Columbia Committee in the House can be seen in the fact that of the 15 Democratic members of the Committee in the Eighty-eighth Congress, 9, or 60 percent, were from the Old Confederacy. Its Chairman, John L. McMillan from South Carolina, is a strong foe of home rule. The Appropriations subcommittee chairman is William H. Natcher from Kentucky, also a foe of home rule.

Two days of the month are set aside for bills coming from the District of Columbia Committee (second and fourth Mondays of each month). When bills are reported from the District of Columbia Committee and placed on the Calendar they may be brought up during these two days. The major purpose and use of this rule is simply to make privileged at regular intervals the business of the Committee.

Committees Privileged to Report

In addition to the special legislative days described above which give privileged status to certain types of legislation without a rule from the Committee on Rules, a few committees are empowered by the rules of the House to report legislation (usually of a certain kind) at any time. This privilege to report carries with it the right of immediate consideration by the House, except for general appropriation bills for which printed reports and hearings must be available for three days prior to consideration. This privilege to report and achieve consideration of bills also means that a rule from the Rules Committee is not necessary.

Committees whose reports are privileged and the legislation on which such reports are privileged are:

1. Appropriations (on general appropriation bills but not on appropriations for specific purposes or resolutions extending appropriations);
2. Ways and Means (all bills relating to revenue);
3. Rules (resolutions involving rules and the order of business);
4. House Administration (on the right of a member to his seat, enrolled bills, printing, and expenditures from the contingent fund of the House);
5. Interior and Insular Affairs (bills affecting public lands, and admission of new states);
6. Public Works (bills affecting rivers and harbors);
7. and Veterans' Affairs (general pension bills).

This rule providing for privileged reports, along with the Consent Calendar, Private Calendar, Suspension of the Rules, and special legislative days for District of Columbia bills, are ways in which the Rules Committee can be avoided under special circumstances (other ways, less used, will be discussed in Chapter Five). All of these procedures establish privilege to take bills from the three calendars (Union, House, and Private) for floor consideration. There are times, however, when committees or sponsors of legislation cannot or will not use these procedures. The Private Calendar, of course, is strictly for private bills. The Consent Calendar and Suspension of the Rules require unanimous consent and two-thirds support respectively. The District of Columbia Calendar is only for District bills. And even if a committee is privileged to report for consideration by the House without a rule from the Rules Committee, some committees under certain circumstances will go to the Rules Committee for a rule anyway.

The Ways and Means Committee, for example, is privileged to report any bill raising revenue. This provision has been broadly construed, giving wide latitude. On most revenue-raising bills that are not handled by unanimous consent or suspension of the rules, however, the committee goes to the Rules Committee for a rule. The purpose, here, is simply that the Committee on Rules is the only body which is empowered to fix terms of debate. Traditionally, and for the purpose of avoiding excessive logrolling on the floor of the House, the Ways and Means Committee has asked for, and received, a closed rule from the Rules Committee which bars all amendments other than committee amendments on the House floor. Therefore, even though the Ways and Means Committee is privileged to report its bills and have them considered by the House without a rule, it almost always goes to the Rules Committee for the purpose of getting a closed rule.

There are times, too, when the Appropriations Committee goes to the Rules Committee for a rule rather than report general appropriation bills directly to the floor for consideration. This is because, for several reasons, it may be in violation of other rules of the House if they did not do so and hence a special rule allowing violation of such rules is necessary. For example, programs must be authorized by law before appropriations may be passed. "Authorized by law" means, in this context, that a bill authorizing the appropriation must have passed the House and Senate in identical form and must have been signed by the President. During 1964 when the Senate was engaged for over three months in a civil rights filibuster, both authorization and appropriation bills were being held up in the Senate. The House, however, was working right along on these measures. Since the Senate could not pass its authorization bills (due to the prolonged filibuster), the House could not pass its appropriation bills. However, they could do so by going to the Rules Committee and requesting a rule waiving points of order against the bill. The Rules Committee granted such rules on several occasions.

It is also a rule of the House that no legislation may be inserted in an appropriation bill. Occasionally, a "rider" is desired by the committee which in fact does legislate. Here again, to get around the rules of the House, a special rule from the Rules Committee waiving points of order against the bill is necessary.

It is also interesting to take more careful note of the kinds of bills which are privileged under the rules. General appropriation bills and revenue bills are, of course, necessary to keep the government going. To have these bills privileged for floor consideration makes a good deal of sense. Bills affecting the order of business in the House as well as rules and procedures (Rules Committee), and matters affecting members and the admission of new states (House Administration) also seem justified. But, in addition to these classes of bills from these four committees, three other committees are allowed to report certain kinds of legislation and have it considered without a rule from the Rules Committee. These are rivers and harbors (the omnibus "pork barrel" bill) from Public Works, bills affecting the use of public lands from Interior and Insular Affairs, and general pension bills from Veterans' Affairs. Each of these bills may be said to be very strongly constituency based and the former two bills especially subject to logrolling. Although bills from these committees are normally sent to the Committee on Rules, to give them special privilege in the rules of the House reinforces the idea of how important these kinds of bills are to congressmen. Rivers and harbors, public land use, and veterans' pensions are given the same privileged status as are appropriation, revenue, and House organization and procedure bills. In terms of the application of the rule giving certain kinds of bills privileged status, it is just as important not to hold up a rivers and harbors bill as it is not to hold up a general appropriation bill or a tax bill. Furthermore, in terms of the rule, it is more important not to hold up a rivers and harbors bill or a public land use bill than to hold up a civil rights bill or an anti-poverty bill, the latter two both requiring rules from the Rules Committee.

RULES FROM THE RULES COMMITTEE

All other bills not privileged in one of the above ways must receive a rule from the Committee on Rules to be taken from the calendar and brought up on the floor of the House. (Discharge and Calendar Wednesday procedures, and the 1965–66 21-day rule, which may be used when the Rules Committee refuses to report legislation referred to it, will be discussed in Chapter Five.) Since the procedures referred to above involve, with some exceptions, non-controversial legislation, most bills of major consequence, and especially those bills which are a part of the President's major requests, must go to the Rules Committee for a rule after being reported from a committee. Even the 1964 tax bill, which was privileged as a revenue bill from the Ways and Means Committee, went to the Rules Committee for a closed rule.

The Rules Committee is a bipartisan committee (as are the other committees) with a fixed ratio of members set at two to one in favor of the majority party. Members on the committee are formally appointed in the usual manner, by the respective party Committee on Committees, but because of the importance of the Rules Committee for the leadership of both parties the choices of the respective party leaders nearly always prevail.

The major powers of the committee are to set the terms of debate on the House floor for resolutions which come to it. This includes setting the number of hours of general debate in the Committee of the Whole House on the State of the Union (a procedure to be discussed in the next chapter), determining whether amendments will be allowed on the floor (an open vs. a closed rule), and determining whether possible points of order against the bill will be in order.

Because of these powers, and because most of the important legislation in any session of Congress must go to the Rules Committee for a rule, the Committee on Rules may exercise considerable influence over the flow of legislation. But probably the best description of the Rules Committee in its activities is that it is, by and large, a body which cooperates relatively closely with the leadership and with the substantive committees which come before it requesting rules for their bills. Occasionally, perhaps two to five times a session, the Rules Committee acts in a fashion which others consider to be grossly unfair or arbitrary. In most instances, however, the activities of the Rules Committee are routine. James A. Robinson gives us some idea of the activities of the Committee and the extent to which they cooperate or do not cooperate with the leadership. The following data is taken from his study.[7]

Of the 150 or so bills which come to the Rules Committee each Congress, the committee denies hearings to about 20 of them. Occasionally the denial of a hearing will be against the wishes of the leadership. For example, in 1964 Judge Smith attempted to deny hearings to both the Civil Rights Bill and the Anti-Poverty Program. In each case, the majority on the committee forced Judge Smith to call hear-

[7] James A. Robinson, *The House Rules Committee* (Indianapolis: Bobbs-Merrill, 1963). See also Robert L. Peabody, "The Enlarged Rules Committee," in Robert L. Peabody and Nelson W. Polsby, eds., *New Perspectives on the House of Representatives* (Chicago: Rand McNally, 1963), pp. 129–164.

ings and in both cases favorable rules were reported. In many cases the Rules Committee will hold up a bill because it is not wanted by the leadership, or it is known by the leadership that the bill will fail on the floor. As an example of the former, the Rules Committee never completed its hearings in 1964 on the so-called Quality Stabilization Bill (national fair-trade bill). This bill was opposed by the leadership although, if brought to a vote on the floor, it might have commanded a majority vote. Also in 1964 the Rules Committee held up the Area Redevelopment Bill to extend the ARA program. Although the leadership supported the bill, several whip polls conducted by the office of the majority whip indicated that the bill would fail if brought to the floor.

The Rules Committee also denies rules, after hearings, to about 12 bills per Congress. For the most part they are bills which have only lukewarm support. In very few cases are they bills which the leadership strongly supports.

There are, of course, many constraints which operate on the Rules Committee preventing it from acting arbitrarily. If the Chairman is acting capriciously, or is out of step with the majority on the committee, the committee itself may call hearings in the absence of the Chairman after seven days' notice. If the committee is out of step, a discharge petition, Calendar Wednesday, or, during 1965–66, the 21-day rule could be used to go around the committee. And, the committee may be challenged in other ways. For example, in 1961 the committee was enlarged from 12 to 15 members allowing for the addition of administration supporters to the committee. In 1963 the size of the committee was permanently made 15 members. Or, in 1949 and again in 1965 a 21-day rule was put into effect allowing the committee to be by-passed if it held up bills for a period longer than 21 days. Often, of course, the threat of any of these occurring may be enough to encourage the Rules Committee or its chairman to take action.

Even though the Committee on Rules is usually cooperative, there are occasions (perhaps three or four times a year) when the Committee refuses to grant a rule, delays hearings, or in some other way harasses the leadership. A battle will often ensue with the outcome dependent upon the extent and intensity of support which the leadership can exert. However, it is rarely clear, when the Rules Committee is successful in blocking further action on a piece of legislation, whether the bill would have passed on the floor of the House, even with strong leadership support. That the Rules Committee can delay action on bills which have wide support within the House and which are supported by the leadership is not in question. They can and they do. The major question is the length of delay. During 1965–66 the leadership had been delegated additional power to deal with a recalcitrant Rules Committee. At that time the House adopted (by a vote of 224–201) a rule allowing the Speaker to recognize a member of the committee whose bill is being delayed for the purpose of bringing the bill directly to the House floor if the Rules Committee had the bill for 21 days without granting a rule, or after 21 days if the Rules Committee voted not to grant a rule.

Most rules from the Rules Committee are open rules, but when a request is made for a closed rule (such requests usually come from the Ways and Means Committee), it is almost always granted. Robinson's data show that between 1939 and 1960 there were 1128 open rules and 87 closed rules granted by the committee.[8] The Rules Committee is also quite cooperative in granting rules which waive points of order, especially under certain circumstances for appropriation bills. And finally, most rules provide for either one or two hours of general debate (approximately 80 percent), with rules for longer general debate given to major bills in the President's program.

Reports from the Committee on Rules are privileged, so there is no trouble bringing them to the floor. They must, however, like other resolutions reported from other committees, lay over one day before consideration unless by two-thirds vote (in effect suspending the rules) the House shall determine otherwise. This one-day delay occasionally becomes important toward the end of the session. For example, in December of 1963 the House was still working on the foreign aid appropriation bill. This bill had come back to the House from conference committee (conference committee reports are highly privileged and do not need a rule), but because the conference report contained legislation not in the House bill a rule was needed waiving point of order against "legislation in an appropriations bill." When the Rules Committee reported the resolution, the leadership tried to bring it up the same day by a two-thirds vote but the resolution was defeated. The resolution was then brought up the next day by a majority vote.

When a resolution is reported by the Rules Committee the rules of the House provide that it shall be reported to the House within

[8] Robinson, *op. cit.*, p. 44.

three days. If the report is not made within three days, the resolution then goes on the calendar and if not called up by the member of the committee making the report (the member making the report is usually assigned by the chairman and is often, on controversial legislation, the chairman himself) within seven days any member of the committee may then call it up. This rule, of course, is to avoid what might happen if the chairman were opposed to a bill but the majority of the committee voted to report a rule. This rule makes it impossible for the chairman to assign himself to report the rule and then not report it. He may, however, delay proceedings for up to ten days. If it is late in the session, or if ten days' delay seems too much, it is possible for the majority of the committee to assign the member to report the rule. This is viewed, however, as an insult to the chairman since it is normally within his power to assign members to report rules. Nevertheless, this was done by Representative Ray Madden, who led the fight in the Rules Committee for the 1964 Anti-Poverty Program. He moved in committee that he be assigned to report the rule, rather than allowing Judge Smith to assign the member reporting. This was to insure that there would not be even ten days of delay. The motion carried, but it was an unusual circumstance.

One power of the Committee on Rules which the rules changes at the beginning of the Eighty-ninth Congress (1965–66) cancelled was the power of the committee to grant or refuse rules to send House-passed bills to conference committees with the Senate. This power meant that any member could block floor consideration of House-passed bills returned from the Senate with amendments. This, in turn, is derived from the fact that both the House and the Senate must pass legislation in identical form before it can become law. When House-passed bills are returned to the House with Senate amendments the House then has a number of alternatives open to it (to be discussed in Chapter Nine), none of which, however, are possible until the bill can come to the floor. Before 1965 it required unanimous consent to take such a bill from the Speaker's table. Barring unanimous consent, the bill had to go to the Rules Committee for a rule making it privileged business. Most bills receive unanimous consent and are immediately taken from the Speaker's table and disposed of either by agreeing to a conference requested by the Senate, agreeing to the Senate amendments, or insisting on its own bill and requesting a conference with the Senate. Robinson reports that between 1939 and 1960 there were 23 rules granted by the Committee

on Rules to go to conference, or an average of one a year.[9] This is
not because the Rules Committee has refused to grant many rules,
but simply because unanimous consent is usually granted.

Occasionally, however, unanimous consent has not been granted
and the bill has had to get a rule from the Rules Committee. Such
requests for a rule have, in the past, been denied and bills once passed
by the House and then passed by the Senate (in different language)
have died without a House-Senate conference to work out the differences. Perhaps the most notable example of this was in 1960 on a
general aid to education bill. The House of Representatives for the
first time in its history had passed an education bill which provided
funds for construction of primary and secondary schools. The Senate had done so twice before. The Senate amended the House-passed
bill and returned it to the House. Objection was heard when unanimous consent to take the bill from the Speaker's table was requested,
and the bill went to the Rules Committee. By a 5–7 vote the Rules
Committee refused to grant a rule and the bill died. It was this action, along with other factors, which led to the move to increase the
size of the committee in 1961 from 12 to 15 members, making it
possible to add two new Democrats more favorable to the President's
program.[10]

The justification for this procedure was that it is possible for the
Senate to add amendments to House-passed bills which have nothing
to do with the topic of legislation as passed by the House. Many
members of the House, especially conservative members, object to
this procedure because it, in effect, by-passes the committee which
ordinarily would have had the non-germane amendment referred to
it. This practice, however, is not very prevalent. The argument against
this procedure is, of course, that both the House and the Senate have
already acted on the legislation and it should not be within the power
of a small group of people to thwart the actions already taken by the
whole House (as happened, for example, with the 1960 education
bill). Occasionally there is a non-germane rider to a House-passed

---

[9] *Ibid.*, p. 51.
[10] For a description and analysis of this change in the Rules Committee see Hugh
Douglas Price, "Race, Religion, and the Rules Committee: The Kennedy
Aid-to-Education Bills," in Alan F. Westin, ed.; *The Uses of Power* (New
York: Harcourt, Brace & World, 1962), pp. 1–72; and Milton C. Cummings,
Jr. and Robert L. Peabody, "The Decision to Enlarge the Committee on
Rules: An Analysis of the 1961 Vote," in Peabody and Polsby, ed., *op. cit.*,
pp. 167–194.

bill, but the logic of sending it to the Rules Committee to get a rule allowing it to be discussed on the floor of the House is not very compelling.

Even Judge Smith, Chairman of the Rules Committee until his defeat for re-election to Congress in 1966, thought the requirement for unanimous consent to take a House-passed bill returned by the Senate from the Speaker's table was too strict. At the end of the Eighty-eighth Congress (1963–64) Judge Smith proposed with tongue-in-cheek that five objections, rather than one should be required to prevent immediate consideration of a House-passed bill with Senate amendments.

This rule is a good example of a point which needs to be made over and over again. There are some rules which operate in favor of those who prefer the *status quo* in the House, but they are employed only sporadically. For example, almost all bills receive unanimous consent to go to conference. Only occasionally, when the Senate adds a non-germane amendment, or when the Senate liberalizes a bill with amendments, a bill which, like the education bill of 1960, received bare majority support to begin with, would the rule requiring the bill to be sent to the Rules Committee in the absence of unanimous consent be invoked. And even when invoked it may not successfully block the legislation. But every once in a while, perhaps once every few years, a major piece of legislation will fail because of one or another of the rules which may be invoked by those in the opposition.

To prevent this particular instance from happening again, the Eighty-ninth Congress adopted a rule which allows the Speaker to recognize the committee chairman or a majority member of the committee who favors the legislation to move that a House-passed bill returned by the Senate with amendments be considered immediately. This motion may then be voted on by the whole House, ending with a majority vote. Hence, a single objection (or as Judge Smith would have liked it, five objections), is no longer sufficient to send such a bill to the Rules Committee. Action may now be taken by a majority in the House.

Perhaps the best way to emphasize the power of the Rules Committee is that the committee is able to report rules which, if adopted by a majority of the House, in effect suspend the rules. There are only three exceptions to this. The Rules Committee may not report a rule dispensing with Calendar Wednesday except by a rule adopted by two-thirds of the House members; nor may the Rules Committee report a rule which denies to the minority the right to make a motion to recommit a bill; nor may the committee report a rule which provides for immediate consideration of the rule without its laying over one legislative day.

The usual method of suspending the rules is to make a motion to that effect. Such a motion requires the affirmative vote of two-thirds of the House and is in order only on the first and third Mondays of each month. Furthermore, the Speaker has absolute discretion in recognizing members to make such motions. But, in fact, the Rules Committee also may report rules which suspend the rules. For example, even by granting a rule for immediate consideration of a bill the committee is, in effect, suspending the rules. But more importantly, rules which bar amendments or which waive points of order are rules which allow for certain rules of the House to be suspended by a simple majority vote. Since the amending process is provided for in the rules, to bar amendments is to suspend the rules; since points of order are made for the purpose of staying within the rules, to waive points of order is to suspend the rules.

An additional power of the Rules Committee, one which is exercised very infrequently, is the power of the Rules Committee to report legislation to the floor regardless of whether or not it has been previously reported by a committee, and even regardless of whether it has been introduced. In other words the committee may report a rule for any legislation which, if adopted by a majority of the House, makes such legislation privileged for immediate consideration. This action occurred twice in 1964. Following the Supreme Court's decisions of Baker v. Carr in 1962, which allowed citizens to file suit against malapportioned legislatures under the "equal protection of the laws" clause of the Fourteenth Amendment, Wesberry v. Sanders in February of 1964, which ruled that congressional districts must be fairly apportioned, and Reynolds v. Sims in June, 1964, which ruled that both houses of state legislatures must be apportioned on the basis of population, many congressmen and senators, especially those whose policy preferences were benefited by rurally dominated state legislatures, wanted to do something to overturn the decision of the Supreme Court. A number of bills and constitutional amendments were introduced in the House and referred to the Judiciary Committee, chaired by Emanuel Celler of New York, a proponent of the stand taken by the Supreme Court. Celler's committee was not disposed to report out the legislation and in August of 1964 the Rules

Committee granted a rule to report to the floor a bill introduced by Representative Tuck of Virginia which would take from the Supreme Court jurisdiction in matters of apportionment of state legislatures, a bill which had not been reported by the Judiciary Committee. The rule and bill both were voted on favorably by the House. And again, in August, the Rules Committee reported a rule to make privileged a constitutional amendment introduced by Representative Patman of Texas which would allow one house of the state legislature to be apportioned on a basis other than population. This rule never came to the floor for a vote.

These two actions by the Rules Committee took many members of Congress completely by surprise. Although the leadership was undoubtedly aware that such actions would take place, many members had never even realized that the Rules Committee could report legislation which had not been reported from a substantive committee. Only twice before since 1937 had the Rules Committee taken such action, once in 1945 on a labor bill, and once in 1953 on a tax bill.[11] This power of the Rules Committee is another example of the ability of the Rules Committee to suspend the rules by majority vote.

Such powers as these should give pause to those who wish to do away with the Committee on Rules. Imagine such power in the hands of the leadership. Being able to bar amendments, to waive points of order against a bill, and to report any legislation regardless of whether a committee has reported it, and even to initiate legislation, are powers of no small measure. I think it is clear that what is "wrong" with the Rules Committee from the point of view of the pro-administration members is not that the Rules Committee should be stripped of its powers, but rather that the locus of that power should be shifted into the hands of the leadership. The reasons why it is difficult to effect this will become clearer as we continue. The 21-day rule (which was in effect during 1965–66) and the majority vote provision to send to conference were significant steps in the direction of by-passing the committee, but what is lacking is the ability or willingness to change the personnel on the committee.

It is also clear, however, that the Rules Committee's negative role is only "now and again," not "all the time." Normally the committee is quite cooperative with the leadership. Normally the votes on the committee are there. However, the committee under a conservative chairman can delay action a good deal, and occasionally defeat

---

[11] Robinson, *op. cit.*, p. 29.

legislation. Such actions do not happen very often, but when they do happen they are usually on quite significant matters, such as civil rights or anti-poverty.

It is also true that the leadership itself will ask the Rules Committee not to grant a rule when the leadership feels it does not have sufficient votes to pass the bill when it reaches the floor. The Area Redevelopment Administration bill, for example, was held up by the Rules Committee for over a year at the request of the leadership, not in spite of it. As usual, however, the Rules Committee was blamed for impeding legislation.

Floor Rules and
Procedures (House)

The floor of the House of Representatives appears, to the casual observer sitting in the gallery, to be a very confusing, noisy, and unexciting place compared with the Senate. There are 435 members of the House and most are little known even, in many cases, in their own constituencies. Members are constantly streaming on and off the floor, talking with one another in their seats or smoking behind the rail, and the unpracticed eye will usually miss the significance of the activities that are occurring on the floor, the reasons for their occurrence, and how they are related to the legislative process in general. Hopefully, from this chapter, a picture will emerge of the House of Representatives as a well-ordered, well-managed, sensible set of activities, as members, having differing preferences about the legislation before them, clash with each other over important matters within a very strict set of rules. The rules are in some cases complicated, and the possible sequence of moves many in number, but nevertheless, like a game of chess, players attempt to win. Unlike chess, however, which turns out to be a gigantic puzzle with only three possible solutions (win, lose, or draw), winning or losing on the floor of the House of Representatives is a good deal more complicated. It is possible, for example, to lose a little and win a little, to win partially, or even, under some circumstances, for almost everyone to win. This chapter will lay out the rules and procedures involved in the game on the floor of the House of Representatives, and will discuss the effects of the rules on the players, and strategies and tactics based on the rules of the game.

The House of Representatives goes into session every day (unless it has, by unanimous consent, determined otherwise) at twelve noon. By a resolution adopted at the beginning of each Congress, daily meetings (except Sunday) are specified. Usually on Thursday the majority leader will ask unanimous consent that when the House adjourns it adjourn to the following Monday. One objection to this request, however, can force the House to meet on Friday and Saturday. Members do not object for a number of reasons. Most members are anxious that the House not meet on Friday and Saturday. Most congressmen are quite busy people with an enormous workload. Much of the workload has to do with constituency affairs (either in Washington or back home). They need and want the time to conduct other business and may wish to have a long weekend in which to go back to the district for meetings, speeches, and other constituency work. Even if they have nothing pressing, the leadership rarely has anything scheduled for Friday and Saturday so there is no particular reason to meet. To object, then, would be pointless as well as irritating to friend and foe.

The reason it requires unanimous consent to adjourn longer than one day is because not meeting is in violation of the rules. In the absence of unanimous consent the rules must be suspended. But a motion to suspend the rules is in order only on the first and third Mondays of the month. A rule from the Rules Committee could make any day eligible for suspension of the rules, but the leadership does not anticipate an objection. Even if there were an objection, however, it would inconvenience mostly the leadership. A *pro forma* session would be held on Friday and Saturday in which a motion, after the reading of the *Journal* of the preceding day's activities, would be made to adjourn.

This ability of the House to adjourn, in violation of its own rules, by unanimous consent is a good example of the fact that, even in a body as large as the House, informal norms and expectations play a very important role. It would be possible for a single member to tie up the House for many hours on any day if he were so disposed. The fact that members employ delaying tactics infrequently, and normally only when many other members support them, is illustrative of the importance of informal as well as formal rules and procedures.

The House has developed, then, with rare exceptions, a Monday to Thursday schedule, with Monday being reserved primarily for noncontroversial legislation. The first and third Mondays of each month

Consent Calendar and bills on Suspension of the Rules are in order. On the second and fourth Mondays District of Columbia business is privileged. Normally, no major legislation comes to the floor before Tuesday or after Thursday.

It is also of interest to note that the threat of a possible Friday or Saturday session looms over the House each week. If the legislative schedule for that week is not finished by Thursday the leadership will want to carry it over to Friday. Since most members do not expect a Friday session they have already scheduled a number of activities for the long weekend. A Friday session would mean that many would have to cancel previous engagements, in many cases engagements out of town. The possibility of a Friday session, then, encourages members not to be excessively dilatory.

At precisely twelve o'clock noon a bell rings throughout the House side of the Capitol and in the House Office Buildings and the Speaker gavels the House to order (at this point there are usually only ten to twenty members on the floor). The House chaplain or visiting priest, rabbi, or minister offers a prayer, and an abbreviated version of the *Journal* of the preceding day is read and approved. Any member may object to this proceeding and demand that the *Journal* be read in full, but this is rarely done except for purposes of delay. Amendments to the *Journal* are also in order, an additional source of possible delay. After the *Journal* is read and approved the Speaker recognizes members for one-minute speeches and insertions into the *Congressional Record*. Bills and resolutions are officially introduced during this period, although it is not necessary for a member to gain recognition for the introduction of bills. Committee reports are received, as well as petitions and memorials, and messages from the Senate and the executive branch. This activity constitutes the morning business of the House and usually lasts from 5 to 35 minutes. It is in the discretion of the Speaker whether or not to recognize members during this period, but it would be a rare occurrence if a member, seeking recognition, did not receive it. A Speaker may occasionally be arbitrary, especially if he has a good legislative or possibly partisan reason, but such factors are not often related to morning business.

At any point after the reading of the prayer a point of order that a quorum is not present is in order and neither the Speaker nor the person who has the floor may refuse to recognize or yield the floor respectively for that purpose. A quorum while the House sits as the

House of Representatives (as opposed to the Committee of the Whole House on the State of the Union) is a majority of the members, or 218. The purposes of a quorum call may be many, but when called at this point in the proceedings it is usually simply to get members to the floor. The leadership, however, may have other uses for this first quorum call. If an important bill is to be considered that day (or even the day after) they will use the quorum call as an attendance check. A list of the absentees is compiled and the names are transmitted by phone to the Congressional Liaison Office of the President's Executive Office, by the Office of the Democratic whip (at least this has been the practice under both President Kennedy and President Johnson). At this point the offices of the absent members who are expected to side with the administration on the bill are called to inquire if they are in town and expected to be on the floor. If not, they will be summoned to return for the expected vote.

There are many other uses for quorum calls which will be discussed as it becomes convenient, but it is useful to observe at this point the general notion that a single rule or procedure may be used for multiple purposes, some not even intended by the procedure, and that such uses may even be simultaneous. In this may lie the key to why rules are difficult to change and why support for change is hard to mobilize. Each rule may serve multiple purposes for members. In some cases it may be more than one purpose for most of the members, in others it may be that it has one purpose for one group of members and another purpose for another group. If the latter is the case the rule may be extremely difficult to change since the function it is serving is different for different members.

A quorum call takes about 25 to 35 minutes. The clerk first reads the entire list of members in alphabetical order. He then reads a list of those who failed to respond on the first roll-call, and he then calls off the names of those standing in the well of the House who either came in late or failed to answer to their names when called.

After this quorum call morning business may proceed, or if morning business is finished, the legislative business may begin. Members, meanwhile, drift out to read the papers which are on racks in the lobby off the floor, read the AP and UP ticker tapes located in the same place, get a bite to eat at the snack bars located in each corner of the back lobbies, converse with other members or journalists, return to their offices, or go downstairs to the members' dining room for lunch.

Assuming it is not the first or third Monday when the Consent Calendar and Suspension of the Rules are in order, or the second or fourth Monday when District of Columbia business is privileged, or the first or third Tuesday when the Private Calendar is read, the Speaker will generally recognize a member of the Rules Committee who has been designated by the Chairman to call up the rule making privileged the next legislative business. What the business for the day is will come as no surprise to the members. Each Friday a whip notice of the following week's activities is circulated to the members informing them of the legislative program. Actually, although the whip notice is circulated above the signature of the Democratic whip it in fact is written in the office of the Majority Leader who, with the Speaker, is responsible for the program. If there are any changes in the program the majority leader will announce them on the floor. Members will often call up the Democratic whip's office as early as Wednesday to try to get the program for the following week so they can schedule their own activities, but rarely is the program known that far in advance. The majority leader usually gets the program made up sometime on Thursday, it is announced on the floor on Thursday afternoon, and received in the members' offices by Friday.

Most important legislation goes to the Rules Committee for a rule which makes the bill privileged business. Such rules, when called up, are debatable for one hour. By custom one half of the time is allotted to the opponents of the bill. Debate on the rule, however, usually does not last the full hour. Normally it is clear that the rule is going to be adopted and members are anxious to get on with the day's activities. Robinson reports that between the years of 1937 and 1960 only 24 rules were defeated, or an average of one a year.[1] However, some rules on bills are quite controversial because the bill itself is controversial.

A recent example of a rule which failed adoption occurred in October, 1964. The fiscal year ends June 30th. If appropriation bills for the coming fiscal year (which begins July 1st) are not passed by that time, the agencies are left with no funds to spend. Congress takes care of this situation by passing "continuing appropriation bills" until the regular appropriation for the new year is passed. These continuing appropriation bills grant to those agencies and departments who have

[1] James A. Robinson, *The House Rules Committee* (Indianapolis: Bobbs-Merrill, 1963), p. 37.

not yet received a new appropriation the power to spend at the same rate as the previous year. In June of 1964 Congress passed such a continuing appropriation to last until September 1. At the end of August Congress passed another to last until the end of October. In October, with some appropriation bills still not passed, the leadership asked for another continuing appropriation to last until the end of November. A rule from the Committee on Rules was reported to bring this continuing appropriation bill to the floor. The members, however, were anxious to adjourn and go home to engage in campaigning for the election due on November 3. To grant such a continuing appropriation was perceived as possibly postponing further the day of adjournment and the rule was voted down. This forced the leadership to act more quickly and Congress did finally adjourn on October 3rd.

Other examples of rules being defeated are just as intrinsically connected with the substance of the legislation. Generally, if a rule is defeated it is because the content of the legislation which the rule is reporting is not acceptable to the House. If the rule cannot command a majority then the legislation probably cannot. On the other hand, because the rule passes (usually by voice vote) does not mean the legislation will pass.

Although rules from the Rules Committee vary somewhat depending upon the nature of the bill and other conditions, the following is a typical form for a rule:

> *Resolved,* That upon the adoption of this resolution it shall be in order to move that the House resolve itself into the Committee of the Whole House on the State of the Union for the consideration of the bill (H.R. ____), entitled, etc. After general debate, which shall be confined to the bill and continue not to exceed ____ hours, to be equally divided and controlled by the chairman and the ranking minority member of the Committee on ____, the bill shall be read for amendment under the five-minute rule. At the conclusion of the consideration of the bill for amendment, the Committee shall rise and report the bill to the House with such amendments as may have been adopted and the previous question shall be considered as ordered on the bill and amendments thereto to final passage without intervening motion except one motion to recommit with or without instructions.

Following adoption of the rule the House immediately resolves itself into the Committee of the Whole House on the State of the Union. This is a device which is intended to make less formal and at the same time expedite the business of the House. Formally what occurs is that the Speaker appoints a Chairman of the Committee of the Whole (the Speaker himself is not allowed to preside), and the rules under which debate takes place change. The Speaker often schedules conferences with the majority leader, whip, committee chairmen, agency heads, and White House liaison staff during the afternoon to discuss legislation which will soon be coming to the floor, and the Committee of the Whole procedure frees the Speaker for such activities.

The time for general debate as provided for under the rule is then divided between the floor manager for the proponents of the bill (usually either the chairman or subcommittee chairman of the committee which reported the legislation) and the minority party (usually a ranking minority party member on the committee). They alternate in their opening remarks, and then yield time in small amounts for others to speak.

During this time, or at any time during debate, a point of no quorum may be raised. A quorum when in the Committee of the Whole is 100 members rather than 218. If a quorum is not present (the chairman of the Committee of the Whole counts), the bells in the House side of the Capitol and in the House Office Buildings ring three times, and the clerk again calls the roll, calls the absentees, and recognizes members in the well who came in late or failed to respond to their names. The Committee then rises, the Speaker returns to the chair, announces that a quorum is present, suggests that without objection further proceedings under the call of the roll be dispensed with (to be discussed), hands the gavel back to the chairman of the Committee of the Whole, and the House is again in Committee of the Whole.

If a quorum is not present, several alternatives are available. No further business may be conducted in the absence of a quorum. Either a motion is made that the Sergeant-at-Arms be instructed to bring in the absentees, or there is a motion to adjourn. It is rare that a quorum cannot be found since the leadership is not likely to schedule activities when members are expected to be out of town and, conversely, members are not likely to be out of town when important legislation is scheduled on the preceding week's whip notice. However, toward the end of the Eighty-eighth Congress (1963–64), when the election was rapidly approaching, quorums were more difficult to come by and occasionally when one was not available the House had to adjourn. Since the number for a quorum in the Committee of the Whole is only 100, and since there was probably a previous quorum call earlier in the day when the House was not in the Committee of the Whole and the number for a quorum was 218, it is unlikely that a quorum cannot be had at this point in the proceedings.

It is also possible for any member to object to "further proceedings under the call of the roll" being dispensed with. These proceedings involve instructing the Sergeant-at-Arms to bring in the absentees. Under the rules all members are required to respond to quorum calls and to be on the floor unless sick or officially excused. Normally, of course, some members are simply busy doing other things and will not respond to some quorum calls. In some cases it may be committee business. In other cases some members may be out of town, visiting with constituents, downtown talking with agency officials, in the gym exercising, or out on a golf course.

If a member objects to dispensing with further proceedings under the call of the roll when a quorum is present it is obviously to delay action. If objection is heard a motion is then made to dispense with further proceedings, but such a motion, although requiring only majority support, may itself require a vote, and more delay will ensue.

This example is illustrative of how the rules, as fair as they may be, can be used by members who wish to delay. When the rules of the House are violated (as in reading an abbreviated *Journal,* or dispensing with further proceedings under the call of the roll) any member may object and delay will be a consequence. It is not that the rules unfairly favor inaction, it is just that action requires operating under a set of rules and the rules themselves may be used to cause delay.

After general debate is concluded, the bill is then read for amendments (assuming an open rule). This is accomplished in one of several ways. Either the bill is read line by line and amendments are submitted at the appropriate point, unanimous consent is asked that the bill be considered as read and open for amendment at any point, or unanimous consent is asked to proceed title by title rather than line by line. The rules specify that the bill should be read line by line with no amendments in order until that part of the bill which is to be amended has been read. Hence there is need for unanimous consent if the floor manager prefers to have the bill read title by title (the usual method for long, complicated bills) or in its entirety (the usual method for shorter bills).

In the House, unlike the Senate, amendments need not be submitted in advance. When a member has an amendment, he seeks recognition and the clerk reads the amendment. If it is long and complicated, or simply technical in nature, the amender will ask unanimous consent to dispense with further reading. The mover of the amendment has five minutes in which to explain his amendment. He can get additional time if he chooses, but only by unanimous consent. The floor manager then has several choices. He can accept the amendment (in which case the amendment will almost always be adopted, usually by a quick voice vote) attempt to change it by proposing a substitute, or try to defeat it. Which strategy he chooses depends upon a host of complicated factors including how much the amendment changes the bill, and how much support he thinks the amendment has. It is at this point that a floor manager needs to be knowledgeable of the ways of the House. The number of mistakes he could make are many. He could, for example, accept an amendment which would not have carried, thereby changing the bill and possibly losing some support for the bill which he had before the amendment was added. The manager could attempt to propose a substitute and perhaps win, but the change would not have been necessary because the original amendment would have lost. And, the manager could attempt to defeat the amendment and lose. This latter alternative is especially costly because when one amendment carries, it opens the possibility that others may also.

Which strategy the floor manager will use on each amendment, and whether he wins or not, is dependent upon a number of complex factors. Generally, a floor manager has several advantages that other members do not have:

1. Many members, and especially the leadership, will support the committee. There is a norm of floor behavior for the majority party which is that, unless there is good reason to the contrary, a doubt should be decided in favor of the committee. The activity of the leadership is also important. For example, even the Speaker votes on teller

votes (but does not vote on roll-call votes unless there is a tie).

2. Many amendments are offered by the minority party and, therefore, party loyalty is easily invoked. This is especially true with non-roll-call votes which often involve issues with which members are not familiar. The most immediate response, under these conditions, is to vote with the floor manager.

3. The floor manager is usually the most knowledgeable person on the floor concerning the provisions of the bill. He is probably also the most knowledgeable about what the House will accept or reject. Unless he has recently assumed his position this is not the first bill he has managed, nor the first time he has managed this particular type of bill. The history of the legislation, and the provisions of the bill currently before the House are quite familiar to him. Also, he has seen the bill through the committee and is familiar with the nature of the opposition against the bill. He will know, probably better than anyone else, what should be accepted, what should be opposed, and what his chances of winning are.

4. The manager of the bill is usually the committee chairman (or at least a subcommittee chairman), and amendments to bills rarely come from other chairmen or subcommittee chairmen. The manager, then, will start with a good deal of support on his side, as well as being able, because he is undoubtedly more senior and more respected than the mover of the amendment, to pick up additional support. A chairman opposed to a non-chairman on the floor of the House is usually an unfair fight.

5. Very often time is also on the side of the floor manager. Members are anxious to get the bill out of the way so they can return to their offices. This kind of pressure works in favor of the floor manager in a number of interesting ways. Members, for example, will be reluctant to vote for amendments for fear that other similar amendments will also be proposed and adopted. A piece of legislation in some cases is a delicate balance of a number of interests already compromised and worked out in committee. And even when this is not true, members can be made to believe it is true. To upset the alleged balance on the floor in favor of one interest invites a rash of attempts to do

the same for other interests. Also, members will be reluctant to pursue a point very far on the floor. Extended,
technical debate is difficult to follow on the floor and it is
presumed that most committees have carefully considered
the bill.

Whether a floor manager will turn these advantages to use will
depend upon his own personal style, how skillful he is at parliamentary maneuverings and floor debate, his status with the House,
whether his committee has reported a bill which accurately reflects
what the House is likely to accept, and who is proposing the amendment. Some examples may be helpful.

On each appropriation bill which came before the House in 1964,
H. R. Gross from Iowa was in the habit of proposing an amendment
to the bill which specified that no funds therein appropriated could
be used to finance a National Service Corps (the Senate had passed
such a bill, and Gross was simply trying to prevent the initiation of
such a program from funds not so designated). Since these appropriation bills had no provisions for such programs most floor managers,
including the now Chairman of the Appropriations Committee,
George Mahon of Texas, would simply accept Gross's amendment.
Not so, however, with John Rooney of New York, subcommittee
chairman of the State, Justice, Commerce, and Judiciary Subcommittee of the Appropriations Committee, and floor manager for its
bill. Rooney decided he would fight Gross's amendment. Rooney is
noted for his insistence that his subcommittee bill be accepted by
the House as it passed the committee, and his success in doing just
that had been excellent. He is also a scrapper, and seems to relish a
good fight.

When Gross proposed his amendment, Rooney spoke against it
and on three votes Rooney won each time; first on a voice vote, then
a standing vote (42–50), then a teller vote (55–64). This marked the
first time that Gross's amendment had ever been defeated. Had
Rooney accepted the amendment, as other floor managers before him
had done, the provision would not have affected the bill at all.
Rooney simply did not want any amendments, and especially an
amendment of the kind proposed by Gross. Although Rooney's status
with the House, combined with his legislative skill, were necessary
qualities in helping him win, this was, as much as anything else, a
matter of style. Most Northern Democrats were delighted that Rooney

was going to fight, and a good deal of enthusiasm and shouting was a by-product. When the result of the teller vote was announced the Northern Democrats burst into applause.

Some floor managers are simply more skillful than others. This skill is dependent upon a number of factors, but by and large it is a product of experience and good hard work. Many bills are recurring issues and a manager has previous years' experience to rely on during the amending process. Also, skillful floor managers will check to see what amendments are to be offered and how much support they are likely to have. Skill, then, is often a matter of adequate preparation and knowledge about what will come up and what might be acceptable to the House.

Another factor which affects the amending process is the status of the floor manager. Some managers have developed the reputation for getting what they want. Floor managers with this kind of reputation would include Wilbur Mills of Ways and Means, George Mahon and John Rooney of Appropriations, Carl Vinson, who retired after the Eighty-eighth Congress (1963–64), Chairman of the Armed Services Committee, Albert Rains, who also retired, Chairman of the Housing Subcommittee of Banking and Currency, among a number of others. Floor managers with poor reputations would include Wright Patman, Chairman of Banking and Currency, Adam Clayton Powell, former Chairman of Education and Labor, and Henry Reuss, Chairman of the International Finance Subcommittee of Banking and Currency. Adam Clayton Powell, for example, did not manage the first anti-poverty bill, turning it over, instead, to Phil Landrum, a Southerner, because it was expected that Landrum would be able to save more of the bill.

A floor manager's success on the floor will also depend to some extent on the committee which is reporting the bill. Some committees are skewed in one direction or another (a point to be discussed more fully in Chapter Ten). It is possible, then, for some bargains which are made in committee not to reflect, accurately, the bargaining position on the floor. Education bills from the Education and Labor Committee fall into this category. Edith Green, a subcommittee chairman of the Education and Labor Committee, for this reason and others will bring a bill out onto the floor only to give most of it up before she is through.

The person who proposes the amendment is also important. If a high status, well-respected member supports an amendment it will cause the floor manager some trouble. If a Democrat, for example, proposed a weakening amendment it is likely to get Southern Democratic and Republican support. During the Food for Peace floor debate Rooney spoke in favor of an amendment proposed by Paul Findley, a Republican from Illinois, restricting the flow of surplus agricultural products to Poland and Yugoslavia. The amendment carried. The very next day after some discussion between Rooney and the White House, the amendment was reconsidered, Rooney switched sides and opposed the amendment, and the amendment lost.

Whatever strategy the floor manager chooses, however, he in turn is allowed five minutes for debate. Additional members may ask for time to speak by proposing *pro forma* amendments to "strike out the last word." This is simply a device by which members may get five minutes in which to speak. Debate, can, therefore, go on for a considerable period of time under the five-minute rule. Debate on an amendment can be stopped by either asking unanimous consent or moving that all debate on this amendment and amendments thereto end in ____ minutes, or end at ____ o'clock. If unanimous consent is not granted the floor manager generally looks to the Republican floor manager (or to the mover of the amendment) to see if time can be agreed upon. The Republican floor manager may then signal the number of minutes desired and the Democratic floor manager will modify his request. If the time can be worked out among the interested parties (respective party floor managers and the movers and opponents of amendments) others will not usually object to unanimous consent requests to close debate. Motions, rather than unanimous consent requests are avoided, if possible, because they have the appearance of shutting off the opposition from debate. Also, a motion may require a teller vote, which would consume about ten minutes. Under the latter circumstance the Democratic floor manager might just as well grant ten additional minutes for debate. It is to be noted, however, that debate on amendments and, as we shall see, on the entire bill, may be closed by simple motion requiring a majority vote. There is no opportunity in the House, as there is in the Senate, to filibuster. There are many opportunities for delay in the House, but not for preventing a bill, once on the floor, from coming to a vote.

When one amendment is disposed of the clerk continues to read and additional amendments are in order. Debate continues under the five-minute rule just discussed.

Voting on amendments in Committee of the Whole may be of three kinds: voice, division (standing), and teller. When debate under the five-minute rule for the amendment is completed, the chair will ask: "As many as are in favor will say aye (pause), opposed no (pause). In the opinion of the chair the ayes (or noes) have it." At that point any member may demand a division (standing vote). It is usually, of course, the losing side that asks for such a vote, and it may be had at the request of a single member. The chair then intones, "As many as are in favor will rise and remain standing until counted (pause while the chair counts). As many as are opposed will rise and remain standing until counted (pause while the chair counts). The results of this vote by division are ayes _____, noes _____, and the ayes (or noes) have it."

At this point one of three things may happen, depending upon how close the vote was and whether the sum of the ayes and nays add up to a quorum (100 or more). Assuming a quorum is present and the vote is relatively close, a demand for tellers is usually made. Any member may demand tellers but the demand must be seconded by 20 percent of a quorum, that is, 20 members. Again, the losing side will usually demand tellers. The chair then appoints the mover of the amendment to count the ayes and the opposition floor manager (or a leading opponent to the amendment) to count the noes. A single bell rings in the Capitol and House Office Buildings to announce a teller vote. The ayes then queue up in one of the side aisles and march up the middle aisle to be counted. The teller then reports the count to the chair and the noes file down the opposite side aisle and up the center aisle to be counted. The teller for the noes then reports his count. Late voters then file past and additional ayes and noes are reported. The chair then reports the vote: "On this vote by tellers the ayes are _____, and the nays are _____. The _____ have it and the amendment is (not) agreed to."

At this point, or at the end of a division, if a quorum is not present (i.e., if the sum of the ayes and noes does not add up to 100 or more) any member may object to the vote on the grounds that a quorum is not present and make a point of order that a quorum is not present. What is called an automatic roll-call vote then takes place. The clerk begins to call the roll, but instead of answering present, as with usual quorum calls, members vote aye or nay on the amendment. This process takes, as do most calls of the roll, about 25 to 35 minutes. As with other quorum calls three rings of the bells sound on the House side of the Capitol and the House Office Buildings. No other notice is given, however, that this is a roll-call vote and not simply a quorum call. Since members like to be recorded on roll-call votes the cloak-rooms are flooded with calls inquiring as to whether the bells mean an automatic roll-call or a simple quorum. Many of them trudge over to the floor anyway, either because they could not get the cloakroom, they want to be recorded on quorum calls as well as roll-call votes, they have some constituents in the office they want to get rid of, things are dull in the office and they would enjoy taking a walk and talking with others, or a number of other reasons. At the end of the automatic roll-call the vote is announced and all voting then ends.

If a quorum is present at the end of a division vote, the only motion that is in order is a demand for the tellers. If a quorum is present on a teller vote, no further voting is in order. Roll-call votes, then, can be had during Committee of the Whole only in the absence of a quorum.

Several points can be made about this system of voting. First, an amendment can be voted on more than once. If one side loses a voice vote it may demand a division. If a division is lost, 20 members may demand a teller vote. So at least three votes are possible if 20 members desire to have them. A roll-call vote is also possible if less than a quorum responded on the division or teller vote.

It is also possible to lose one vote and win the subsequent vote. That is, one side may win by voice vote, lose by standing vote, and win by tellers. The order is always voice to division to tellers (although division may be skipped) and never the reverse. The most important vote, of course, is the last vote by tellers. If a quorum is present, the teller vote is the last vote taken on the amendment. This is especially crucial because amendments which lose in the Committee of the Whole may not be voted on further. Amendments which win in Committee of the Whole may be voted on again when the Committee rises and reports back to the whole House. Not all votes go through the series of voice, division, and teller. Often, when an amendment either wins or loses by voice vote, voting will end there. Also quite often voting will end with a division. Teller votes are usually reserved for important amendments and amendments which are won or lost by close votes by either voice, division, or both.

Given this system of voting in Committee of the Whole, several interesting strategies are available to the members. In all cases except possibly a Republican President and a Democratic Congress (that is, a Democratic President and either a Democratic or Republican Congress, or a Republican President and a Republican Congress), a bill which is reported from a committee is usually a more conservative bill than the bill introduced at the request of the Administration. There are several exceptions to this including the 1964 and 1965 Civil Rights Bills as reported by the Judiciary Committee, and Medicare as reported by Ways and Means. All three were stronger than originally requested by the Administration. But generally, when changes are made by committees, they reduce rather than expand what the Administration requests. Changes have been made, amendments added, provisions deleted, in such a way that a majority of the committee found it acceptable. Usually those who are in opposition are located so that they can delay or possibly even prevent passage if their preferences are not taken into account.

Once the bill is reported, the floor manager is typically the chairman of either the committee or subcommittee having major responsibility for the bill. Very few floor managers are willing to see their bills changed on the floor. Even if they are opposed to certain provisions in the bill they may not want amendments to carry. It is a mark of skill and prestige for the committee (and floor manager) if the floor manager can get the bill accepted without many or major changes. There are, of course, exceptions to this generalization, such as Otto Passman and the President's annual foreign aid request, but normally floor managers honestly attempt to get the committee's bill through the floor with as few changes as possible.

Amendments will be offered to all major bills (assuming an open rule). With minor exceptions, these amendments will be suggested by those who wish to weaken the bill. In some instances liberals who lost in committee will attempt to restore parts of the bill which were deleted or changed, or will attempt to delete provisions which were added by the committee but which they feel weaken the bill. But for the most part the amending process is a process by which floor managers attempt to fend off and defeat weakening amendments.

Proponents of amendments, then, at least under Democratic Presidents, are usually Republicans and Southern Democrats. Opponents of amendments are usually Northern Democrats (plus some Southern Democrats and a few Republicans). Northern Democrats are notoriously poor attenders on the floor during Committee of the Whole proceedings. They are often in their offices seeing constituents or attending to other business. Republicans and Southern Democrats, on the other hand, are proportionately better attenders during Committee of the Whole proceedings. Hence, during the amendment process an advantage goes to the more conservative Republicans and Southern Democrats simply on the basis of numbers of people who are on the floor. The best strategy for proponents of amendments, then, is simply to have more people on the floor than the opponents of amendments. One of the most difficult tasks of most floor managers is in seeing to it that proponents of the legislation will stay around during Committee of the Whole to vote against weakening amendments.

Because of this "conservative bias" in Committee of the Whole several different mechanisms have been established to insure that Northern Democrats will be alerted to votes on the floor. The Democratic Study Group, a loose-knit organization of about 125 Northern Democrats (175 during the Eighty-ninth Congress), has a whip system of its own, independent of the Democratic whip office, which attempts to alert its members to important teller votes. This system operated quite effectively during the 1964 Civil Rights debate. Members are stationed on the floor and are responsible for alerting a certain number of other Democratic Study Group members to come to the floor for teller votes. The regular Democratic whip system also functions somewhat in this capacity. However, because teller votes take only about ten minutes, members must be alerted in advance if they are to come to the floor from their offices. On occasion, for example, the Speaker will ask the whip office to put out a whip call asking all Democratic members to come to the floor. Such a procedure probably requires 15 to 20 minutes. The offices of 18 assistant whips are alerted, and they in turn call the offices of the members within their zones.

On other occasions, when time is short, the Speaker will ask the head of the Democratic cloakroom to call the Capitol operators. The Capitol operators are then instructed to call every Democratic office and tell them that the Speaker requests their presence on the floor. Such a procedure would take about 5 to 10 minutes.

There are several ways in which all debate may be closed in Committee of the Whole. One is simply to allow debate to continue in its normal course. If the bill is short, or non-controversial, and few amendments are proposed, debate on amendments will simply come to an end relatively quickly. If, however, the bill is lengthy or controversial, and many amendments are proposed, the question of ending debate becomes important. Since most members are on tight schedules, the question of timing becomes quite important. If, for example, there is a meeting to which many supporters of the bill are planning to go, or if it is a Thursday afternoon when Northern Democrats are anxious to get to the airport or train station for their long weekend back in the district, then to prolong debate on the bill may mean that many of the supporters will not be there when it comes time to vote. If time is running short, the floor manager may limit debate in one of two ways. Either he can ask unanimous consent (or, if that fails, move) that debate on the present amendment and all amendments thereto end at a time certain. Or, if he chooses, he may ask unanimous consent (or move) that debate on this amendment and all amendments end at a time certain. When that time is reached amendments may still be voted on but they cannot be debated. The only notion that members have of what is being voted on is from the clerk's reading the amendment, and through informal discussion among the members. This procedure gets very involved and members are even more in the dark about what they are voting on than they usually are. The practice probably favors the committee bill since members are reluctant to support amendments to the committee bill (majority party members, anyway) unless they have good reason. In the absence of debate, "good reason" is difficult to establish. It is possible, however, for the majority to end debate and often, as time gets short toward the end of the day, the floor manager makes several motions to limit debate on specific amendments. Since it is rare for the House to spend more than one day on a bill, limited debate is used fairly often.

When all debate is ended and all amendments are disposed of, the Committee of the Whole rises and reports back to the House.

Several other rules and procedures in the Committee of the Whole bear on this discussion. First, amendments must be germane. The House has rather strict rules about attaching riders to bills, and has developed rather elaborate criteria for distinguishing between germane and non-germane amendments. When the leadership wishes to attach a non-germane amendment to a bill it must do so by a rule from the Rules Committee waiving points of order against the bill or by making a specific amendment in order. The Parliamentarian, who sits on the right-hand side of the Speaker just below the Speaker's dais, is present at all times to give counsel. Although the Speaker himself (or Chairman of the Committee of the Whole) rules on points of order, he rarely does so without consulting with the Parliamentarian. Rulings from the chair may be appealed in most instances, but such appeals are rarely made, and even more rarely successful. An appeal from the ruling of the chair would be considered an attack on the Speaker (or Chairman of the Committee of the Whole), and a vote on such an appeal would be, unless there were a revolution, a straight party vote.

It is also possible to defeat the bill outright in Committee of the Whole. A motion to recommit the bill is not in order in Committee of the Whole, but a motion to strike the enacting clause is in order. This is a preferential motion which must be considered immediately after it is made. Ten minutes of debate follows the motion (five minutes to each side), and then a vote. If the motion to strike the enacting clause carries (such a vote will undoubtedly be taken by tellers), the Committee of the Whole must raise. The House as a whole may then vote on the action by the Committee of the Whole, and if upheld, the bill is dead. If the House overturns the action of the Committee, the House then resolves itself back into the Committee of the Whole.

A motion to strike the enacting clause is an unusual event, but when used is surrounded with drama. During the floor debate in 1964 on the President's Anti-Poverty Bill, objection was heard to Phil Landrum's motion (the floor manager for the bill) to dispense with further reading of his substitute bill. The bill which Landrum wished to substitute for the bill approved and reported by the House Education and Labor Committee was a slightly modified version of the Senate-passed bill. The strategy was simply to put before the House a bill which had already been modified by the Senate in such a way that it would be more acceptable to Southern Democrats. It would then be possible to avoid a number of fights on the House floor over amendments which had already been accepted by the Senate. Avoiding such fights would not only save time, but might also prevent further amendments or amendments which cut even further into the Administration's proposals.

Landrum's substitute bill, however, was 67 pages long. Since a substitute bill is in the nature of an amendment, and since amendments must be read except if by unanimous consent the House determines otherwise, the substitute bill had to be read when objection was heard. It was known that it would take a reading clerk approximately three hours to read the entire bill. At this point, most Northern

Democrats drifted from the floor and back to their offices, expecting a long hiatus in the day's activity.

Landrum tried twice again to dispense with further reading of the substitute bill, but objection was heard each time. Unknown, however, to the Democratic leadership during the first hour of reading, the Republicans had a whip call summoning all Republican members to the floor. Judge Smith, who was strongly opposed to the bill, summoned opposition Southern Democrats to the floor. On the next attempt by Landrum to dispense with further reading of the substitute bill, the opposition was ready and waiting. No objection was heard to Landrum's request and further reading was dispensed with. Judge Smith then immediately sent a preferential motion to the desk to strike the enacting clause. Judge Smith spoke for five minutes against the bill, Landrum five minutes for the bill. On the vote by tellers, Judge Smith's motion to strike the enacting clause carried 170–135.

Finally alerted by Judge Smith's preferential motion, the Democratic leadership frantically sent out a whip call of its own, and slowly Northern Democrats began to appear on the floor. Not soon enough, however, to defeat the motion on tellers.

The Committee of the Whole then rose and reported their action back to the House. The leadership was now in full gear attempting to get its supporters back to the floor for a vote. The motion before the House was whether to accept the action taken in Committee of the Whole. On that motion Landrum demanded the yeas and nays, 20 percent of the members assented, and the clerk began to call the roll. If the motion carried on a roll-call, the bill was defeated.

The leadership needed time to get supporters to the floor. There are two reading clerks for the House, a clerk chosen by the Republican leadership and one chosen by the Democrats. Normally they alternate in the duty of reading. The Speaker designated the Democratic reading clerk to call the roll.

A roll-call vote normally takes about 25 minutes. On this roll-call, 50 minutes were consumed, as the Democratic reading clerk called each name slowly and deliberately. The result of the vote was announced by the Speaker, 197 for striking the enacting clause, 225 against. The leadership had won, but not without some trying moments.

This story is illustrative of a number of points. First, the Democrats had taken a poll on the Anti-Poverty Program and the poll indicated that although the vote would be close the leadership would probably win. But the poll was on what the members would do on final passage, not on a motion to strike the enacting clause. It was important for the opponents to try to defeat the bill on some motion other than on final passage.

Second, Landrum's substitute bill (a weaker bill than the one reported from Education and Labor) was not yet adopted by the House and amendments had not yet been offered and voted on. If the opponents could get a vote before the amending process made the bill more acceptable, they would have a better chance of winning.

Third, Northern Democrats, as we have already mentioned, have a bad habit of drifting off the floor. One can hardly blame them in some cases. To sit on the House floor for three hours while a bill is being read is not the most fruitful activity. The Southern Democratic-Republican conservative coalition knew this and tried to strike quickly in defeating the bill. And, of course, while in Committee of the Whole they did strike quickly. The teller vote was over before enough Northern Democrats had come back to the floor. It was only after an additional 50 minutes that enough supporters could be found to reverse the action taken in Committee of the Whole.

Fourth, this strategy worked out by Judge Smith with the Republicans was carefully planned and deftly executed. In this case, it required a delaying tactic on the part of the leadership to insure that enough Northern Democrats would return to the floor. It should also be reported that the action taken by the Southern Democrats and Republicans was a well-coordinated action which required planning and a good deal of communication. The so-called "conservative coalition" is, in some cases at least, more than an accident.

There are also less dramatic uses to which the preferential motion to strike the enacting clause may be put. During the amending process it sometimes occurs that many members want to speak on particular amendments. The Chairman of the Committee of the Whole recognizes members, giving preference to the leadership of both parties, the floor managers, and committee members before recognizing others. H. R. Gross, Republican of Iowa, became impatient one day, felt he was not given ample opportunity to talk, and to gain recognition sent a preferential motion to the desk to strike the enacting clause. This maneuver gave him the right to the floor, and he spoke against the pending bill. This is simply another illustration of how the rules may be used for purposes other than those intended.

When the bill has been read (and amended) in the Committee of the Whole, the Committee "rises," the Chairman steps in the well of the House, the Speaker returns to the dais, the mace is placed back in its pedestal (indicating that the Speaker is now in the Chair) and the House is now in the House of Representatives. A quorum reverts to 218. It is at this point that the House acts on the recommendations made in the Committee of the Whole.

It is interesting to note, in this respect, that amendments which have been rejected in Committee of the Whole are not reported, but amendments which have been accepted are reported. This means that once an amendment is defeated in Committee of the Whole it may not be voted on again (except as incorporated in a recommittal motion). Amendments which are adopted in Committee of the Whole may be voted on again and may be defeated by the House. Because this procedure gives special advantage to the committee reporting the legislation, an elaboration of the procedures involved will prove fruitful.

Section 336 of Jefferson's Manual (which, under Rule 42 of the House, states procedures for the House except as the Rules themselves amend or contradict them) specifies that "amendments rejected by the committee are not reported." The key word is "reported." Rejected amendments, because they are not reported by the Committee of the Whole, have no privileged status. Amendments accepted by the Committee are reported, and may, on the demand of any member, be voted upon separately. The usual practice, however, is for all of the amendments accepted by the Committee of the Whole to be voted upon *en bloc.*

Section 337 of Jefferson's Manual further specifies that "the fact that a proposition has been rejected by the Committee of the Whole does not prevent it from being offered as an amendment when the subject comes up in the House." So, theoretically at least, it is possible for rejected amendments to be brought up again in the House. However, they never are for the following reasons.

Rules from the Rules Committee generally take the following form: "That upon adoption of this resolution, etc. . . . At the conclusion of the consideration of the bill for amendment, the Committee shall rise and report the bill to the House with such amendments as may have been adopted, and the previous question shall be considered as ordered on the bill and amendments thereto to final passage without intervening motion except one motion to recommit." In

other words, the order for the previous question has already been
entered by the rule from the Rules Committee and no intervening
motions, such as motioning up defeated amendments, are in order.
When the Speaker assumes the chair and the House is in the House
of Representatives the first order of business as proposed by the
Speaker under the rule is: "Under the rule, the previous question is
ordered. The question is on the amendments" (if there are any). It is
at this point that amendments adopted in the Committee of the
Whole are voted on. The next order of business as put by the Speaker
is: "The question is on engrossment and third reading of the bill." It
is at this point that a motion to recommit is in order (to be discussed shortly). Hence, debate has been cut off immediately after the
Committee of the Whole rises because the rule from the Rules Committee orders the previous question. In this way only amendments
adopted in the Committee of the Whole may be voted on in the
House.

As we have suggested, however, not all bills need rules from the
Rules Committee for privilege to the floor. For example, general
appropriation bills do not require rules and, in fact, are usually considered without a rule unless special circumstances require a closed
rule or a rule waiving points of order. In a situation where a rule from
the Rules Committee is not involved, the procedures are somewhat
different, but with the same effect. Section 337 of Jefferson's Manual
specifies that "when a bill is reported with amendments, it is in order
to submit additional amendments, but the first question is on the
committee amendments; but the opportunity to debate or make additional amendments depends on the will of the House as expressed on
a motion for the previous question." Here again, theoretically, additional amendments (including defeated amendments) are in order
after the Committee of the Whole rises, but again in practice the
previous question cuts off additional amendments. What happens is
that after the Committee rises the Speaker recognizes the floor manager (who, by custom, is privileged to first recognition). The floor
manager for the bill then moves the previous question. This motion
is usually adopted *pro forma* by unanimous consent. If a person or
group wanted to vote on defeated amendments, however, they would
have to defeat this motion for the previous question. The motion for
the previous question has the effect of cutting off debate, and thus
further amendments (besides those already adopted by the Committee) are not in order. After voting on amendments accepted by the

Committee of the Whole the question is then on engrossment and third reading of the bill, and then a recommittal motion is in order before final passage. It is possible for the recommittal motion to incorporate as instructions amendments which have been defeated in Committee of the Whole.

The fact that rejected amendments are not voted on in the House, but amendments adopted in Committee of the Whole are, gives a double advantage to the leadership. As we have previously indicated, most amendments are weakening amendments. Amendments are usually attempts to give special treatment to some group or groups, to cut the amount of money authorized or appropriated, to add conditions under which the money may be spent, to take out whole titles of bills, etc. If the leadership can defeat these moves in Committee of the Whole, they are defeated for that bill. If, however, they are adopted in Committee of the Whole, they may be rejected by the whole House. It should be noted, however, that rarely are amendments adopted in Committee of the Whole defeated in the House. Occasionally, if the amendment is particularly serious (such as striking the enacting clause of the Anti-Poverty Program) the House will reverse the action taken by the Committee of the Whole, but such reversals are the exception rather than the rule.

This whole set of procedures just described, however, is probably the most glaring example of how the rules and procedures of the House can favor the leadership. Most discussions of rules and procedures point out how the rules are unfair to the leadership. This is one example where clearly the reverse is true.

After the amendments adopted in Committee of the Whole have been voted on (usually *en bloc* and *pro forma*), the question before the House is on engrossment and third reading of the bill. An "engrossed" copy of the bill is a copy on parchment exactly as it passed the House, with amendments included. Before the rules changes adopted at the beginning of the Eighty-ninth Congress (1965–66) any member could demand that an engrossed copy be physically present. If such a demand were made, a delay of several hours would ensue while the bill was being prepared on parchment, and usually the House would adjourn until the following day. For example, Representative Goodell (Republican of New York) demanded an engrossed copy of the 1964 Anti-Poverty Bill, and the House had to adjourn until the following morning (which was a Saturday).

This demand for an engrossed copy often puts the leadership in a quandary. Either they could wait the number of hours necessary to prepare an engrossed copy (and possibly lose a number of supporters of the bill) or adjourn until the next day (and again possibly lose a number of supporters of the bill). Unless it is clear that the bill will not pass, the demand for an engrossed copy works against the leadership. Although it is rare for such a demand to be made, it does occur occasionally on important pieces of legislation.

If, as is usually the case, an engrossed copy of the bill is not demanded, the motion for engrossment and third reading of the bill is usually approved *pro forma*.

On January 4, 1965 when the First Session of the Eighty-ninth Congress convened the House of Representatives put an end to the ability of a single member to delay passage of a bill by insisting upon an engrossed copy of the bill. Among the three rules changes which were adopted by a vote of 224–201 was a rule, proposed by the Speaker and adopted earlier by the Democratic caucus, to allow engrossment of the bill by a majority vote and taking away the privilege of a single member demanding a physically engrossed copy. Hence this delaying tactic, seldom used but a nuisance to the leadership and an inconvenience to members, was abandoned.

After the vote on engrossment and third reading of the bill (third reading is by title only) a motion to recommit the bill to the Committee from which it was reported is in order, and may be offered by anyone who is opposed to the bill. A motion to recommit is a highly privileged motion and may not be abridged, even by a rule from the Rules Committee.

There are two forms of recommittal motions: (1) a simple motion to recommit the bill, and (2) a motion to recommit with instructions to report back to the House "forthwith" the bill with amendments. A simple motion to recommit, if it carries, defeats the bill at that time, although it is possible for the committee, at a later date, to re-report the bill to the House for another try. For example, on February 26, 1964 the House voted, 208–188, to recommit H. R. 9022 to amend the International Development Association Act to authorize the United States to participate in an increase in the resources of the International Development Association. The Banking and Currency Committee re-reported the bill, and on May 13, 1964, a motion to recommit the bill a second time was defeated 247–132. The bill then passed on a voice vote.

A motion to recommit a bill with instructions to report back forthwith, with amendments, is a motion often used by the Republicans to offer an alternative program. The motion very often will incorporate a number of the amendments which have been offered to the bill in Committee of the Whole but which have been defeated. However, a motion to recommit with instructions is not limited to defeated amendments, and any changes, as long as they are germane, are in order in such a motion.

An interesting situation occurs when a bill is being considered under a closed rule. No amendments, except Committee amendments, are in order under a closed rule, including possible liberalizing amendments by Northern Democrats who will support the bill but would prefer a stronger bill. However, as has been mentioned, the right of the opposition to offer a motion to recommit is highly privileged. What occurs, then, is that the opposition has an opportunity to amend the bill but the proponents do not. Normally, however, motions to recommit, with or without instructions, are defeated. The International Development Association bill was the only bill in 1964, for example, to be recommitted.

If a motion to recommit with instructions carries, the bill as amended by the instructions is reported back to the House immediately and is then voted on. If the recommittal motion is defeated, as is usually the case, the question is then on final passage of the bill.

Most pieces of major legislation which come before the House are made subject to a recommittal motion, usually with instructions. This motion is offered by the opposition in an attempt to modify the program. It is sometimes the case that a motion to recommit is considered more important than the vote on final passage. For example, in 1962 on the Republican motion to recommit the Trade Expansion Bill with instructions simply to continue the reciprocal trade program for another year, and in 1963 on the Republican motion to recommit the tax bill and tie the $11-billion tax cut to reduced governmental spending, the recommittal vote was considerably closer than the vote on final passage.[2] Often there are roll-call votes on the motion to recommit, and when that fails, a simple voice vote on final passage. Defections will often occur among Southern Democrats who, although on final passage will support the bill, would prefer the Republican alternative.

[2] Lewis A. Froman, Jr. and Randall B. Ripley, "Conditions for Party Leadership: The Case of the House Democrats," *American Political Science Review*, vol. 59 (March, 1965), pp. 52–64.

After the motion to recommit (assuming it fails), the next order of business is final passage. If there has been a roll-call on the recommittal motion, if it is late in the day, and if a number of members are restless and anxious to leave, there may not be a roll-call vote on final passage. However, if 20 percent of the members demand it, a roll-call vote may be ordered. It is also possible, as we mentioned earlier, to have an automatic roll-call if a quorum is not present on a non-roll-call vote. An interesting case took place on the second round of the pay-raise bill in 1964. The first time the pay-raise bill was brought before the House it included increases for executive officials, federal judges, and congressmen and their staffs. There were attempts to strike out the pay increases for congressmen while the bill was being amended in Committee of the Whole. Since such votes are non-record votes, attempts to do away with congressional increases failed. But when the bill was reported back to the House a roll-call vote was demanded by 20 percent of the members and, on this record vote, the pay-raise bill failed.

The second time it was brought to the floor (slightly changed but still including a $7,500 pay raise for congressmen rather than the original $10,000), attempts were made to avoid a roll-call vote. Very near the end of the Committee of the Whole the floor manager for the bill, James Morrison of Louisiana, suggested the absence of a quorum. The roll was called and most members came to the floor. The purpose of this quorum was to avoid an automatic roll-call vote because of the absence of a quorum on a vote when the Committee of the Whole rose and reported to the full House. The move was successful. An attempt was then made by the opponents to demand a roll-call, but the Speaker ruled that an insufficient number had risen. Some observers felt that it was quite close, but on a count of the House, the chair's ruling is never appealed. A roll-call was avoided and the bill passed easily by a voice vote. This is another example of how quorum calls may be used for purposes other than those intended.

After the vote on final passage, most members leave. There are usually, following the end of legislative business, a number of "special orders." Some time during morning business before the start of the legislative day members may address the chair and ask unanimous consent to speak for a certain length of time on a specified day. These speeches are usually discussions of various problems which members would like to have recorded in the *Congressional Record*. Occasionally there will be a controversial speech, but it may be stopped quite simply by suggesting the absence of a quorum. Most members will have left for the day and a quorum would be impossible to muster. These speeches, then, are simply statements by members to be read in the *Congressional Record*. The Republicans, for example, have developed the practice of giving weekly speeches on various contemporary domestic and foreign problems. After special orders, the House adjourns.

CHAPTER FIVE

Alternative Procedures
in the House

In the last two chapters we have attempted to describe what might be called the "normal" legislative process in the House of Representatives. By "normal" is meant that this is the way things usually happen. Through unilateral action, anticipated reaction, simple and time logrolling, compromise, and side-payments, coalitions are formed and perhaps reformed at each legislative stage.

But what happens when an intense minority within one of these legislative steps is able to delay or prevent a bill from coming to the House floor? The two major points at which such delay or defeat may take place are the legislative committees and the Committee on Rules. Assuming that the normal methods of bargaining fail, proponents of legislation must turn to extraordinary methods, procedures which will allow them to bring to the attention of the whole House legislative proposals which are being held up at these two crucial points in the normal decision-making process.

DISCHARGE RULE

There is, essentially, only one procedure by which the whole House may prevent delay or defeat by legislative committees (aside from various forms of bargaining or other informal pressures which may help to dislodge bills from reluctant committees). This is the procedure of discharging a committee of a bill. If a bill has been referred to a legislative committee for 30 days without its having been reported, it is in order for any member to file a discharge petition. The petition lies at the desk for signatures of members. A discharge petition requires the signatures of a majority of the House membership (218) before further action may take place.

If 218 members sign a discharge petition it then goes on the Discharge Calendar which is privileged business the second and fourth Mondays of each month. When the bill has been on the Calendar of Motions to Discharge Committees for seven days, it is in order on the correct Monday for any member who has signed the petition to move that the committee be discharged of its consideration of the bill in question. Debate is for 20 minutes, divided equally between proponents and opponents, after which a vote is in order. If the motion to discharge the committee is adopted, it is then in order for any member who has signed the petition to move the immediate consideration of the bill which has been discharged. If the motion carries, it shall then be in order to consider the bill under the general rules of the House. If consideration of the bill is left unfinished at adjournment, it shall become the unfinished business of the House until disposed of. If the House votes against immediate consideration, or the motion for immediate consideration is not made, the bill goes to the appropriate calendar to which it would have been referred had the committee reported the bill and it has the same privilege as if it had been reported. If the motion to discharge the committee is defeated, no further motion to discharge any committee of a substantially similar bill may be acted upon during that session of Congress.

The utility of the discharge rule is very difficult to assess. Measured by the number of times it has resulted in legislation, it has not been of much use at all. For example, Robinson reports that between 1937 and 1960 more than 200 discharge petitions were filed. Of these, 22 received a sufficient number of signatures to go on the Calendar. Fourteen of the 22 were passed by the House, but only two, the Fair Labor Standards Act of 1938 and the Federal Pay Raise Act of 1960, became law.[1] Indeed, since the discharge rule first came into effect in 1910, these are the only two instances of bills becoming laws via this route.[2] In September, 1965, 218 signatures were collected to discharge the District of Columbia Committee of a bill

---

[1] James A. Robinson, *The House Rules Committee* (Indianapolis: Bobbs-Merrill, 1963), pp. 6 and 33.
[2] George B. Galloway, *The Legislative Process in Congress* (New York: Crowell, 1953), p. 540.

which would provide home rule for Washington, D.C. Passed by the Senate five times in recent years, home rule for the District of Columbia has been bottled up in the southern and conservative controlled House District of Columbia Committee. The bill was successfully discharged but a considerably weakened substitute was adopted on the floor and the issue was essentially buried for another year.

There may be three interpretations of the apparent lack of success of the discharge petition. First, it may be that it is simply not a very effective technique whereby a majority may take a bill away from a minority (a committee) which is blocking it. Second, it may be a very effective technique but its major use is not in actually discharging committees but in threatening to discharge committees. In this case it would be useful to know the number of times members have threatened to use the discharge and the number of times the committee chairman or other committee members have given in to the threat. And third, it may be that the discharge petition is not successful because minorities in the House seldom hold up bills which a majority would pass. Many of the bills which have had discharge petitions filed against them may be bills which a minority in the House favors.

To test each of these alternatives is not possible within the confines of this book and indeed such tests would present very difficult obstacles. How, for example, would a person know whether a majority favored a bill, or whether it was simply favored by a minority, if there were no action taken on the floor of the House? A lack of 218 signatures may be *ipso facto* evidence that a majority did not favor the bill, but then the proposition that the discharge petition is an effective method of majority rule becomes little more than a tautology. In addition, such an argument does not take into account either the problem of intensity of preference or informal restraints which may be at work in the House to prevent the use of "unusual" procedures such as the discharge petition. It is important, however, to raise the question of interpretation of this data, since it is not clear exactly what the data mean.

At this point, however, we can say that each of the three previously stated interpretations probably has some substance. First, the discharge petition probably is not a very effective way in which a bill may be taken away from a committee which is blocking it. Such action is opposed to the reciprocity principle which is of great importance as a system of coordination in the House. The requirement of 218 signatures is a stiff requirement, and members are naturally reluctant to sign unless they feel quite intensely about the bill and are willing to alienate members of other committees, and especially the chairman of the committee which is holding up the bill.

Second, it is undoubtedly the case that the threat of a successful discharge petition often spurs committees to action. A most recent example of this occurred in 1964 with respect to the prayer amendment. Since the Supreme Court decision in 1962 that prayers in public schools violated the first amendment of the Constitution there have been many bills and constitutional amendments introduced in Congress to try to overturn this decision. The Judiciary Committee in the House, chaired by Emanuel Celler of New York, a champion of the Supreme Court decision, refused to hold hearings on these bills and amendments. Representative Becker of New York filed a discharge petition for his constitutional amendment to allow prayers in the public schools and the petition collected approximately 170 signatures. At this point Chairman Celler called hearings. As it turned out, the testimony by religious and other groups was heavily against the Becker amendment or indeed any interference with the decision of the Supreme Court, so the matter was dropped for lack of support. However, Chairman Celler was goaded into calling hearings by the existence of the discharge petition.

Third, on inspection of the many bills which have had discharge petitions filed against them, many would probably not have majority support, at least intense majority support. But this is simply a matter of conjecture since no data are available concerning the support among House members for or against these bills.

Additional Methods of By-passing Legislative Committees

The discharge petition is the major instrument whereby majorities, at least under certain conditions, are able to by-pass or threaten to by-pass legislative committees. There are two other methods, however, by which legislative committees may be circumvented.

First, the Rules Committee is empowered to report to the floor any legislation which it chooses to report, whether or not a committee has reported it, and whether or not it has even been introduced. This route of bringing bills to the floor, as one might expect, has been little used. The major reason being that, by and large, the

Rules Committee is a somewhat conservative body and, by the very nature of its being so, usually does not favor legislation. The major function of conservative bodies is, on the whole, to protect the *status quo*. Thus, one of their activities is to try to block legislation, not promote it.

However, occasionally, positive legislative actions may promote the cause of conservatism rather than hinder it. There were two such cases in 1964. These two actions followed the decision by the Supreme Court that both houses of state legislatures must be apportioned on the basis of population. This action by the Supreme Court struck at one of the strongholds of the conservatives, to wit, over-representation of rural areas in state legislatures. Two bills were discharged by the Rules Committee which the Judiciary Committee refused to report: (1) the Tuck Bill, which would take from the federal courts jurisdiction to hear cases involving apportionment of state legislatures, and (2) a constitutional amendment introduced by Wright Patman of Texas which would overturn the decision of the Supreme Court by making it constitutional for one house of the state legislature to be apportioned on criteria other than population. The Tuck Bill was reported favorably by the Rules Committee 10–4 and passed the House 218–175. A motion to consider it in the Senate was defeated, 56–21. The constitutional amendment was reported by the Rules Committee on a vote of 8–3, but because two-thirds rather than a simple majority is required to pass constitutional amendments and because the conservatives knew they did not have the necessary votes, it was never called up in the House.

These examples do illustrate, however, what the Rules Committee *can* do, and what a difference it can make whether the Rules Committee is controlled by the leadership or by a possible conservative coalition. If the Rules Committee were controlled by the leadership essentially *any* bill desired by the leadership could reach the floor for a vote, whether or not it had been reported by a committee, and even regardless of whether it had been introduced.

But this power of the Rules Committee to discharge legislative committees is little used. Besides these two cases in 1964, only twice before since 1937 had the Rules Committee exercised this power. Once in 1946 on a bill which would allow the drafting of striking workmen into the armed services, and again in 1953 on the Excess Profits Extension Bill.[3]

[3] Robinson, *op. cit.*, p. 29.

A third way in which legislative committees may, in effect, be discharged of bills under their jurisdiction (besides the discharge petition and action by the Rules Committee) will be the subject of considerable discussion in Chapter Nine. Briefly, however, it is by adding to a House-passed bill a non-germane Senate amendment. Such a bill, when it is returned to the House, may be sent directly to a conference committee with the Senate without having to go to a legislative committee.

BY-PASSING THE RULES COMMITTEE

The second point at which most criticism of rules and procedures is directed is the Rules Committee. The Rules Committee is able to prevent bills from going to the floor for a vote. In some cases they may do this as a favor to the leadership, in other cases as a favor to some other group. And, it is undoubtedly true that occasionally the Rules Committee will hold up a bill that is preferred by a majority of the membership. Under such circumstances what alternatives are open to the proponents of the legislation in question?

There are a number of ways in which bills may by-pass the Committee on Rules in the normal legislative process. Private bills, for example, do not go to the Rules Committee. Non-controversial bills on the Consent Calendar or under Suspension of the Rules also avoid the Rules Committee. Some bills of some committees are privileged without a rule. But aside from these "normal" methods, there are essentially three methods by which bills, which must ordinarily be given a rule from the Committee on Rules to be privileged on the floor, may reach the floor without such a rule.

As with legislative committees, the Committee on Rules may be discharged of bills pending before it. The procedure is the same as with legislative committees except that only 7 rather than 30 days are required before the discharge petition can be filed. Such a procedure requires 218 signatures on a discharge petition and then a majority vote on the floor, the same procedure as with legislative committees.

Calendar Wednesday. A second way in which non-privileged bills may be brought to the floor without going to the Committee on Rules is through the procedure known as Calendar Wednesday. Each Wednesday immediately after reading the *Journal* a call of the committees is privileged business. Committees are listed in alphabetical order. When a committee is reached it may call up a bill on either the Union or House Calendar which is not otherwise privileged. Bills on the Union Calendar are considered in the Committee of the Whole. There are two hours of general debate, equally divided, and then amendments are in order under the five-minute rule.

There are several difficulties connected with the procedure which make it cumbersome and little used. Actually, Calendar Wednesday is usually dispensed with by unanimous consent. Such a request is almost always agreed to. For example, in 1964 there were no calls of the Calendar under Calendar Wednesday. In 1963 unanimous consent to dispense with Calendar Wednesday was refused only once. This was an attempt by the Republicans to use Calendar Wednesday to bring up the Civil Rights Bill. Since only two hours of general debate are allowed, and since the bill must be finished the same day (it cannot become the unfinished business unless debate has been concluded and the previous question has been ordered), the Democrats perceived this as an attempt to bring up the bill under very unfavorable circumstances. Carl Albert, the majority leader, moved to adjourn, and the motion carried along straight party lines. During the Eighty-seventh Congress (1961–62) an education bill was brought to the floor under Calendar Wednesday proceedings but was defeated. The last time the procedure was used successfully was in May of 1960.

The formal difficulties connected with Calendar Wednesday are many. First, since the committees must be called in alphabetical order the committee which is eleventh in order may have to wait eleven weeks for its turn. Committees further down the list may have to wait even longer.

Second, the bill must be taken up and considered in one day. The large number of delaying tactics which are available to the opposition (reading the *Journal* in full, quorum calls, votes to dispense with further proceedings under the call of the roll, points of order) plus the fact that the bill must also survive a motion (and hence a vote) to consider it even after the committee has been reached, all militate against the use of Calendar Wednesday as a practical procedure.

Third, if a committee has had one Calendar Wednesday it may not have another until all other committees have been called. Hence, if more than one bill is being delayed, it is a long wait.

Fourth, not every member is privileged to call up the bill. Generally, the chairman may call up any bill not otherwise privileged which has been reported by his committee. For any other member of the committee to do so, he must have approval by the committee. The cooperation of the chairman, therefore, is usually required in using this procedure.

For these reasons, Calendar Wednesday is little used and a not very successful method of circumventing the Rules Committee.

The 21-Day Rule. On January 4, 1965, besides adopting the rule which allows a majority of the House to send a bill to conference with the Senate, and the rule which does away with the necessity of an engrossed copy of a bill being physically present, the House adopted a third rule change which strengthens the hand of the Speaker and the leadership and will help to prevent delay and obstruction. This is the so-called "21-Day Rule" which allows the Speaker, in his discretion, to recognize the chairman, or any member of the committee so authorized, to call up a resolution which has been pending before the Committee on Rules for 21 days but which has either been acted upon negatively by the Committee, or which has not been acted upon by the Committee. Recognition by the Speaker would be in order on the second and fourth Mondays of each month, the same days as discharge motions.

Most observers of the House of Representatives feel that this is an extremely important and powerful change in the rules of the House. And for good reason. This rule makes it easier to by-pass the Committee on Rules if it is either delaying *or* obstructing bills reported from legislative committees to be reported to the floor. And, unlike the 21-Day Rule which was in effect for the Eighty-first Congress (1949–1950), it places discretion in the hands of the Speaker, not the committee chairman, to determine which bills will be reported to the floor by this procedure and which bills will not.[4] The Rules Committee is not entirely uncooperative with the leadership and many bills which are held up by the Committee are held up at the request of the leadership, not against the wishes of the leadership. Some of these bills are favored by the leadership but the votes for their passage are not yet available. Others are bills which the leadership does not support. The Quality Stabilization Bill previously dis-

[4] See Robinson, *op. cit.*, p. 34 & Chap. 4, for a discussion of the old 21-Day Rule, and Joseph S. Clark, *Congress: The Sapless Branch* (New York: Harper & Row, 1964), p. 135.

cussed, which, in effect, is a national fair trade or price-fixing act, was held up by the Committee on Rules at the request of the leadership because the leadership did not want the bill to come onto the floor. It was opposed by President Kennedy and it was opposed by President Johnson. Under the old 21-Day Rule, which lasted from 1949 to 1951, the Chairman of the Interstate and Foreign Commerce Committee, from which the Quality Stabilization Bill was reported, would have been empowered to call up the bill. Under the present, revised rule, it is in the Speaker's discretion to determine recognition for such a purpose.

The adoption of this rule, and placing the discretion for its use in the hands of the Speaker, was felt to be significant for two major reasons. First, the 21-Day Rule is a very simple procedure which undoubtedly reduced the power of the Committee on Rules to delay and obstruct bills favored by the leadership. Even the old 21-Day Rule, which was a good deal less "leadership oriented" than the present rule was directly responsible for eight bills, seven of which passed, reaching the floor in opposition to the Rules Committee. These bills included anti-poll tax legislation, Hawaiian and Alaskan statehood, minimum wage, and housing. It is also quite possible that, indirectly, the 21-Day Rule forced the Committee to report other legislation which it might not have wanted to except for the threat of a successful 21-Day Rule use.

The second major reason for the importance of the 21-Day Rule, especially in its present form, is the increased power of the Speaker which the rule grants. Most criticisms of the distribution of power within the House center around the high degree of decentralization of power which exists, both because of the existence of weak political parties at the national level and the power of the committees over legislation. Interestingly, many look with fondness back to the day of Speaker Cannon and the immense centralization of power which existed in the Speakership until 1910. Any reform, then, which "returns" power to the Speaker and works against the decentralized power structure is greeted by many with enthusiasm.

During the First Session of the Eighty-ninth Congress (1965), the first year under the newly adopted 21-Day Rule, six bills successfully came to the floor of the House via this route. These six were the repeal of section 14b of the Taft-Hartley Act which permits state "right to work" laws, a school construction bill, a bill to broaden the 1964 Civil Rights Act in the field of employment discrimination, a government employees' salary increase, an amendment to the Bank Holding Company Act, and a bill to establish a National Foundation on the Arts and Humanities. Five of the six passed the House, but due to Senate inaction only three became public law.[5]

The high probability that the 21-Day Rule would be an effective deterrent and antidote to the power of the Committee on Rules, plus the increased power which was placed in the hands of the Speaker, made the new 21-Day Rule an important event.

On January 10, 1967, the opening day of the Ninetieth Congress (1967–68), the House of Representatives voted 233–185 to repeal the 21-Day Rule. The major factor producing this outcome was the large Republican gain in congressional seats in November, 1966. Republican support (157–26 for repeal), combined with a large contingent of Southern Democrats (69–18) brought about repeal. Only 7 of 148 Northern Democrats voted with the majority.[6] As in 1949–50, the 21-Day Rule remained in effect for only two years.

[5] *Congressional Quarterly Weekly Report,* #46 (Nov. 12, 1965), pp. 2323–2325.

[6] *Congressional Quarterly Weekly Report,* #2 (Jan. 13, 1967), pp. 39 and 84.

CHAPTER SIX

Pre-floor Rules
and Procedures in the Senate

In this and the following two chapters we shall discuss the effects of rules and procedures in the Senate, strategies and tactics based on these rules and procedures, and comparisons between how things are done in the Senate and how things are done in the House of Representatives. This chapter will be concerned with the normal legislative process up to floor consideration of legislation. The next chapter will discuss the normal legislative process on the floor of the Senate, and Chapter Eight will be concerned with what happens when the so-called "normal" legislative process breaks down and "unusual" rules and procedures are employed.

INTRODUCTION OF BILLS

Bills are introduced in the Senate during the morning hour (to be explained in the next chapter) just after the Senate convenes. Senate practice, however, requires that the members introducing bills be on the floor, gain recognition, and formally introduce bills. The smaller size of the Senate makes this a more feasible practice there than in the House where members need only drop their bills into the hopper for introduction. Senators also introduce fewer bills because, unlike House members, senators may co-sponsor legislation thus avoiding the necessity of many senators introducing identical bills.

When a senator introduces a bill, he will often attempt to get as many co-sponsors as he is able. Co-sponsorship, it is felt, will help the bill along its legislative journey as well as allow senators themselves to claim credit for legislation as "sponsors." Before introducing a bill a senator will often circulate it among interested colleagues for their support. At the time of formal introduction on the Senate floor he may ask that it lie at the desk for a specified number of days before referral to a committee so that additional co-sponsors may sign it. After the bill has been referred, additional co-sponsors may be added by unanimous consent.

This practice of co-sponsorship of legislation can produce a number of interesting situations. It may happen, for example, that a senator will co-sponsor a piece of legislation and then be forced (for one reason or another) to vote against it on the floor. Such happened on one bill to Hubert Humphrey when he was majority whip. An early co-sponsor, Humphrey found that his role as majority whip (where he was subject to strong Administration pressures) and his own personal preferences conflicted. The Administration did not support the bill which Humphrey co-sponsored and Senator Humphrey voted against the bill he had originally helped to introduce.

Senators, for other reasons, also have certain restraints placed on them in this co-sponsorship of legislation. It is possible for an opponent in an election, for example, to find out what legislation the senator has co-sponsored. A simple tally of the amount of money involved in such sponsorship may prove embarrassing to a senator in his campaign. Since a senator knows that very few bills which are introduced will become law he may prefer to put his approval on a bill only after it seems to have a reasonable chance to succeed.

Even with the practice of co-sponsorship, an enormous number of bills are introduced in the Senate each year. In the Eighty-eighth Congress (1963–64), for example, senators introduced a total of 3,947 bills and resolutions.

Senators, like House members, will introduce bills for a wide variety of reasons. In many cases bills are introduced simply because influential constituents would like them introduced. This is especially true if such bills would cost little or no money. Major pieces of legislation, however, are introduced by committee or subcommittee chairmen for the Administration. As in the House, these are the bills which receive the major attention of the Senate.

REFERRAL TO COMMITTEES

Rule XXV of the Senate sets out the jurisdictions of the sixteen Senate Standing Committees. Bills are referred to the Standing Committees by the President of the Senate (the Vice President), the President Pro-Tempore, or whoever happens to be presiding officer at the time. Because committees have relatively fixed jurisdictions there is little dispute over which bill goes to which committee. Occasionally, however, bills may overlap jurisdictions. This occurred in 1964 when the Agriculture Committee reported a Food For Peace bill involving disposal of surplus food. The House had amended the program to the effect that loans to buy food for Poland and Yugoslavia must be paid back in U.S. dollars rather than in local currency. The Senate accepted the House amendment in conference committee. Senator Fulbright, Chairman of the Foreign Relations Committee, objected to the conference report on the grounds that this was a matter of foreign affairs and the Agriculture Committee had no business determining policy in such matters. However, on a motion to refer the bill to the Foreign Relations Committee for study, the Senate voted against Fulbright's motion.

There is inevitably an occasional dispute as to committee jurisdiction. These disputes, if not settled informally among the chairmen of the committees involved, may break out into a floor fight. In this case the presiding officer makes a ruling and it may be appealed to the whole Senate, in which case a majority of the Senate determines which committee gets the bill. To avoid this type of showdown a bill will sometimes be referred to several committees (a practice not allowed in the House). This practice not only avoids open breaches, but also helps to build a consensus around the bill. If committees differ as to the provisions which ought to be in the bill, votes on the floor settle the differences.

Since there is some discretion in the referral process there are, as in the House, attempts to write bills so they will be sent to one committee rather than to another. A large portion of the Civil Rights Bill of 1964, for example, was sent to the Commerce Committee rather than to the Judiciary Committee because the interstate commerce clause of the Constitution was used as a justification and legal backing for the bill. This was to avoid having the bill delayed in the Judiciary Committee, chaired by Senator Eastland of Mississippi.

Committees and Subcommittees

As in the House of Representatives, nearly all bills are referred to committees (exceptions will be noted in Chapter Eight). But unlike the House, senators are members, on the average, of three committees rather than just one. And often the number of subcommittees reaches six to eight. Senator Clark gives this description of his day between the hours of 10:00 and 12:00 A.M. when most committees meet.

One morning late in November, 1963, I had four committee meetings at ten o'clock. One was a hearing before the Subcommittee of the Labor Committee on Manpower and Employment, of which I am chairman, where witnesses from the Defense Department were to testify on the impact of defense contracts on employment and unemployment. Another was a hearing at which Senator Fulbright and Secretary of the Treasury Dillon were to appear in opposition to the Mundt bill prohibiting the Export-Import Bank from insuring credits extended by banks to grain dealers selling wheat to Russia. While this hearing was before the full Committee on Banking and Currency, it ordinarily would have been held before the Subcommittee on International Finance, of which I am chairman. Since Senator Robertson, the chairman of the full Committee, favored the Mundt bill and I opposed it, and the vote on the bill in the committee was sure to be close, I felt it important to hear all the testimony and interrogate the witnesses.* [*The vote was 8–7 against the bill, which was reported to the Senate with a recommendation that it not pass and was defeated by a vote of 55–37.]

The third meeting was an executive session of the Rules Committee on the Bobby Baker case, where important questions of procedure were to be decided. The fourth was a meeting of the Special Committee on Problems of the Aging.

In the end I persuaded Senator Randolph to chair the Employment hearings, and I read later the prepared statements of the witnesses. I notified the Aging Committee staff that I could not be present, and spent the morning running back and forth between the fifth floor of the New Senate Office Building and the third floor of the Old Senate Office Building, picking up as much about wheat sales to Russia and Bobby Baker's fabulous career as I could.

Enough has been said to make the point that the present committee assignment load on Senators, even as far down the seniority list as I—and I am No. 50 as these words are written—is heavier than it ought to be. On senior Senators it is much too heavy to permit effective service.[1]

[1] Joseph S. Clark, *Congress: The Sapless Branch* (New York: Harper, Row, 1964), pp. 187–88.

Because of this huge workload a single senator or a small number of senators on a committee or subcommittee will handle most of the work connected with any given bill. Other senators will participate when they can, but unless there is strong and intense interest in a bill, most members will specialize on only a few of the many bills which come before their committees and subcommittees. It is not uncommon to attend a hearing before a Senate committee at which only one or two senators are present. Other members of the committee are not home sleeping; it is more likely that they are attending committee meetings too, with only one or two of their colleagues present there.

Table VIII provides a list of committees, committee ratios, committee chairmen, and number of subcommittees in the Senate for the Eighty-ninth Congress (1965–66).[2]

As in the House of Representatives, committee chairmen in the Senate have a great deal of power. But for a number of reasons the difference in power between chairmen and non-chairmen in the Senate is not as large as it is in the House. Although chairmen are empowered to call meetings, determine the agenda, schedule witnesses, recognize members, establish subcommittees, and appoint members of the committee to subcommittees, their actions are much less likely to be arbitrary or to violate the interests of other senators. The major reason for this greater equality in the Senate has already been suggested. Almost all senators are in some position of influence: each is a member of at least one important committee; each (except for very junior members) is probably a subcommittee chairman; each may have control over some staff. The rules of comity are also stricter in the Senate than in the House. Senators are not usually denied or cut short in the questioning of committee witnesses, for example. Nor will chairmen deny recognition to other committee members. They may attempt to delay by scheduling an inordinate number of witnesses, or by postponing and canceling committee hearings and meetings, but a persistent senator, if he is supported by a majority of the committee, can usually get consideration of his measures before the committee.

The principle of seniority with respect to subcommittees is also followed more strictly in the Senate than in the House. Senators are often appointed to a subcommittee of their choice, for example,

---

[2] *Congressional Quarterly Weekly Report,* #18 (April 30, 1965), Part I (Washington, D.C.: Congressional Quarterly Service, 1965).

TABLE VIII
SENATE COMMITTEES — EIGHTY-NINTH CONGRESS

Senate Committees	Committee Ratios	Committee Chairman	Number of Subcommittees
Aeronautical & Space Sciences	D 11–R 5	Clinton Anderson (N.M.)	none
Agriculture & Forestry	D 10–R 5	Allen Ellender (La.)	5
Appropriations	D 18–R 9	Carl Hayden (Ariz.)	13
Armed Services	D 12–R 5	Richard Russell (Ga.)	5
Banking & Currency	D 10–R 4	Willis Robertson (Va.)	6
Commerce	D 12–R 6	Warren Magnuson (Wash.)	9
District of Columbia	D 5–R 2	Alan Bible (Nev.)	4
Finance	D 11–R 6	Russell Long (La.)	none
Foreign Relations	D 13–R 6	J. W. Fulbright (Ark.)	10
Government Operations	D 10–R 4	John McClellan (Ark.)	5
Interior & Insular Affairs	D 11–R 5	Henry Jackson (Wash.)	6
Judiciary	D 11–R 5	James Eastland (Miss.)	14
Labor & Public Welfare	D 11–R 5	Lister Hill (Ala.)	7
Post Office & Civil Service	D 8–R 4	Mike Monroney (Okla.)	5
Public Works	D 12–R 5	Jennings Randolph (W. Va.)	4
Rules & Administration	D 6–R 3	Everett Jordan (N.C.)	6

and once on it the same rule of seniority which applies to full committees will apply to subcommittees. Hence committee chairmen have less discretion in manipulating the subcommittee system within their own committee. The rules and procedures of the Senate also make it easier to discharge committees of bills which are being held up by a committee chairman. Hence chairmen will be less successful in preventing bills from reaching the floor even if they do attempt to act arbitrarily.

As in the House, however, committees are essentially in control of the flow of legislation. If a bill cannot pass a committee it probably will not be brought out onto the floor and is even less likely to pass.

BRINGING A BILL TO THE FLOOR

As in the House, most bills which reach the floor of the Senate are first reported by the appropriate committee. There are ways in which committees may be by-passed (which will be discussed in Chapter Eight), but by and large bills must first be reported from committees to receive floor consideration.

When a bill is reported by a committee it goes on the Senate Calendar. The Senate is much less elaborate in its rules and procedures governing the bringing of bills to the floor. And even what rules it has are used flexibly and loosely. There is, for example, no special calendar for bills under suspension of the Rules, no special Consent Calendar or Private Calendar, no special District of Columbia Calendar or Discharge Calendar, and no Rules Committee to give legislation privileged status. (The Senate does have a Committee on Rules and Administration, but it is not granted the same power as its namesake in the House.)

In place of these elaborate procedures there are essentially two calendars in the Senate, a Calendar of Business, or General Orders, to which all legislation, whether public or private, involved or not involved with money, controversial or non-controversial is assigned, and an Executive Calendar for nominations and treaties. Under the Calendar of Business there are several other sub-headings, but General Orders is the Calendar from which almost all legislative business comes.

There is one special procedure which the Senate does have, however. Every Monday a call of the calendar (meaning a call of the General Orders Calendar) is privileged business after the morning hour. This simply means that the non-controversial bills on the Calendar (similar to the House Consent Calendar Bills) may be brought up. If there is no objection to a bill, debate proceeds under a rule limiting debate by each senator to five minutes. If, however, there is one objection to a bill it is either passed over or may, by motion, be considered. If the majority decides to consider the bill, the five minute rule no longer applies. The call of the Calendar may take place after the morning hour each day, but it has privileged status each Monday. Often, the call of the Calendar on Monday is dispensed with by unanimous consent, and, again by unanimous consent, it is called once or twice a month at the convenience of the members.

Unlike the House, then, the rules and procedures governing the privileged status of bills and resolutions in the Senate are extremely simple. This simplicity in structure, however, masks a complexity of informal procedures.

Simply knowing the formal rules in the case of scheduling bills for Senate floor action is not very helpful in explaining what actually is involved in scheduling. What makes scheduling in the Senate different from the House of Representatives is an elaborate set of clearing procedures so that all senators will be informed. Before looking at the reasons behind this practice, it may first be useful to make several comparisons between House and Senate scheduling.

First, when bills are reported from Senate committees, they are *rarely* held up for floor action. There is no similar institution in the Senate to the Committee on Rules in the House. Scheduling for floor action is done, when the Democrats are the majority party, by the Democratic Policy Committee, a committee of nine Democrats chaired by the majority leader Mike Mansfield. Besides Mansfield there are three other senators who are members of the Policy Committee *ex-officio*, Russell Long (Whip), Carl Hayden (President Pro-Tempore), and George Smathers (Secretary of the Conference). These are the same three who are also *ex-officio* members of the Steering Committee. In addition to these members, the majority leader appoints five others.[3] The Policy Committee advises Mansfield as to scheduling, but it rarely acts arbitrarily in not scheduling a bill, and there is very little feeling that the Policy Committee is unfair.

---

[3] The members in the Eighty-ninth Congress were Lister Hill (Alabama), Warren Magnuson (Washington), John Pastore (Rhode Island), Richard Russell (Georgia), and Stuart Symington (Missouri).

Normally the Policy Committee does not meet at all, and scheduling is left to the majority leader.

A second major difference between House and Senate scheduling of legislation is that there is more cooperation between the majority leader and the minority leader in the Senate. Senator Dirksen, minority leader, is consulted before any bill is brought to the floor. This does not mean that Dirksen can exercise a veto over the scheduling process. It simply means that Mansfield lets Dirksen know what is going to come up next, and inquires as to whether this suits the Republicans. If, for some reason, Dirksen asks for a postponement of a bill, such a postponement will usually be granted. This cooperation, however, is merely a special case of the next point to be made.

Third, in the Senate, all senators, Democrats as well as Republicans, have some say in scheduling. This is in sharp contrast with the House where scheduling is a matter for the principals to decide, chiefly the Speaker, majority leader, and floor manager for the bill (the committee or subcommittee chairman, or both) and, on most occasions, the chairman of the Rules Committee.

Fourth, it is very often the case that the Senate will juggle anywhere from two to five bills at the same time, going from one to another by unanimous consent. This again is in sharp contrast with the House which never has more than one bill before it at any one time.

The reasons for these differences between the House and the Senate in scheduling legislation for floor action lie mainly with the differences between the two bodies which we have already discussed in Chapter One. The Senate is a smaller body where everyone is relatively equal in power (as compared with the House). Senators are also quite busy men with full schedules. The scheduling of legislation becomes an informal process suiting the conveniences, if possible, of most of the members. Time and again when Senator Mansfield announces the forthcoming schedule (after consultation with the interested members of the Policy Committee as well as the minority leader and others principally involved), a member will request some slight change to fit his own schedule, and if that change is convenient to the members it is granted. Accommodations of this kind, of course, are not made to the extent of postponing floor action indefinitely. It is simply a matter of convenience, not conviction on the substance of the legislation, which promotes attempts to accommodate to the Senators' varying and busy schedules.

After a committee reports a piece of legislation, that legislation goes on the Calendar of General Orders. There is no attempt by the leadership to detain major legislation, nor would such attempts be successful. The presiding officer of the Senate, unlike the Speaker of the House, has very weak powers. Senators must be recognized in the order in which they seek recognition (except that the majority leader, by custom, may always get the floor when he wants it), and any senator, when he has the floor, may move that the Senate take up certain legislation. It would be futile, therefore, for members to attempt to block legislation by refusing to schedule it.

CHAPTER SEVEN

Floor Rules and Procedures (Senate)

Bills reported from committees are placed on the Calendar of General Orders and are then scheduled for floor action by the majority leader in consultation with the Democratic Policy Committee, the minority leader, and other interested senators. There is usually no difficulty in getting a bill scheduled once it has been reported from a committee. How bills are then handled on the floor of the Senate is the subject of this chapter. What we shall be concerned with here, with the exception of the cloture rule, is the "normal" flow of legislation. In Chapter Eight we will be concerned with rules and procedures which are employed when the normal political process breaks down.

There are, theoretically, two different ways in which the Senate starts the day. In practice, however, the two procedures have the same result. The Senate, unlike the House, usually recesses from day to day rather than adjourning from one day to the next. A recess is technically simply a break in the day's proceedings. When the Senate reconvenes the following day after a recess (usually at twelve noon, but by simple motion, and usually by unanimous consent, the Senate may recess to an earlier hour) the unfinished business of the previous day is immediately in order following the prayer and the reading of the *Journal*. In practice, however, the majority leader (or someone designated by the majority leader to act for him if he is not there) asks unanimous consent to dispense with reading the *Journal*, and asks unanimous consent that there be a "morning hour" with statements limited to three minutes. Unless it is expected that a filibuster will be started that day, such requests are usually agreed to. Rarely, for example, is the Senate *Journal* read. Only if senators wish to delay action will such a demand be made, and this happens only on the first day of a proposed filibuster.

During this morning hour following a recess, senators may present petitions and memorials, report bills from committees (which are then referred to the Calendar) and introduce bills and other resolutions. Senators also use this period to insert material into the *Congressional Record*. When the morning hour is completed, that is, when senators have completed their insertions into the *Record*, or by the hour of two o'clock, the unfinished business of the previous day is then laid before the Senate.

When the Senate has adjourned rather than recessed, the only difference in procedure is that the practice is more fully sanctioned by the rules of the Senate. The Senate, after an adjournment, must meet at twelve noon (unless it has determined otherwise), and after the prayer and reading of the *Journal* (the latter usually dispensed with by unanimous consent) there is officially a period, not to exceed the hour of two o'clock, for "morning business" (presentation of petitions and memorials, reports of standing and select committees, and introduction of bills and resolutions). After the hour of one o'clock, any bill on the Calendar may be brought up for debate. When the hour of two o'clock passes, the morning hour is officially closed, and the Senate goes on to other business. If a bill has been brought up between the hour of one and two o'clock and has not been disposed of, it goes back on the Calendar.

In practice, it makes little difference in terms of the morning hour whether the Senate recesses or adjourns. It does make a difference, though, in terms of other rules and procedures. For example, many of the rules of the Senate specify that some action must lay over one legislative day. By "legislative day" is meant the length of time from one adjournment to the next adjournment. If the Senate recesses rather than adjourns, several calendar days may go by but the Senate will be in the same legislative day. When, for example, a bill is reported from a committee it must lay over one legislative day before a motion to consider is in order. If the Senate recesses rather than adjourns it may be many days, and even weeks, before the next "legislative day." The practice of recessing rather than adjourning, then, is used by the majority leader as a way of controlling what will and will not be permissible under the rules of the Senate. Recesses, of course, also avoid the less flexible rules concerning the morning hour when the Senate adjourns. For example, during a filibuster proponents of the bill will desire a recess rather than an adjournment, since the previous business of the day before is then immediately in order after the prayer, and the morning hour may be dispensed with. Thus, opportunities for delay of the pending business may be avoided.

The Senate, in early 1964, passed a rule change which also has a bearing on the morning hour. Before 1964 committees could not meet while the Senate was in session except by unanimous consent. The effect of the rules change was to allow committees to meet during the morning hour of the Senate. This change in the rules was simply designed to give the committees an additional period of time to conduct business while the Senate was conducting less important business, and reflects the increased business which committees must handle. This additional time which committees have varies from no time at all (if the Senate has recessed, there then being no official morning hour, and someone has objected to the unanimous consent request to allow a "morning hour"), to two hours in length (if the whole time for morning business is taken up). Normally, the morning hour will last anywhere from fifteen minutes to an hour and a half, depending upon how many senators have insertions to make in the *Record* and how long they take to make them. It is frequently the practice, for example, for senators to make speeches during the morning hour which, although required to be within three minutes in length, may go on longer than that. It also sometimes occurs that a discussion will develop between two or more senators if the speech is controversial, and the participants will continue to talk until someone objects.

This last point illustrates a broader generalization that can be made concerning rules and procedures in the Senate. A senator may violate a rule of the Senate (such as speaking longer than three minutes during the morning hour) as long as another senator does not demand "the regular order." That is, the Presiding Officer normally will not announce that a rule of the Senate is being violated. The Presiding Officer in the Senate is not an active, potent force. Occasionally he can make rulings concerning points of order which have some effect, but usually what the Senate does is determined by who has the floor. Unless some other senator makes a point of order that a rule is being violated, the rules of the Senate may be violated at will. Often, this violation of the rules is made legitimate by asking unanimous consent to violate the rules, and for a number of reasons which we will discuss such unanimous consent requests are almost always granted. However, quite often a senator will not ask unanimous consent, usually because he either forgets he is breaking a rule, or possibly because he does not realize he is violating a Senate rule.

At the close of the morning hour, bells on the Senate side of the Capitol and in the Senate Office Buildings ring five times signalling that the legislative business of the Senate is about to begin, and that committees may no longer meet without unanimous consent of the Senate.

What happens after the morning hour is by no means predictable. It depends upon what action the majority leader has scheduled for that day, and whether or not other senators have speeches, not necessarily connected with the pending legislation, which they would like to make. If the Senate recessed the previous day the unfinished business is laid before the Senate, but the majority leader may ask unanimous consent to go into executive session to consider appointments by the President in which the Senate is asked to "advise and consent." Or, the majority leader may ask unanimous consent to consider an entirely different bill. Or, discussion of the unfinished business may take place. Which choice the majority leader makes will depend upon the schedule he has worked out with other senators.

Whatever does happen, however, will usually be done by unanimous consent. Unanimous consent is not required in some instances, and if there is objection the majority leader may move to take up a certain bill, cast aside the pending business, or go into executive session. Occasionally, however, what the majority leader wishes to do, such as having a morning hour after a recess the day before, is in violation of the rules of the Senate and does require unanimous consent. It is extremely rare that such unanimous consent requests are objected to. Partially this is because if objection is made, a motion to do what was asked by unanimous consent will almost certainly carry (or else the majority leader really is not the leader of the majority party). But this is partially true because other senators, unless they have a very good reason, feel restrained to object. To object to a unanimous consent request by the majority leader is not simply to object to the whim of the majority leader, it is to object to a schedule which has been carefully worked out among the interested senators, including the minority leader. Most members would not find it very useful for their own concerns to object to scheduling primarily involving others unless they had an understandable and over-powering reason. Therefore, much of what takes place on the floor of the Senate, especially with respect to the flow of legislation, takes place without difficulty under unanimous consent.

There are several rules and procedures of floor debate which, in themselves, need explanation. To watch the Senate in action from the galleries is not at all the same as watching the House in action. The rules of the Senate are simpler in the sense that there are fewer of them, and they are also quite different from those in the House, but the effects of the rules are no less important in determining the nature of debate in the Senate or the decision to pass or reject a bill or amendment.

One rule, honored more in the breach than in practice, is the rule of germaneness adopted in January, 1964. This rule specifies that after the morning hour debate must be germane to the legislative business for three hours. In other words, when the morning hour is completed and legislative business is in order, senators must talk germanely to whatever business is before the Senate for a period of three hours.

Before 1964, of course, speeches and debate on the floor did not have to be germane for any period of time. The reason why a rule of germaneness was so late in coming to the Senate, and the reason why it is very often ignored, is that senators themselves want it that way. Often they will have a speech prepared or a topic they wish to discuss, but they must give it at a certain hour. Earlier in the day, perhaps, they have commitments back in the office, and later in the day they must leave town on constituency business, or meet with executive officials downtown. They have a tight schedule which may not fit in with the rule of germaneness. They will come to the Senate floor, nevertheless, because these speeches are at least important to them, if not to others, and either ask the senator who has the floor to yield to them or, if they can get the floor in their own right, give their speech. If the speech is not germane, seldom will other senators object. After all, they will also, at some time, be in the same predicament and they would like the same courtesy extended to them. Occasionally the senator giving the speech will acknowledge that it is not germane and ask unanimous consent to waive the rule. In any case, the senator will probably not be challenged. Such a challenge would violate the informal rule of comity which is so important among a small group of extremely busy men. A senator understands better than anyone else the problem of scheduling, and he is at least sympathetic to the plight of another senator who feels that he must make some short speech or insertion into the *Record* before going off to other business. It is annoying, of course, and this annoyance is why there was a change in the rules. But annoyance or not, things go on pretty much as they did before the rule of germaneness.

The Senate, by the adoption of the germaneness rule, has allowed for several interesting situations in terms of the way in which the rule of germaneness relates to other rules and procedures. It is still the case, for example, except for general appropriation bills, that amendments to bills need not be germane to the bill. That is, excluding appropriation bills, the Senate has no rule of germaneness with respect to amendments. Hence, if need be, a senator wishing to make a non-germane speech could propose a non-germane amendment and then speak germanely to the non-germane amendment and not violate any rules of the Senate. This may be one reason why it was possible to adopt this rule of germaneness. Senators knew that it could be violated, and because such a violation would make the Senate look foolish, violating the rule by implicit unanimous consent would occur.

A second rule which pervades all that goes on in the Senate is the rule which allows senators to speak almost indefinitely on the business which is before the Senate. This is the cloture rule (Rule XXII) which requires two-thirds of those present and voting to cut off debate. More will be said of this rule later. Here, however, it is enough to point out that the implication of the rule is that senators may not be shut off from debate by anything less than the concurrence of two-thirds of their colleagues. This feature of the rule, quite obviously, makes it difficult to predict when the Senate will finally decide to vote on the bill pending before it. It is difficult to tell in advance how many senators will want to speak on the bill, how long each will take, and whether discussion will develop prolonging even further the final resolution of the bill.

The ability of any senator to speak for as long as he chooses is one of the most sacred institutions of the Senate and distinguishes it quite sharply from the House of Representatives, or indeed, any other legislative body in the world. As we have seen, debate is severely limited in the House (both by the five minute rule for debate in Committee of the Whole, and in the ability to move the previous question, thereby ending debate), and in no debate will every member of the House have an opportunity to speak. Also, in the House, most bills are scheduled and voted on the same day (except for very controversial legislation, which is scheduled for more than one day). The Senate, on the other hand, is less rigid and less predictable. One does not necessarily know when a bill will come to a vote, and a senator need not fear that he may not be able to speak on the bill. Any senator can speak for as long and often as he likes, as long as he is physically able to speak. The only limitation, which is not really a limitation at all, is that no senator may speak more than twice on the same subject on the same legislative day. As we recall, a legislative day may stretch into days, weeks, or possibly even months. To avoid the two-speech rule, however, requires only that a senator propose an amendment to the pending business. Amendments are always in order, and amendments are considered to be "different subjects" for the purposes of the two-speech rule. Therefore, even during a filibuster when the Senate recesses from day to day (thus continuing the same legislative day) all a senator need do to speak more than twice is to offer an amendment. And he may, of course, offer as many amendments as are necessary to continue to speak.

UNANIMOUS CONSENT AGREEMENTS

In the Senate there are only two ways in which debate may be involuntarily closed and a vote had on a bill. One is by unanimous consent agreements to limit debate, the other by a successful cloture petition. Each, however, is used for quite different purposes.

The purpose of a unanimous consent request to close debate and vote is simply to expedite the business of the Senate and allow senators to schedule their time to leave open the appointed hour of voting. These requests, because they require unanimous consent, are obviously not used to close debate against the wishes of any single intense senator.

When debate has been going on for some time on a bill, and it looks as though it may continue for some time, the majority leader will begin to consult with all interested parties (especially the minority leader) about the possibility of mutually agreeing to close debate and vote. If the majority leader feels that unanimous consent can be reached, he will take the floor and ask for unanimous consent to end debate and vote at a time certain. Usually the time selected is one or two days later. A quorum call must take place before the propounding of such a request. This is to insure that senators who may feel constrained to object will be given warning to be present. When quorum calls are requested in the Senate, two bells ring throughout the Senate side of the Capitol and in the Senate Office Buildings. In the senators' offices it is usual practice for a designated person on the senator's staff to call the respective party cloakroom to ask the purpose of the quorum. In this way the senator can be alerted, and if time is not available for him to be there, his objection will be relayed to the majority leader or another senator who will object for him.

The timing of such unanimous consent requests is crucial in determining their success. A single objection, of course, defeats the request. Therefore, clearance with interested senators is necessary. Also, many senators do not like to limit debate. If the request comes too early in the debate it will probably be defeated. Members, when they come to the floor, may attempt to get the majority leader to postpone the time or even the day of voting. If they are unyielding in their wishes, the majority leader has no other choice but to try for another hour or possibly another day.

Debate on many controversial bills is ended by such unanimous consent requests. But it can be done only if all members are willing to have the issue come to a vote. It can also be done only if all senators feel that their rights are protected and that they will be allowed to speak for at least a short period of time. In the absence of such a unanimous consent agreement, a cloture petition is the only alternative to voluntary consent if debate is to be closed.

The importance of unanimous consent agreements to limit debate is simply another example of the loose way in which the Senate operates. It is also an indication that senators must be tolerant of one another and must be willing to go along with what others want unless the reason for opposition is compelling. A body of 100 men that operates in large measure by unanimous consent has to insure that the rights of each member are constantly protected. One alternative to comity and mutual respect is a strongly hierarchical organization which could force members to agree. There is no evidence, however, that this latter alternative would ever be adopted. Senators, perhaps even more than congressmen, are fiercely independent men. The organizational structure of the Senate is highly decentralized, dispersing power among a number of people, and the party system itself, like the party system in the House, is very weak indeed.

There is one other point which can be made about the practice of unanimous consent. If unanimous consent requests were not honored, there would probably be more pressure on the Senate to change its rules. That is, the Senate is able to have such loose and flexible rules primarily because no senator takes advantage of them, at least not very often. It would be possible for a senator or a small group of senators to delay and postpone action in the Senate time and time again. But such action would undoubtedly create a situation in which other senators simply could no longer tolerate the delays.

Therefore, we have somewhat of a paradox: Senate rules can be loose and flexible because, by unanimous consent, they are constantly violated. If the rules were enforced by its members, it would probably be necessary to change them. It is only by informal pressures that the loose formal rules are able to work.

CLOTURE

The second way in which debate may be shut off is by the invocation of Rule XXII. When a group of senators engage in debate for the purpose of not allowing a bill to come to a vote (a filibuster) the only way in which debate may be closed and a vote had is through a successful cloture motion. The mechanics of cloture are quite simple; the politics of cloture are extremely difficult.

Any senator may circulate a cloture petition. When 16 senators have signed the petition, the petition is filed with the presiding officer and is read to the Senate. On the second calendar day after the filing of the petition, and one hour after the Senate convenes, the motion to close debate is put to the Senate for a yea or nay vote. If two-thirds of those present and voting vote yea, the cloture motion has been successful. If one-third plus one of those present and voting vote nay, the cloture motion fails. In case of the latter, debate either continues as before or the bill is withdrawn. A second cloture petition may be filed at any time.

If the motion secures the necessary two-thirds majority, several things are allowed under the rules. First, each senator may speak for one hour on the bill or on any amendments already proposed. Second, no additional amendments may be filed. Third, only germane amendments may be considered for a vote. When the amendments have been voted on, and all senators have had an opportunity to speak for one hour (some, of course, may not want to do so), the bill then comes to a vote.

Whether a cloture motion will be successful or not, then, depends upon the ability of the proponents of a bill to get the necessary two-thirds vote. This is usually not an easy matter. To build a coalition that large will often take a number of concessions to luke-warm opponents of the bill. When such concessions are made, the proponents run the risk of losing the initial support of those already in the coalition. There are also some senators who, regardless of the issue, are reluctant to support cloture motions. Included among these are, of course, Southerners who find that they are able to use unlimited debate to such good advantage that they do not want to jeopardize their own use of the filibuster by voting against its use by others. Some senators from small states are also reluctant to vote for cutting off debate, simply on the theory that someday they may want to use the filibuster themselves and would prefer that others not vote to cut off their debate. In fact, there are few people who do not feel that at some time the ability to filibuster will be useful to them. Included among these are Northern Democratic liberals who, as we shall see, have used the filibuster to good advantage. Being for or against the filibuster, then, is a matter of perceived relative advantage, not absolute advantage.

The cloture rule was first adopted in 1917. Prior to this date unlimited debate with no means at all of ending filibusters was the rule in the Senate. In 1949 the rule was changed from two-thirds of those present and voting to two-thirds of the entire membership, but it excluded cloture petitions on motions to change the rules themselves. In 1959, the present cloture rule, two-thirds of those present and voting, on any motion whatsoever, including motions to change the rules, was adopted.

From the adoption of the cloture rule in 1917, through the Eighty-ninth Congress (1965–1966), there have been 36 cloture votes, of which 7 have been successful. The successful 7 were: Versailles Treaty (1919), World Court (1926), branch banking (1927), prohibition reorganization (1927), communications satellite (1962), civil rights (1964), and voting rights (1965). Of the 36 cloture votes,

15 have been on civil rights bills. The 12th and 15th attempts, in 1964 and 1965, were the only successful ones.[1]

In 1964 in the Senate there were two filibusters. One, on which cloture was successfully negotiated, was the Civil Rights Bill of 1964, and the second, on which cloture failed, was the Dirksen amendment to the foreign aid authorization bill to delay enactment of the ruling of the Supreme Court that both houses of the state legislature must be apportioned on the basis of population. These two filibusters illustrate a number of interesting points concerning how cloture is used and what the difficulties are in invoking it.

Debate on the Civil Rights Bill began on March 9, 1964, cloture was voted on June 10, and the vote on final passage was taken on June 19. All in all, the Senate debated the Civil Rights Bill for 83 days. The major opponents of the bill were, of course, Southern Democrats. But when Senator Dirksen and his bloc of about seven votes finally decided that the bill was changed enough to be acceptable (no major changes were actually made), the proponents had enough votes for cloture.

The second filibuster in 1964, interestingly enough, was led, not by Southern Democrats, but by a small group of Northern Democrats under the direction of Senator Paul H. Douglas of Illinois. This filibuster was occasioned by the attempt of Senator Dirksen, also of Illinois, to attach a non-germane amendment to the foreign aid authorization bill which would delay the implementation of the decision of the Supreme Court that both houses of state legislatures must be apportioned on the basis of population. A cloture petition was circulated by Senator Dirksen and it picked up the necessary signatures, but the motion for cloture failed by a ratio of more than two to one. A quite watered-down version of the amendment, making it simply a recommendation and not a directive to go slow in apportionment cases, was then substituted for the Dirksen proposal and was accepted by Senate. Later, in a conference committee with the House, the amendment was dropped.

As these two cases illustrate, a filibuster may be used to advantage by any group of senators, conservative or liberal, Northern or Southern. It is also true, however, that the liberals have been attempting

---

[1] Data in this paragraph are from *Current American Government* (Washington: Congressional Quarterly Service, 1963), pp. 85–86, *Congressional Quarterly Weekly Report*, #24 (June 12, 1964), p. 1169, and *Congressional Quarterly Weekly Report*, #6 (Feb. 11, 1966), p. 355. There were two unsuccessful cloture motions on a civil rights bill in 1966.

to change the rule. In 1959 they were actually able to have the number necessary to invoke cloture reduced from two-thirds of the entire Senate to two-thirds of those present and voting. It was also made possible to invoke cloture on attempts to change the rules themselves; before 1959 cloture could not be invoked on proposals to change the rules.

Since 1957 liberals in the Senate have been attempting to change the cloture rule from two-thirds of those present and voting to three-fifths, or 50 percent, depending upon whose motion is being considered. Senator Anderson from New Mexico has been the leader in the fight to reduce the requirement to three-fifths. Senators Douglas and Clark are the leaders to reduce the requirement to a majority. The proposal which has had the greatest support is Senator Anderson's, and in 1963, although cloture on a filibuster against Senator Anderson's rule change was not successful, the liberals, for the first time, were able to muster a majority of the Senate on their side. In 1965 the resolution to change the cloture rule was sent to the Committee on Rules and Administration where it did not receive enough votes to be reported to the floor. In 1967 the attempt to change the rule was again defeated.

The question now arises about the effects that Rule XXII has on the Senate. The consequences of Rule XXII cannot be over-estimated. The ability of a senator or a group of senators to talk for as long as they are able, physically, to keep up the pace unless cut off by two-thirds of their colleagues is obviously of immense importance when considering decision-making in the Senate.

What this means is a number of things. (1) If there exists a relatively large minority opposed to a bill or resolution (one-third plus one), the majority in the Senate is unable to act. This has been the case, for example, with a number of civil rights bills. (2) If a large minority exists which is opposed to a bill they will usually be able to exact concessions from the proponents in return for bringing an end to the filibuster. That is, the filibuster can be used as a threat. (3) The job of the proponents in building a coalition is simply increased enormously by having to put together a coalition of two-thirds rather than a simple majority. (4) The cloture rule increases the importance of intensity in the decision-making process. That is, in the face of a majority, an intense group of senators may still prevail. (5) The existence of this "ultimate weapon" enormously facilitates bargaining within the Senate. The knowledge that a filibuster may be used, and used legitimately, by any group of senators forces other senators to plan their legislative strategies and tactics carefully, and to anticipate some objections which may be intense. It encourages senators, because filibusters are exhausting and hard on everyone, especially those opposed to the filibuster since they must be there constantly to make quorums, to negotiate with those who are strong enough in opposition to threaten or actually use a filibuster. In other words, the existence of the cloture rule pervades almost everything that is done, at least legislatively, within the Senate.

Voting in the Senate

A bill or amendment, then, comes to a vote in the Senate under one of three conditions: (1) senators have simply stopped talking on their own accord, (2) a unanimous consent request has been entered into specifying the time of a vote, or (3) cloture has been invoked. The prevalence of each as a debate-closing procedure is also in the same order. That is, senators normally simply run out of things to say. On many major, controversial bills when senators wax enthusiastic and when much controversy will be engendered, a unanimous consent agreement is often necessary simply to bring the debate to an end. With no deadline on discussion, senators are prone to engage in relatively lengthy discussion. Unanimous consent agreements are not attempts to force anyone to stop talking. They are simply mutually agreed upon stopping points. Occasionally, however, there is a group of senators who wishes to use unlimited debate in the Senate not simply as a means of debate and attempting to win other senators to their cause, but rather to try to prevent a vote from taking place at all. In such a case neither of the first two debate-closing procedures will be successful. A cloture petition must be circulated and a motion to end debate endorsed by two-thirds of the senators.

When debate has come to a close, there are three methods of voting in the Senate: (1) voice vote, (2) division (or standing vote), and (3) roll-call (yeas and nays). The Senate does not have a system of Committee of the Whole, as in the House, nor does it have a teller vote. Also, as differentiated from the House, a bill in the Senate can only be voted on by one method of voting. For this reason if a Senator wants a roll-call vote, he must ask for it, because once a vote has been taken, a roll-call vote may not then be demanded.

The major form of voting in the Senate, as in the House, is by voice vote. This is because, as in the House, most bills are relatively non-controversial and are passed by unanimous consent. But the Senate does have many more roll-call votes than does the House. This is almost entirely explained by the fact that the Senate is a smaller body and roll-call votes do not take much time. Roll-call votes are usually planned and announced in advance so that senators are aware that a roll-call vote will take place.

The method of getting a roll-call in the Senate is the same as in the House—one-fifth of those present, assuming a quorum, may demand a roll-call vote. It is not always easy, however, to get enough senators to the floor to get a roll-call vote ordered, as Senator Clark's following story suggests.[2]

> On Tuesday, November 26, 1963, I was prepared to call up an amendment. . . . I was anxious to get as many Senators as possible to the floor to hear my argument. Since I was going to ask for a roll-call vote I needed at least eleven Senators on the floor to join in my request for the "ayes and nays."
>
> The . . . resolution was called up at around one o'clock, when most Senators were eating lunch. To prevent immediate passage of the resolution by voice vote I had to call up my amendment right away. There were half a dozen Senators on the floor. I suggested the absence of a quorum. The clerk called the roll. . . . A few Senators drifted into the chamber, answered their names and departed.
>
> Mike Mansfield said to me, "Joe, do you want a 'live' quorum?"
>
> I said, "Yes." With a look of only mild pain he departed without asking that the quorum call be suspended, knowing that if he did so I would object to his unanimous consent request.
>
> [Finally, after a call of the absentees, the Presiding Officer announced that a quorum was present.]
>
> There were only seven Senators in the chamber, four less than the number necessary to get the "ayes and nays."
>
> I was on my feet. "Mr. President, the Senator from Pennsylvania takes judicial notice of the fact that a quorum is not present and asks the clerk to observe that there are only seven Senators present in the chamber," I said.

[2] Joseph S. Clark, *Congress: The Sapless Branch* (New York: Harper & Row, 1964), pp. 193–195.

[The Presiding Officer consulted the Parliamentarian] and announced, "The record shows that a quorum responded."

I was in a quandary. Under the rules I could not ask for another quorum call until the Senate "transacted business." I searched my mind for a quick way out and began to talk rather aimlessly, hoping some bright idea would come to me.

Relief came from an unexpected quarter. Everett Dirksen broke in.

"Mr. President, is it the transaction of business to address a parliamentary inquiry to the chair?" he said. [The Presiding Officer, after conferring with the Parliamentarian, said that it was not.]

"Is it the transaction of business to ask unanimous consent to insert a matter in the *Record*?" Dirksen said.

[The chair announced that it would be if the request were granted.]

Dirksen asked me to yield, which I was glad to do. He then got unanimous consent to make an insertion in the *Record* and turned to me.

"Go ahead, Joe, get your quorum call," he said, "but call it off when you get enough Senators here to give you the ayes and nays."

I was happy to comply. Sixteen Senators showed up a few minutes later, I got the ayes and nays ordered, and we went ahead with a two-hour debate on my amendment. It failed to pass 20–63.

This story illustrates a number of points; one is that when a quorum call is requested senators are counted as they enter the chamber and may then depart before the end of the call. It is possible, then, to have fewer senators on the floor after a quorum call than before the quorum call.

Because it is difficult to get a large number of senators to the floor at any one time, the practice has developed for senators to ask for the ayes and nays on amendments for which they wish record votes when, for some other purpose (such as a roll-call vote on some other amendment) senators are present on the floor. If a senator wishes a yea and nay vote, the practice of the Senate is to support his request. It is rare indeed for the Senate to deny such a request of a senator. The leadership may attempt to talk a senator out of demanding a yea and nay vote, especially a junior senator and when the Senate is pressed for time, but if a senator decided to press the matter he would not be denied.

After the result of the vote is announced (whether it be by voice, division, or yea and nay) it is in order for any senator on the winning side to move to reconsider the vote. Usually this is simply a *pro forma* way of "nailing down" the decision. It is in order, by the rules of the Senate, for any member on the side which prevailed to move to reconsider a vote within two days of that vote. To avoid this occurring at an unfortunate time (for example, when the members of the winning side are no longer on the floor), a motion to reconsider is usually made immediately. Another senator then moves to table the motion to reconsider. This has the effect of ending debate as a motion to table another motion is not debatable. If the previous vote has not been close, the motion to table usually passes *pro forma* on a voice vote. Occasionally, however, after a close vote, a member will move to reconsider in the hopes of changing the outcome of the vote. Such an event occurred, for example, on July 23, 1964 when the Senate was considering President Johnson's Anti-Poverty Bill. The story is an interesting one involving a reversal of a vote, numerous attempts to stall until absent senators could reach the floor, and other parliamentary maneuverings.

Senator Prouty of Vermont offered a substitute amendment to an amendment by Senator Javits of New York. Prouty's amendment would have prohibited work-study and work-training programs unless the states themselves had worked out plans for such programs. Javits's amendment would have allowed the federal administrator, in the absence of state plans, to work out plans for the states.

Senator Prouty asked for the yeas and nays, and Senator Prouty's amendment was agreed to, 45–44.

Senator Javits then moved to reconsider the vote by which the amendment was agreed to. Senator Prouty moved to table the motion to reconsider by Javits. The yeas and nays were ordered, and on the motion to reconsider two senators who would have voted against Prouty's amendment but who were late getting to the floor for the first vote finally showed up (Cannon of Nevada and Hayden of Arizona). Senator Hart, who had voted against the Prouty amendment, due to a further mix-up, was not recorded on the motion to table. Nevertheless, with Cannon and Hayden now present (but Hart temporarily absent), the vote to table failed 45–45 (tie votes are always insufficient to pass motions).

The motion then reverted back to the Javits motion to reconsider the vote on the Prouty amendment. At this point Senator Tower of

Texas informed the Presiding Officer that Javits was not on the prevailing side on the original vote on the Prouty amendment and hence was not eligible to make the motion to reconsider. The Presiding Officer ruled, however, after consultation with the Parliamentarian, that Tower's observation came too late.

The yeas and nays were ordered and the motion to reconsider carried 46–45 (Hart now back in the chamber and voting for reconsideration). The Presiding Officer announced the vote incorrectly, however, as 45–46 against reconsideration and two recapitulations by the Presiding Officer were necessary before finally establishing the vote as 46–45 in favor of reconsideration.

Since the Senate had voted to reconsider, the motion was once again what it had been approximately one hour earlier, on Prouty's amendment. After more debate the yeas and nays were again ordered and the amendment was defeated 45–46.

After the motion to reconsider has been tabled or otherwise disposed of, the Senate continues with other amendments or other legislative business. The usual practice in the House of Representatives for the opponents to move to recommit the bill with or without instructions is allowed, but not often practiced in the Senate. The greater flexibility in the amending process in the Senate is probably responsible for this. Amendments in the nature of substitutes are relatively common in the Senate (but not in the House), and these substitutes are often full-blown alternatives to the bill. Acceptance or rejection of these substitutes in the nature of amendments, then, accomplishes the same thing as a motion to recommit with instructions accomplishes in the House.

The Senate, like the House, also uses the practice of pairing. The procedure is the same in both houses. A "live pair" occurs when a senator who is present withholds his vote and pairs with an absent senator on the opposite side. A simple pair occurs when two absent senators on opposite sides pair with each other. A general pair occurs when two absent senators pair, but do not announce on which side they would vote. As in the House, the most useful form of pair to the leadership is a "live pair," when a senator against the leadership who is present pairs with a senator for the leadership who is absent. This has the effect of subtracting one vote against the leadership. For example, on the four series of votes on the Prouty amendment just referred to, Senator Walters of Tennessee had a "live pair" with the absent Senator Edward Kennedy of Massachusetts. Senator Kennedy in each case would have voted against the Prouty amendment (and thus for the leadership). Senator Walters would have voted for the Prouty amendment (and against the leadership). Had Senator Walters voted on each of the first two votes, the Prouty amendment would have carried.

The "normal" rules and procedures in the Senate, then, are more flexible than in the House. There are fewer calendars and less rigid rules of debate. But the major difference is in the closing of debate. In the House, a majority may cut off debate. In the Senate at least two-thirds is necessary if the opposition is strong enough to conduct a filibuster. This difference gives a minority in the Senate more power than it has in the House once the bill has reached the floor for a vote.

Alternative Rules
and Procedures

In the last chapter we discussed the "normal" ways of doing business in the Senate of the United States. Except for the cloture rule, which is pervasive in its effect if not in its use, these rules and procedures are followed for all but a small fraction of bills in the Senate. Normally, as in the House of Representatives, bills proceed slowly from the time they are introduced in the Senate, through the committee and subcommittee system, and, if reported favorably by a committee, are considered on the floor for amendments and a vote up or down.

There are also several procedures which may be used if bills are sent to a Senate committee but are not reported out of that committee. That is, as in the House, there are a number of rules and procedures which may be employed if for one reason or another the "normal" legislative process breaks down. Before discussing these rules and procedures, however, a few general remarks may be helpful.

First, Senate committees are less likely to block legislation which a significant segment of the Senate desires to discuss and vote on than are committees in the House of Representatives. Put another way, legislation which is desired by a majority of the Senate membership, or even an intense minority of the membership, will usually find its way out of Senate committees. In part this lesser degree of committee obstruction has to do with the stronger rules of comity in the Senate as compared with the House. But more important than comity is the fact that "discharging" a committee in the Senate is so much easier than it is in the House. As we shall see, in the face of a recalcitrant committee a single determined senator may bring a bill to the floor of the Senate. This does not mean that the Senate must then debate the bill, let alone vote on its merits, but committees in the Senate, as compared with the House, do not have the same degree of power to keep bills from reaching the floor.

The second general point to be made about "unusual" procedures is that the Senate has no counterpart to the House Committee on Rules. The majority leader, the Policy Committee, and the minority leader are primarily responsible for scheduling, and most often this scheduling is fair to all senators. If a bill is reported from a committee it will undoubtedly be scheduled if a senator or group of senators wants it to be scheduled.

As compared with committees in the House of Representatives, then, committees in the Senate are less apt to hold up legislation which is desired by a majority of its members, and a bill reported from a committee will not be denied floor consideration.

This is a matter of degree, however. There are occasions when Senate committees will delay or reject legislation which an intense minority or a majority wishes to be passed. There are also occasions when a senator or group of senators will expect that a Senate committee will not report a bill (for example, Civil Rights in the Judiciary Committee). And, there will be some occasions when a senator or group of senators will want to act more quickly than sending a bill to a Senate committee first would allow them to act, especially late in the session. But, under any of these conditions a bill may be brought onto the floor in spite of the refusal of the committee to act. In fact, one generalization about the Senate which is not true of the House is that it is *always* possible to bring a bill onto the floor, regardless of whether it has been considered favorably by a committee, considered at all by a committee, or even whether or not it has been introduced in the Senate.

THE DISCHARGE RULE

One procedure which may be used to circumvent recalcitrant committees is the Discharge Rule. In the Senate any member, during the morning hour, may introduce a motion to discharge a committee of a bill or resolution which has been referred to it. Such a resolution then lies over one legislative day (the day after the Senate next adjourns) and may then be brought up when the senator is recognized following the adjournment. A majority vote will then discharge the committee and place the bill on the Calendar.

Such a procedure, although seemingly simple, is actually quite cumbersome, rarely used, and even more rarely successful. In Howard Schuman's account of the 1957 Civil Rights Bill he explained why this is the case.[1] If there is an intense group of senators against discharging a committee, and more especially if the leadership is against the use of the discharge procedure, there are a number of alternatives which are available to block or stall the procedure. First, a senator must be recognized to introduce the motion to discharge during the morning hour. Assuming an adjournment the day before, other senators may consume the time during the morning hour by, for example, amending the *Journal*, repeated quorum calls, or introduction of other business. This would have the effect of postponing further opportunities to introduce the discharge motion until after the next adjournment. Given the Senate's practice of recessing rather than adjourning from day to day, it may take some time before a senator may be able to get the floor during the morning hour. This is especially true if the leadership does not support the motion to discharge. By practice in the Senate senators are recognized in the order in which they rise to be recognized, except for the majority leader (or a person acting in his place) who, by tradition, may be recognized first. Hence, if the majority leader supports the motion to discharge it will have a good chance of being introduced. Since the majority leader also determines whether the Senate will recess or adjourn (subject to a *pro forma* vote by the Senate), he may easily establish a morning hour for the next day or not, as he sees fit.

Assuming that the motion to discharge a committee has been introduced during the morning hour, after one legislative day it is then in order to bring up the motion to discharge. If, however, the motion to bring up the discharge motion is not made during the morning hour, or if it is made during the next morning hour and not concluded during the morning hour, the discharge petition is placed on the Calendar. Once on the Calendar the motion to discharge faces two possible filibusters: one on the motion to consider the discharge motion, and the second on passage of the motion. And, of course, all of this activity is just on the motion to discharge. If a bill is discharged successfully, it then faces two more possible filibusters:

[1] Howard E. Schuman, "Senate Rules and the Civil Rights Bill," *American Political Science Review*, vol. 51 (December, 1957), 955–75.

one on the motion to consider the bill itself, and the other on passage of the bill. Obviously, then, the procedure for discharging a committee will not be very useful in the face of an intense minority who are willing to carry on a filibuster.

For these and other reasons, a motion to discharge is not made very often. The last time such a motion occurred on an important bill was in 1962 when Senator Mansfield, the majority leader, moved to discharge the Government Operations Committee of the bill to establish a Department of Urban Affairs. It was not filibustered, but even with Senator Mansfield's support, the motion lost by a vote of 58–42. Part of the reason had to do with the poor chances of any discharge petition. Some senators, as with the cloture petition, do not like to "tamper" with the committee system, regardless of the substance of the bill. Hence, even senators who may favor the bill may vote against a motion to discharge a committee of that bill. In return, of course, they hope that other senators will reciprocate when someone attempts to discharge a bill from their committee. In addition there was a good deal of evidence that President Kennedy, although making a Department of Urban Affairs one of his campaign pledges, really did not want such a department established, at least not as a top priority item on his agenda.

But even when a bill wins on the motion to discharge, it simply goes to the Calendar. It must then survive a motion to consider (subject to a filibuster) and a motion on final passage (also subject to a filibuster). If there is strong opposition to discharging a bill from committee, opponents have many devices at their disposal to prevent it from happening. Also, there are "easier" ways by which committees may be discharged, an additional reason why the discharge procedure is little used. Since 1789 there have been only 14 motions to discharge a committee in the Senate, and only 6 have been successful.

One of these successful motions to discharge a committee occurred in 1964, and the details of the action will illustrate the kinds of circumstances which are necessary for a discharge motion to be made successfully. Senator Douglas had a bill before the Senate Banking and Currency Committee which his subcommittee had just reported to the full committee by a vote of 4–3. Senator Robertson, Chairman of the full committee, was opposed to the bill and was reluctant to hold hearings. Senator Douglas announced that he would act to prevent other Banking and Currency bills from coming before the committee until his Truth-in-Lending Bill was given a hearing.

Senator Holland had before the committee a non-controversial bill which would allow the United States Treasury to use its facilities to strike a medal for use in a celebration in the State of Florida. Such facilities would be made available to Florida for cost. Holland's bill engendered no opposition on its merits, but time was short and Senator Douglas stood firm. Senator Douglas would not mind, however, if the Holland bill were discharged from the Banking and Currency Committee. Senator Robertson, the chairman, also did not object to such a procedure, nor did Senator Mansfield, the majority leader, although he was reluctant to do so because of the precedent it might set. Nevertheless the Holland Bill was discharged from the Banking and Currency Committee without objection.

This bill, only the 6th of 14 ever to be successfully discharged in the whole history of the Senate, was also the first to result in a law. The previous five successful discharge motions failed because the House, for one reason or another, did not act favorably on the bill.

NON-GERMANE AMENDMENTS

There is a more important reason, besides the complexity of the Discharge Rule, which makes it a little used procedure, and that is the fact that there exists a much easier way to "discharge" committees. This procedure is derived from the rule in the Senate that only amendments to general appropriation bills need be germane to the bill. What this means, in effect, is that any matter, whether it has been previously introduced or not, whether it has been referred to committee or not, and whether it is germane to the pending business or not (except general appropriation bills) may be introduced as an amendment. This was, in fact, the manner in which the 1960 Civil Rights Bill was brought to the floor in the Senate. Senator Lyndon B. Johnson, then majority leader, in motioning up an obscure bill to aid a school district in Missouri which was federally impacted, announced that the bill would be open to civil rights amendments.

Such a procedure has a number of advantages. First, hostile committees are by-passed. It is not even necessary that the bill be sent to a committee before it is introduced as an amendment to another bill. But if there is a bill lodged in a committee, proposing the bill as a non-germane amendment is perfectly within the rules of the Senate. There are a number of informal norms and expectations which work against its use very often, but "riders" are more prevalent than discharge motions.

Second, non-germane amendments, like other amendments, are not subject to the motion to consider. That is, when an amendment is moved there is no need, as there is with bills which come off the Calendar, to make a decision as to whether they should be considered or not. Hence, there can be no filibuster on the motion to consider as there can with bills which come off the Calendar. A filibuster may occur on the passage of the amendment itself, however, since amend-ments are subject to unlimited debate, and, of course, on the bill to which the amendment is being attached.

Moving a non-germane amendment, then, has the effect of im-mediately bringing to the floor of the Senate for discussion any mat-ter at all. This does not mean that a non-germane amendment need be made the subject of prolonged debate. A non-germane amend-ment, like other motions, is subject to a motion to table. A motion to table is a non-debatable motion which has the effect of putting an end to the discussion of whatever it is that is being tabled. If a mo-tion to table succeeds, the bill or motion fails and no vote on the merits is in order.

If a non-germane amendment does not have the support of at least a relatively large minority of the Senate it may be tabled immediately. This rule prevents single senators from unnecessarily taking the time of other senators by bringing to the floor bills which obviously could not pass and have been delayed in a committee precisely for that reason. It also means that if a bill does not have the support of the leadership it is usually tabled. The majority leader is essentially in charge of the schedule for the Senate. It is the majority leader who determines, in consultation with other senators, and especially the Policy Committee, the minority leader, and the committee and sub-committee chairmen of the committee from which the bill is re-ported, a time for the discussion of that bill. Moving a non-germane amendment is, of course, taking the control of scheduling away from the majority leader, unless the majority leader himself supports such an action.

Also, besides the formal restraint of a possible tabling motion, non-germane amendments are subject to the same kind of informal con-straints as have already been discussed with respect to cloture and the discharge motion. Non-germane amendments are not a part of the regular order. Although they are allowed by the rules, they are not considered to be a legitimate practice unless they have the support of the leadership or the committee chairman whose committee is being by-passed. Generally senators understand the advantages to themselves that certain bills must go to the committees on which they sit. This provides them with a certain amount of leverage with the Administration as well as with other senators. If they support by-passing other committees, what is to prevent members of other committees voting to by-pass their own committees? If such a practice became prevalent it would lead to a complete breakdown of established relations. Senators, even those who feel that the present system is not the "best of all possible worlds" are reluctant to take such action.

In 1964 the most important non-germane amendment brought to the floor was an amendment by Senator Dirksen to the foreign aid authorization bill which would delay the implementation of the Supreme Court's ruling that both houses of state legislatures must be apportioned on the basis of population. This non-germane amendment led to the filibuster, previously discussed, in which a relatively small group of liberals led by Senator Douglas prevented action in the Senate for a month while a compromise "sense of Congress" resolution was drawn up. The liberals then allowed a vote on the "sense of Congress" rider, which was adopted but subsequently dropped in the conference committee between the House and Senate. Senator Dirksen attempted to attach a substantially similar rider on a relatively minor bill in 1965 but a cloture motion to end a liberal filibuster failed by seven votes.

At the beginning of the Eighty-ninth Congress (1965–66) several interesting developments occurred with respect to riders. Although technically not non-germane amendments, the Senate and the House agreed to include in a supplemental appropriation bill which provided $1.6 billion in fiscal 1965 to reimburse the Agriculture Department's Commodity Credit Corporation for price support programs and other activities, two peripherally related amendments. One such legislative "rider" would prevent continued surplus food shipments to Egypt unless the President decides that it is in the national interest to do so; the other would prevent the Administration's plans to close down certain Veteran Administration facilities and agricultural stations until May 1, 1965. The House had made the ban on shipments of surplus food to Egypt absolute, but the Senate had added the escape clause at the insistence of the Administration. In return, however, the Administration had to agree not to implement its plans to close down certain VA and agricultural facilities until May 1, 1965.

Many such legislative riders, although only technically non-germane, are attached to bills in an attempt to tie the President's hands with respect to certain actions. The Senate, of course, finds it easier than the House to attach such riders since it is not bound, as is the House, to germaneness. An interesting consequence of this difference will be discussed in the next chapter.

SUSPENSION OF THE RULES

A third way in which bills may be brought to the floor in the Senate is by suspension of the rules. This procedure is much simpler than in the House and requires only a majority vote. To suspend the rules a senator must, in writing, give one day's notice. On the next legislative day the senator giving notice then may move consideration of his proposal. Such a motion, however, is debatable and is subject to a filibuster if strenuously opposed.

Almost all motions to suspend the rules in the Senate concern amendments to appropriation bills. As we have seen, amendments to bills in the Senate need not be germane except amendments to general appropriation bills. Further, appropriation bills may not, under the rules, be increased, provide new items of appropriation, or provide new legislation. These restrictions are in addition to the ban on non-germane amendments. Because of these restrictions, if a senator wishes to violate any of these rules with an amendment to a general appropriation bill, he must serve one day's notice that he intends to move to suspend the rules. Such motions are quite common, but generally the amendment proposed has some relevance to the bill under discussion. Given the absence of a rule of germaneness for other than general appropriation bills, legislative riders incorporating whole bills are more common on authorization bills.

HOUSE-PASSED BILLS

An additional route in which some bills may by-pass Senate committees occurs when a House-passed bill is sent to the Senate. The rule is somewhat complicated but relatively easy to apply, especially with the cooperation of the leadership. Rule XIV of the Senate provides that: "bills and joint resolutions from the House of Representatives, shall be read once, and may be read twice, on the same day, if not objected to, for reference but shall not be considered on that day nor debated, except for reference, unless by unanimous consent."

What this section of the rule means is that normally, when bills are passed first by the House of Representatives and sent to the Senate they are read once and by unanimous consent read twice and referred to a Senate committee. If a senator wants to keep a House-passed bill from being referred to a committee, however, he may, at this stage, object to second reading of the bill. The bill then remains on the Presiding Officer's desk and must lay over one legislative day.

After an adjournment and the beginning of a new legislative day, the rule then provides: "and every bill and joint resolution of the House of Representatives which shall have received a first and second reading without being referred to a committee, shall, if objection be made to further proceeding thereon, be placed on the Calendar." The force of this provision is that on the next legislative day, after the bill has been read a second time, any senator may object to "further proceeding thereon" (that is, reference to a committee), and the bill goes directly on the Senate Calendar. The most interesting aspect of this rule is that a single senator may place a bill on the Senate Calendar simply by objecting once to second reading and then objecting to further proceeding thereon on the next legislative day and after second reading of the bill.

The strategy with respect to this rule, then, is obvious. If a senator or group of senators feels that a bill, if referred to a Senate committee, will be bottled up in that committee, the rules provide that if the House passes the bill it may then be placed directly on the Senate Calendar. This is how both the Civil Rights Bill of 1957 and the Civil Rights Bill of 1964 were placed on the Senate Calendar. It was expected, in both cases, that the House of Representatives would pass a civil rights bill. Few thought, in either year, that the Senate would pass a stronger bill than that passed by the House. For many reasons, including the fact that the coalition necessary to pass such a bill in the Senate is two-thirds rather than a simple majority (because of the cloture rule), the normal expectation is that some changes in the House-passed bill are necessary in the direction of weakening the bill rather than strengthening it.

Since the committee in the Senate which handles civil rights bills is the Judiciary Committee headed by Senator Eastland of Mississippi, and since that committee has never in its history reported a civil rights bill, the strategy by the proponents of civil rights is clearly to avoid the Judiciary Committee. If the bill were sent to the Judiciary Committee the discharge route, as we have seen, would be available but time-consuming and risky. The bill, of course, could always be brought up as a non-germane amendment (as was the 1960 Civil Rights Bill) but this was considered unnecessary since a more "legitimate" procedure was already available. Although non-germane amendments are clearly possible under the rules of the Senate, the rules of the Senate also provide for placing a House-passed bill directly on the Calendar. Although this procedure still raises the question of by-passing committees, it is clearly provided for by the rules.

However, bringing up a bill by a non-germane amendment is still easier than placing a House-passed bill directly on the Calendar. Most importantly, the non-germane amendment route does not require that the House act first. Second, by placing a bill on the Calendar two filibusters may take place, one on the motion to consider and the second on the bill itself. With amendments, only one filibuster, on the amendment, is probable although a filibuster on the bill itself, with the amendment, may still take place.

Strategies Related to the Four Methods

In these four ways, then, discharge, non-germane amendments, suspension of the rules, and placing House-passed bills directly on the Calendar, Senate committees may be by-passed and bills may be considered which are being blocked by Senate committees. It is probably because of the existence of these four procedures that bills are not often held up in the Senate if there is a sizeable and intense group of senators that wants them considered. There are still, of course, a number of informal pressures not to by-pass committees, including the very strong norm of reciprocity. But nevertheless the ease with which committees in the Senate can be by-passed as compared with the House contributes to the generalization that the Senate, unlike the House, rarely blocks floor consideration when it is desired by a majority of members.

The greatest restraint on the use of these procedures, as is true in the use of normal procedures, is the possibility of a filibuster. If an intense minority opposes legislation, none of these procedures will be of any use unless they are also coupled with one or more successful cloture petitions requiring the affirmative vote of two-thirds of those senators present and voting.

A further observation which can be made concerning these procedures has to do with the conditions under which they will be used. The difficulty of using the procedures, from most difficult to least difficult would be: (1) discharge motion, (2) suspension of the rules, (3) placing a House-passed bill on the Calendar, and (4) non-germane amendment, with the latter being far and away the simplest procedure. When the leadership chooses the discharge route for a controversial bill (which is seldom), one can be fairly certain that the leadership is not very serious about its success. In 1962, for example, when Senator Mansfield attempted to discharge the Government Operations Committee of the bill to establish a Department of Urban Affairs one could guess that the leadership was not greatly concerned about its passage. The leadership could more easily have chosen to bring the bill up as a non-germane amendment on a non-controversial bill. The fact that it was brought up at all was because President Kennedy, during the previous campaign, had made a promise that he would attempt to establish such a department at cabinet level. The Senate merely went through the motions of complying with the President's request, in the weakest way it could.

CONCLUSIONS

Several major observations about rules and procedures in the United States Senate could benefit from added emphasis.

First, rules and procedures in the Senate are simpler than in the House of Representatives. The major reason for this is that the Senate is a smaller body than the House and is able, because informal norms are more powerful and because clearing procedures are easier, to operate on less strict rules.

Second, in comparing the Senate with the House, *except for the cloture rule*, the rules and procedures of the Senate allow majorities to act if there are majorities. The major reason for this is that it is more difficult in the House for a member or group of members to get bills onto the floor if they are not reported by standing committees or given a rule by the Committee on Rules. One of the distinguishing marks of the Senate is that any bill may be brought to the floor of the Senate by a single senator. All that senators need do is to move the bill as an amendment to another bill (except for general appropriation bills). The informal rules of the Senate, as the informal rules of the House, still prescribe that bills go through the "normal" legislative channels, which include committees. But if a Senate committee acts adversely on a bill or refuses to report a bill, it may easily be brought to the floor. By-passing House committees is not as easy. Excluding methods to discharge the Committee on Rules (Discharge Rule and Calendar Wednesday), discharging a standing committee in the House requires a discharge petition (218 signatures) or suspension of the rules (two-thirds vote plus recognition by the Speaker). The rule of germaneness in the House excludes the possibility that bills may be discharged from committees through the amendment process.

Third, what is of crucial significance in the Senate with respect to the protection of intense minorities is the possibility of a filibuster requiring two-thirds of those present and voting to bring an end to debate. On a controversial bill it is simply more difficult to build a coalition of two-thirds than to build a coalition of 50 percent plus one.

In summary, then, the Senate rules, like the House rules, provide numerous occasions for delay and defeat of legislation. Even more than in the House, informal norms of behavior are important in keeping the legislative machinery running. Most bills are referred to committees and subcommittees and it is in these small units that the major work on legislation is done. Chairmen have immense power over the operations of their committees, although probably less so than in the House given the ease with which Senate committees may be "discharged."

But in the Senate, as in the House, intense minorities are well protected. Although in the House an intense majority may finally prevail through, for example, a discharge petition, in the Senate, in the face of an intense minority, something greater than an intense majority is required. One could say that in the Senate, on some bills, an intense extra-ordinary majority is needed for final passage.

The House and the Senate, then, in the way in which they conduct their legislative business, are quite different bodies. But the fact that their rules and procedures are quite different should not obscure a major point which they have in common, and that is the possibility for relatively small minorities to delay and defeat legislation which an apathetic majority, if given the opportunity, might approve. It may in fact be a good idea that intense minorities be allowed to prevail over apathetic majorities. Such a question is strongly related to problems of political stability within the larger society in which the Congress acts. But it is clear that Congress, like most organizations, has developed within its two bodies a system of division of labor and, unlike some organizations, dispersal of power which makes it necessary for either extraordinary or intense majorities, or both, to form before some actions may take place. The evaluation of this conclusion depends essentially upon how one feels about the desireability of certain changes in the American society. Generally speaking those who favor more liberal policies which the President proposes are opposed to the current operation of Congress which essentially requires something more than simple majority approval. Those who favor more conservative policies usually support an institution which permits an intense minority to delay, defeat, and modify executive proposals.

CHAPTER NINE

Rules and Strategies in Adjusting House-Senate Differences

We have, to this point, been discussing the House and the Senate as two separate political institutions. And indeed they are. But Congress as a whole is empowered to legislate. This presents several problems since the two houses are so different from one another but on most matters must act together.

Bills, to become law, must be passed in identical form by both the House and the Senate before being sent to the President for his signature. Because the two houses are different political systems, and because the kinds of pressures operating on the House and Senate are somewhat different, it is rare for the two houses to pass legislation in identical form as the bill first goes through each body. This is especially true of controversial legislation which requires considerable bargaining among the interested parties within each house in order to pass. It is to be expected, then, that the differences between the two houses that we have enumerated will have varying consequences on the substance of legislation as it passes through each house. Our major concern in this chapter will be with what alternative routes are available when the House and Senate pass different versions of the same bill, and what strategies and tactics arising out of these alternative routes are available to opponents and proponents.

HOUSE-PASSED BILLS

If the House of Representatives acts favorably on a bill before action is completed in the Senate, the House notifies the Senate of its ac-

141

tion and sends the House-passed bill to the Senate. When the Senate receives the bill as passed by the House, one of two things may occur. On more than 99 percent of all bills, the bill is read twice and referred to the appropriate committee. Occasionally (as with the Civil Rights Bills of 1957 and 1964) the bill goes directly to the Senate Calendar if there is objection to second reading, a new legislative day, and objection to "further proceeding thereon." The Senate, then, has a procedural mechanism whereby House-passed bills may skip the committee stage and may be placed directly on the Calendar for floor action.

Whether the bill is placed directly on the Senate Calendar or referred to a committee, however, changes in the bill usually take place. For example, on appropriation bills changes are almost inevitable and in a predictable direction. The Constitution grants to the House of Representatives the initiative in revenue bills. This grant of authority to the House has, by custom, been extended to include appropriation bills as well. Members of the House Appropriations Committee view themselves, among other things, as guardians of the nation's purse.[1] It is probable that the House committee, on nearly every appropriation bill except possibly defense, will appropriate less money than the Administration requested and, in some cases such as foreign aid, considerably less. And on other than appropriation bills the House tends to be a more conservative body than is the Senate. Bills which the Administration wants will be modified in the direction of providing less than the Administration requests if and when they are finally cleared by the House.

When the bill is sent to the Senate, then, there often is a lot of pressure by the Administration, as well as by the groups and organizations which have been affected by the cuts made by the House, to restore, at least partially, the funds and provisions which have been deleted or reduced in the House bill. On appropriation bills the Senate has developed a reputation of being a "court of appeals" for those groups and agencies which have been particularly "mistreated" by the House.

These pressures for restoration of the original features of the bill prior to the changes made by the House, as well as the generally more

---

[1] Richard F. Fenno, Jr., "The House Appropriations Committee as a Political System: The Problem of Integration," *American Political Science Review*, vol. 56 (June, 1962), pp. 310–24. See also his *Power of the Purse* (Boston: Little, Brown, 1966).

liberal pressures represented in the Senate, mean that when a bill is passed by the House of Representatives and sent to the Senate, the Senate will probably increase the appropriation or "liberalize" the authorization more nearly in tune with Administration requests and liberal interests. The result is, of course, that the Senate bill and the House bill are different from each other not only in the amount of the program but also in terms of the interests who are benefited.

When the Senate passes its version of the bill it can do one of two things. It can either return the bill to the House with its amendments, thereby giving the House an opportunity to accept the Senate version of the bill, or it can send a message to the House insisting on its amendments to the House-passed bill and requesting a conference with the House. Whether the first or the second alternative is chosen will depend, in part, on whether the managers of the Senate bill think the House will accept the Senate amendments and on how insistent the Senate is on its amendments being accepted.

If the Senate sends the amended bill back to the House without a message requesting a conference, the House may then either accept the Senate amendments, or insist on its own version of the bill and request a conference with the Senate. It is at this point, however, prior to the Eighty-ninth Congress (1965–66), that criticism has been directed at the House for the manner in which it has handled bills which it has passed but which are returned to it by the Senate with amendments.

When the Senate returned the bill to the House, normally with a message asking for a conference, the bill was not privileged for floor action. The usual course of action for non-controversial bills (and some controversial ones) is to ask unanimous consent to take the bill from the Speaker's table and either accept the Senate amendments, reject the Senate amendments and ask for a conference, or accept the Senate's request for a conference. Prior to 1965, if there was one objection to this procedure, the bill had to go to the Rules Committee for a rule granting the bill privileged floor status.

Knowing what we now know about the Committee on Rules, and especially that it often over-represents conservative interests on some types of legislation, a more liberal Senate bill may run into trouble in the Rules Committee. The most notable example occurred in 1960 when the House, for the first time in its history, passed a general aid to education bill (with modest provisions for primary and secondary school construction). The Senate returned the bill to the

House with a number of liberalizing amendments. Unanimous consent was asked to take the bill from the Speaker's table and ask a conference with the Senate. Objection was heard and the original House-passed bill with Senate amendments went to the Rules Committee for a rule. The Committee on Rules, by a vote of 5–7, refused to grant a rule to send the bill to a conference. It was late in the session and little could be done. The House adjourned finally without the education bill, passed in different forms by both the House and the Senate, being allowed to go to conference.

This action by the Committee on Rules provoked such a storm of protest that it led, along with other factors including the election that fall of Senator Kennedy to the Presidency and the consequent expectation of a more liberal program, to a severe fight in 1961 to enlarge the Committee on Rules from 12 to 15 members. This increase in size of the committee would allow for the appointment of two new liberal Democrats (although not necessarily making the Committee on Rules friendly to education bills). It was expected that the Republicans would add an additional conservative, but that with the increased size of the committee liberal legislation would probably be reported out of the committee by at least an 8–7 vote. After an intense struggle between Speaker Rayburn and Judge Smith the motion to enlarge the committee, temporarily, was successful 217–212.[2] In 1963 the increased size of the committee was made permanent.

In 1965 the House passed a rule change which would no longer allow a single objection to prevent a House-passed bill with Senate amendments from coming directly to the floor. By a vote of 224 to 201 the House changed the rule to the effect that the Speaker, in his discretion, may recognize a member of the committee to move that the bill be taken from the Speaker's table. Such a motion, like other motions, would then be subject to a majority vote. Therefore, it is now possible for a majority of the House to send a House-passed bill with Senate amendments to a conference with the Senate, avoiding the Committee on Rules.

[2] See Milton C. Cummings, Jr. and Robert L. Peabody, "The Decision to Enlarge the Committee on Rules: An Analysis of the 1961 Vote," in Robert L. Peabody and Nelson W. Polsby, eds., *New Perspectives on the House of Representatives* (Chicago: Rand McNally, 1963), Chap. 7; and Hugh Douglas Price, "Race, Religion, and the Rules Committee: The Kennedy Aid-to-Education Bills," in Alan F. Westin, ed., *The Uses of Power* (New York: Harcourt, Brace & World, 1962), pp. 1–71.

Prior to the adoption of this rule in 1965, a number of interesting problems arose when unanimous consent to take a House-passed bill from the Speaker's table was refused. The Rules Committee could either grant or deny a rule, and if it granted a rule it could be one of three kinds. (1) Either the Committee could simply propose a rule giving the bill privilege to the floor at which point the House could, by majority vote, accept the Senate amendments or move to send the bill to conference, or (2) it could grant a rule which specifies that the bill must go to conference, and if the latter the rule could instruct the House delegation to the conference committee either to refuse to accept the Senate amendments, or (3) it could instruct the delegates to accept the Senate amendments, or even to refuse some and accept others. Since the adoption of the new rule in 1965, the same alternatives are open but they are no longer in the power of the Committee on Rules to structure. The Speaker, in conjunction with the floor manager for the bill, is now the major person involved in the type of motion which will be made. Several examples prior to 1965 may be helpful in understanding how the rule worked with respect to the Committee on Rules and help in gauging the magnitude of the change that took place in 1965.

In early December, 1963, the House of Representatives passed, by a vote of 216–182, a cotton subsidy bill. This was not a very popular bill and it is said that Speaker McCormack personally changed 40 votes in favor of the bill. The Cotton Bill was the first major piece of legislation to come before the House after the death of President Kennedy and the leadership was anxious that the new President not suffer a defeat.

In the Senate the Cotton Bill was also in deep trouble. Even the Chairman of the Agriculture Committee, Senator Ellender from Louisiana, was opposed to it. To insure a more favorable vote the Senate Agriculture Committee added to the Cotton Bill a large additional section dealing with wheat. This was done in the hopes of adding to the support which Southern Senators would give to the bill the support of those Senators to whom wheat was an important commodity. After a long and lengthy debate, the Cotton-Wheat Bill passed the Senate 53–35.

The Cotton Bill was returned to the House with the wheat amendments and unanimous consent to take the bill from the Speaker's table was denied. The bill then went to the Rules Committee for a rule. At the time the Rules Committee also had before it a food-stamp bill to continue the program of selling to poor families stamps for six dollars which could be redeemed at grocery stores for ten dollars worth of food. This program was strongly supported by Northern Democrats.

Northern Democrats had, in the past, supported agricultural subsidy programs even though, by and large, they have no constituents who receive the benefits of these subsidies. Most Northern Democrats are elected from urban, not rural areas. However, many of them gave their support to farm programs for a variety of reasons, some ideological (helping the poor, whether on the farm or in the city), some having to do with attempting to handle the farm surplus problem. For the first time since agricultural subsidies, however, it became apparent to the Northern, liberal Democrats that they might be able to get something in return for their support of agricultural subsidies. They decided that they would withdraw their support for the Cotton-Wheat Bill unless they received Southern Democratic and Republican support for the food stamp plan.

The bargain was struck. The Cotton-Wheat Bill was sent to a conference with the Senate and the food stamp plan was given a rule and passed the House. The House conferees accepted the Senate wheat amendments, and the bill, now in identical language, was returned to the House and Senate where it was passed and sent to the President for his signature.

This bill is perhaps a classic example of the legislative logroll. Not only was a whole new section (wheat) added to the bill to increase its chances of passing the Senate, but when returned to the House an additional logroll took place with another bill lodged in Rules Committee.

A second interesting issue in 1964 was the beef import bill. It is an example of a problem alluded to earlier in Chapter Eight when we discussed the germaneness rule in the Senate.

There had been in the period 1963–64 falling beef prices and Western, Midwestern, and some Southern Senators were especially interested in attempting to block the importation of beef, primarily from Australia and New Zealand. What these "beef" senators and congressmen wanted was a quota placed on beef imports. The fact that a very difficult and tedious set of tariff negotiations was then taking place in Geneva under the new Kennedy trade law of 1962 placed the Administration firmly against a quota on the importation of beef. Besides, many observers thought the problem had been created by domestic beef producers who were simply increasing their production, causing a surplus of beef and lowering prices.

Given the opposition of the Administration and of many Northern Democrats and "free trade" supporters, it became necessary for the supporters of a quota on beef imports to devise a carefully planned strategy. First, it was felt that getting the quota bill through the Senate would be a good deal easier than attempting to get the bill through the House of Representatives. Not only because Mike Mansfield from Montana (a beef producing state) was the majority leader and thus subject to at least some cross-pressure from his constituents and the beef industry, but also because the Senate is traditionally an easier institution in which cattle and beef interests can negotiate. Essentially this has to do with the fact that senators from beef states have as many votes as senators from more populous industrial states.

In addition to the greater likelihood that the Senate would pass such a bill, it was felt that the difficulties of getting a beef quota bill through the Ways and Means Committee, the Rules Committee, and the House floor would be almost insurmountable. A strategy had to be devised to attempt to "skip" the House of Representatives.

Proponents of the beef quota bill decided on the strategy of taking a bill from the House of Representatives which had already been passed, amend it to include the restrictions desired on the importation of beef, and return the bill to the House with the new amendments. It will be recalled that such a strategy relies on the lack of a germaneness rule and that any amendment on any subject may be in order on any bill before the Senate, except a general appropriations bill. The proponents then felt that perhaps they would be able to get the Committee on Rules to send the bill to conference and get the House conferees to agree to the Senate amendments. Such a strategy would avoid a whole series of fights in the House of Representatives.

The House of Representatives during the Eighty-eighth Congress (1963–64) passed a bill having to do with the free importation of certain wild animals for sale in the United States. This bill was so non-controversial that it passed the House on the Consent Calendar where one objection could have prevented its passage. H.R. 1839 was then sent to the Senate and there referred to the Finance Committee. The Finance Committee then actually struck out of the bill the provisions relating to the importation of wild animals and in its place "amended" the bill with a restriction on the importing of beef. The only thing the bill had in common with the House-passed bill when it was reported from the Senate Finance Committee was the House number.

The beef quota bill, after rather lengthy debate in the Senate, passed the Senate 72–15. The bill then came back to the House of Representatives—a completely different bill than had originally passed the House. Objection was heard to a unanimous consent request to take the bill from the Speaker's table and it went to the Rules Committee for a rule.

Representative Olsen of Montana proposed a resolution to the Rules Committee which would instruct the House conferees to accept the Senate amendments. Representative Mills, Chairman of Ways and Means Committee, from which the original bill came, was less enthusiastic about a bill which would restrict beef imports. Mills was also under pressure from the Administration not to accept a bill which would adversely affect our reciprocal trade program or which would hinder our bargaining position at the trade negotiations then going on in Geneva. Chairman Mills countered Representative Olsen's request to the Rules Committee, simply asking the Rules Committee for a rule which would allow the House to meet in conference committee with the Senate, but with no instructions. Others argued against any rule at all. Many of the latter were Northern Democratic liberals who are strong supporters of free trade. The interesting point, however, is that, not too uncommonly, Northern Democratic liberals were asking the Committee on Rules not to report a resolution, but rather to let the bill die in Committee.

The Rules Committee granted a rule for a conference without instructions (the rule favored by Chairman Mills) by a vote of 8–7. However, to get this rule Mills had to promise that he would try to work out some kind of compromise. The conferees were appointed, a compromise was worked out which kept the idea of quotas but set the quotas at a high enough level that no one really thought they would ever be reached. In case they were, however, the President was granted authority to raise them even further if to do so would be viewed by him as in the national interest. After some grumbling among senators and congressmen who wanted more, the conference report was accepted by both the House and the Senate and the bill was signed into law by the President.

The procedures which were followed in this bill illustrate a most important strategy. One way of avoiding a whole series of pitfalls in the House of Representatives is for the proponents to use some non-controversial bill already passed by the House, and, because the rule of germaneness does not apply in the Senate (except for general appropriations bills), attach another bill to it. The bill is then returned to the House, with the Senate amendments, and several legislative stages in the House have been avoided. First, committee and subcommittee hearings, consideration, and votes have been avoided; then a request for a rule from the Committee on Rules has been by-passed; and, of course, the strategy avoids an initial floor fight. Prior to 1965 the bill would at least have been sent to the Committee on Rules, and then a floor fight on the adoption of the rule could be expected. Since the rule change in 1965 which allows a majority to send a bill to conference without a rule from the Rules Committee only a floor fight can be expected.

This, in fact, was one of the major arguments used by those who did not want the rules changed to allow a majority to send a bill to conference. The argument, propounded by Judge Smith and other conservatives, was that since the Senate can attach non-germane matters to a House-passed bill, some committee consideration is necessary. Giving the Rules Committee an opportunity to pass on the bill is better than no committee action at all. Too many people, however, recalled what had happened in 1960 with the general aid to education bill and other Rules Committee efforts to block legislation from going to conference. Generally, such blocks were thrown at liberal legislation, not conservative legislation. Changing this rule, then, was viewed as an effort to change the rules slightly more in favor of liberal legislation.

A third interesting example of conference committee politics and the effect conference committees can have on the course of legislation is the 1964 social security and "medicare" bill.

On July 29, 1964 the House passed and sent to the Senate a bill increasing by 5 percent the monthly payments under social security and, to pay for such increases, the bill also provided for an increase in the employer and employee payroll tax and base to which the tax was applied. The bill was heavily supported by a bipartisan majority and on the roll-call vote there were only 8 votes against the bill.

Social security bills, because they are tax bills, traditionally have gone to the Ways and Means Committee in the House and its counterpart, the Finance Committee, in the Senate. Medical care for the aged, because the program is tied to the social security system, has also been handled by these two committees. The Chairman of Ways and Means, Wilbur Mills, up until 1965 had opposed a medical insurance program under the social security system. He had not, however, opposed these kinds of programs in principle, being co-author of the only medical insurance program then in force (but not part of the social security system), the Kerr-Mills program. Representative Cecil King of California, second-ranking Democrat on Ways and Means, with several other liberal Democrats wanted, in committee, to attach to the social security bill a medicare bill financed under social security, but lacking the votes to pass such a proposal the attempt was shelved. Since the social security bill, as almost all Ways and Means bills, went to the floor under a closed rule, an amendment on the floor to include the medicare bill was not in order. Since the bill could not be reported out of the Ways and Means Committee there seemed little hope for House action on medicare during the Eighty-eighth Congress (1963–64).

After passing the House, the social security bill then went to the Senate Finance Committee where attempts were made by liberal Democrats on the Committee to add the medicare provisions as an amendment to the social security bill. These attempts, however, were soundly defeated. It will be recalled earlier in our discussion of Senate committees and the distribution of power on the committees, that the Finance Committee is heavily weighted in a conservative direction. Not only is it one of the few committees in the Eighty-eighth Congress which had less than a two-to-one ratio in favor of Democrats, it was the only committee in the Eighty-ninth Congress (1965–66) with less than a two-to-one majority (11 to 6). The Senate Finance Committee is also the committee with the most conservative Democratic Presidential Support Score average and the most conservative Republican Presidential Support Score average. In other words, not only are Democrats not represented "fairly" on the committee, but liberal Democrats and liberal Republicans are not equitably represented. It comes as no surprise, then, that the medicare amendment failed of adoption in committee.

When the social security bill, without medicare, was reported by the Finance Committee to the Senate floor, a number of interesting strategies were employed. For example, it is felt by many that the social security tax probably cannot be raised above a certain level.

At the time the bill was being considered in 1964 the tax rate was three and five-eighths from the employee and an identical percentage matched by the employer. Many tax experts felt at the time that a combined 10 percent tax (5 percent by the employee, 5 percent by the employer) is as high as this form of taxation will be tolerated. Senator Russell Long of Louisiana, an opponent of medicare at that time, proposed increasing the benefits of social security beyond the 5 percent proposed in the bill and, to pay for this increase, Senator Long also proposed increasing the social security tax even higher than that proposed in the bill (eventually reaching very close to the "magic" 10 percent figure). Had Long's amendment been adopted, most observers felt that it would have had the effect of freezing out the possibility of including in the social security system a medical care for the aged program. The attempt failed, with many Senate liberals opposing an amendment they normally might have supported.

After this attempt to "freeze out" the medicare bill failed, the medicare amendment was then proposed. The Senate, unlike the House, does not have a rule which may be invoked to bar amendments from the floor. After lengthy debate, the Senate, for the first time in history in either House, passed a medical care for the aged program by a vote of 49–44. The social security bill, with medicare, was then returned to the House.

Again, as with our other two examples, unanimous consent to take the bill from the Speaker's table was refused. The bill then went to the Committee on Rules for a rule. Representative King proposed before the Rules Committee that they report a rule which would instruct the House conferees to accept the Senate amendments. A rule was also proposed which would instruct the House conferees not to accept the Senate provision, and Chairman Mills asked for a simple rule to send the bill to conference with the Senate but without instructions of any kind. Mills' proposal was adopted by the Committee on Rules.

Representative King then tried to take the fight to the floor of the House. When the rule came to the floor Representative King wanted to amend the rule adding instructions to accept the Senate medicare amendment. However, he found that he did not have the votes and so dropped the plan. On analysis, he found that this would have been very unfavorable grounds on which to fight for medicare. The vote would not have been on the medicare amendment but rather on a procedural motion to amend the rule reported by the

Rules Committee to instruct the House conferees to accept the Senate amendment. The House seldom instructs its conferees, and many House members are reluctant to support such a motion, regardless of the issue involved, for fear that an attempt to instruct the conferees of their own committee may one day be at stake.

Not only, then, did Representative King find that the fight would be fought over procedure and not entirely over the medicare provision, but he found that procedure to be extremely complicated. It would not be just one vote that the pro-medicare forces would have to win, but rather four votes. First, a motion to instruct the conferees not to accept a Senate amendment has precedence over a motion to instruct the conferees to accept a Senate amendment. King's forces would have to defeat this first motion. Second, the opponents of medicare would then move the previous question, ending debate and prohibiting further amendments. Medicare proponents would have to defeat this motion. Only after these two initial skirmishes would King's amendment to the rule be in order. That motion would have to pass, and then a motion on the adoption of the rule, as amended, would have to pass. This was indeed a quagmire of rules and procedures which King found quite to his disadvantage.

The House adopted the rule as proposed by Mills to send the bill to a conference with the Senate without instructions to the House conferees. In conference, the Senate conferees stuck to their medicare amendment and the House conferees insisted on their opposition to medicare. No agreement was reached in conference and medicare, *along with the social security bill,* died in conference. The conferees could not agree on a bill in identical form, although they had no disagreement about the original House-passed bill increasing benefits under social security. Lacking such agreement, there could be no bill at all.

These three examples illustrate the kinds of problems which can arise when the House and the Senate pass bills in different forms. These particular problems occur when the Senate adds amendments or makes changes in House-passed bills. Since 1965, it is no longer necessary to send a bill to the Rules Committee if unanimous consent to take the bill from the Speaker's table is refused. However, the House does confront the same problem. It will be the leadership, primarily the Speaker, majority leader, and relevant committee chairman, rather than the Committee on Rules, who will decide under what circumstances the bill should be sent to a conference committee with the Senate. Thus, the problem remains the same; the locus of the decision, however, has changed. As with a rule from the Rules Committee sending a bill to conference, the decision taken by the leadership is subject to majority approval, and may be amended. The major difference between the procedure before the rules change and after the rules change is that bills desired by the leadership cannot be held up from a conference committee by Rules Committee inaction. It will always be possible for the leadership to get to the floor a House-passed bill with Senate amendments which needs to be passed in identical form by both Houses before being sent to the President for his signature.

SENATE-PASSED BILLS

The discussion to this point has related primarily to House-passed bills sent to the Senate and returned to the House with amendments or changes. The reverse, of course, also occurs. The Senate passes some bills first and sends them to the House. Under these circumstances, *unless the House has a similar bill already on the Calendar*, the bill must be sent to a committee. The House, unlike the Senate, does not have a provision in its rules in which Senate-passed bills can go directly on the Calendar unless a similar House bill has already been reported from a committee and is on the Calendar.

For example, in 1964 the Senate passed the Administration's Anti-Poverty Bill before the House. The bill was then sent to the House. But, since the House Labor and Education Committee had already reported an Anti-Poverty Bill, and since the bill was already on the Calendar, the Senate-passed bill did not have to be referred to committee. Eventually, when the House bill was taken from the Calendar, Representative Landrum of Georgia, the House floor manager for the anti-poverty program, offered the Senate-passed bill as a substitute for his own committee's bill. The strategy here was to accept the already negotiated compromise embodied in the Senate bill to avoid unnecessary fights on the House floor which might endanger the entire bill. It was at this point that Judge Smith offered his preferential motion to strike the enacting clause, a tactic which, fortunately for the bill, failed.

When Senate bills are sent to the House of Representatives, then, the normal route is to refer them to one of the House committees (this is also true, of course, with House-passed bills which are sent to the Senate). If the bill is then reported from the House committee, it is often already amended and changed from the version which passed the Senate. The bill is then frequently amended further on the House floor. If the Senate-passed bill is not reported from a House committee, it may be dislodged by a motion to discharge the committee.

If the Senate-passed bill is reported from a committee and passed on the House floor with amendments, it is then returned to the Senate. The House, however, has two options. Either the House itself can ask for a conference with the Senate, or it can simply send the bill to the Senate. The Senate can either then accept the House amendments or itself ask for a conference. The usual strategy, if the House members in charge know that the Senate is probably not going to accept the House amendments, is for the House to ask for the conference. The reasoning here is obvious. If the House returns the bill to the Senate and the Senate does not accept the House amendments, it will return the bill to the House and ask for a conference. Prior to 1965, to agree to such a request would have required either unanimous consent or a rule from the Committee on Rules. Since 1965 such a request requires the affirmative action of the House.

To avoid this additional stage the House will often itself ask for a conference if the Senate is expected not to accept the House amendments. Prior to 1965 this avoided having to go unnecessarily to the Rules Committee. Since 1965 it avoids unnecessarily bringing the bill back out onto the House floor. The Senate, of course, may still agree to the House amendments even if the House has asked for a conference. So no harm is done for the House to ask for a conference prematurely with the Senate. The advantage is to avoid the possibility that the bill will come back to the House before going to a conference anyway, and the possibility that the House would not, at that later time, authorize such a conference. The danger of this happening is less under the new rule than under the old rule, but it is a possibility nevertheless.

Since the Senate does not have a Rules Committee, Senate-passed bills which are amended by the House and returned to the Senate have not run into the same kinds of problems as some House-passed bills returned to the House. Senate-passed bills returned to the Senate with House amendments simply go onto the Senate Calendar and are scheduled by the majority leader in consultation with other interested senators.

Senate-passed bills returned by the House with amendments, when placed on the Senate Calendar, are subject to a filibuster—in fact, two filibusters, one on the motion to consider and the second on final passage. This means, then, that once the Senate has handled a bill, the House must accept the Senate version of the bill if a filibuster is threatened in the Senate when the bill is returned. For example, on a civil rights bill, if the House has passed a bill and sent it to the Senate and the Senate has amended it and returned it to the House, the House must accept the Senate amendments unless it is willing to return the bill to the Senate for a possible filibuster.

Since the House, unlike the Senate, has a rather strict rule of germaneness regarding amendments, the strategy of attaching onto a Senate-passed bill an entirely different bill is not common. It is possible, however, for the House to strengthen or weaken various portions of the bill, or even to add whole new titles to the bill, as long as they are germane. The bill is then returned to the Senate for action there. However it is not possible, as it is with House-passed bills being returned to the House with whole new bills attached as non-germane riders by the Senate, for this practice to occur in reverse. A strategy to try to skip Senate committees by attaching a non-germane amendment to an already Senate-passed bill is not practical under House rules.

However, it is possible for Senate committees to be skipped in a quite different way. House-passed bills may be placed directly on the Senate Calendar without being referred to Senate committees. In fact, a single senator need only object twice on different legislative days to place a House-passed bill directly on the Senate Calendar. So, although the rules and procedures are quite different in each house, each house does have a mechanism whereby its own committees may be by-passed if action is taken in the other body. House committees may be by-passed by a non-germane amendment to a House-passed bill. Senate committees may be by-passed by placing a House-passed bill directly on the Calendar.

General Strategies and Tactics

Since the United States Congress is composed of two houses rather than just one, and since both houses of Congress must pass legislation in identical form before it can become law, a number of interesting problems arise with respect to strategies and tactics to determine which house of Congress should consider the legislation first, which second, and which house should call for a conference. That is, will it make any difference in legislative outcomes which house acts on a bill first? Will the Administration get a stronger bill if one house rather than another house acts first? Is the Administration more likely to get a bill if one house acts before the other house? These are important questions involving general congressional strategies and tactics. The answers vary somewhat, depending upon what kinds of difficulties are expected in each house.

Usually if a bill will have an easier time passing in the House than in the Senate, the advantage is in having the House pass the bill first. It is advantageous for several reasons, one being that once the bill is passed by the House it is always possible to put the bill directly on the Senate Calendar, by-passing the Senate committee, if this is what is delaying the bill. For example, on a civil rights bill, it is always better for the House to act before the Senate. Not only will the House pass a stronger bill, but the bill can then be placed directly on the Senate Calendar. Also, if the bill originates in the House only one filibuster in the Senate is likely. On the other hand, if the bill originates in the Senate, there is opportunity for more delays and possible defeat. There may be a filibuster when the Senate considers the bill, and then, if the bill is to be made stronger in the House, a second filibuster on the bill produced by the conference committee. A stronger bill usually results if the Senate is confronted with the strongest bill the House is able to produce.

If, on the other hand, the bill will have an easier time passing in the Senate than in the House, or if the Senate might pass a stronger bill than the House, then the advantage is in having the Senate pass the bill first. It may be necessary, under some circumstances, for the Senate to take an already House-passed bill and attach a non-germane amendment in the form of a bill to the House-passed bill. As we have seen, this would have the effect of skipping the committee stage of consideration in the House. This would be desirable if a House committee were not likely to report the bill. If it is simply a question of the Senate's passing the stronger bill, it is still an advantage to have the Senate pass the bill first. A number of parliamentary procedures would then be open, such as substituting the Senate-passed bill for the bill reported by the House committee when the House bill reaches the floor.

In general, then, what is being suggested here is that the strategy most likely to succeed is to have the house which is either more likely to pass any bill, or the house which is more likely to pass a stronger bill pass the bill first. If the more favorable house should go first this opens up the possibility of either skipping the committee stage in the other house, or forcing the other house to deal with a bill already passed. The house which is less likely to act, or to act more weakly, is then confronted with a different problem. The question is no longer whether there will be a bill or no bill, the probability of there being a strong bill versus a weaker bill becomes one of the alternatives. If committees in the house which acts second do not act at all, a stronger bill might pass the floor of that house than if the committees in that house had an opportunity to work out a weaker bill.

In addition, once a bill has passed one house the pressure for passage in the other house is greater. The members of one house have committed themselves to a bill. Once having made the commitment they will want to fulfill that commitment. For example, let us assume that to vote for a controversial bill will cost votes at home (as well as, perhaps, gain votes). If one chooses to vote for the bill, one has paid the cost. But let us assume that the bill fails in the other house. Then, generally speaking, the cost has been for naught (this is not quite the case since credit can be given even though a bill has not resulted). An example of this would be the 1964 Civil Rights Bill. Many Republicans in the House voted for the strongest Civil Rights Bill in history. Many of them did not want to be left out on a limb. If the Senate did not pass a bill, or if the Senate dropped several important provisions in the bill, the Republicans who voted for the bill might feel that they had done so at their own risk with no payoff. Thus, there was a great deal of pressure on the Senate, and especially on Senate Republicans, to accept most of what the House Republicans had committed themselves to.

Although the best legislative strategy may determine that one house should act before the other, there are a number of factors which, in fact, promote the opposite result. It takes time and energy to pass a piece of legislation. Many hours of hard work, and many resources which could be used in other ways have to be diverted in the enterprise. If it is felt that the other house will not pass a bill, there may be reluctance for the other body to use its resources in what its members may feel is a bootless endeavor. This will be especially true if, at one time, they had passed a bill and found that the other body did not do so. In the future they would feel that when the other body acts then they will act, but that it is useless to act first.

What strategies will be employed, then, depends upon a number of factors including what the bill is about, which body will more probably pass the bill, and the parliamentary strategies and tactics which are available. Given knowledge of these factors, however, we can probably specify what the "best" strategy would be to pass a particular bill. For example, what would be the strategy most often successful on a general aid to education bill? Since the Senate has passed a general aid bill four times, and the House only once, and since when they both passed a bill the Senate bill was stronger (and the House finally killed the bill anyway through its Rules Committee which refused to grant a rule to go to conference), we would suggest that the bill should start in the Senate. If a weaker bill passes the House (it is expected that the House will pass, if it passes a bill at all, a weaker bill), the House should ask for a conference with the Senate. A problem then arises, however, if the conference goes beyond the House bill. What are the chances that the House will not accept the conference report? A compromise in the conference must be negotiated very carefully to insure that a conference report will not be rejected by the House. But even if the conference agreed upon the House-passed bill, the argument here is that it will be a stronger bill because the Senate acted first than it would have been had the House acted first.

The strategy in 1960 on the education bill, then, was headed for trouble from the start. The House passed a weak bill and sent it to the Senate. The Senate then strengthened the bill through amendments and returned it to the House. This gave the Rules Committee an opportunity to deny a rule for a conference and, because it was late in the session, the bill died. The strategy in 1965, although successful, was also the reverse of what is being suggested here. The pressures to let the least favorable house act first are strong indeed.

COMPOSITION AND ACTIVITIES OF CONFERENCE COMMITTEES

Not all bills require that a conference committee meet. For example, of the 1,026 public and private bills which were passed in the Eighty-eighth Congress (1963–64), 89 bills were sent to conference.

Of these 89 bills, 85 finally became law. We can say, then, that when both houses of Congress pass bills in different language, one house usually accepts the language of the other house. Normally, the language of the house which passed the bill second is the language which is adopted. Only on controversial bills, or on bills where the two versions differ significantly from one another will a conference committee be necessitated. This occurs on approximately a tenth of all bills which are passed. We can also say that usually when a bill is sent to conference differences will be resolved and a bill which both houses can agree on will be reported. Only occasionally will a bill be stranded in conference. The most significant bill left in conference in the Eighty-eighth Congress (1963–64) was the bill to increase the benefits and taxes under social security, with an amendment adding a medicare program which was attached to the bill in the Senate. So, although not many bills are left in conference, it may occur that the bills which are left in conference are relatively important bills.

When a conference committee is necessary because one house or the other will not accept the amendments of the other body, a conference committee is appointed. In the House of Representatives, the conferees are appointed by the Speaker. In the Senate, the conferees are appointed by the President of the Senate. Those appointed as conferees are almost always those who have had major responsibility for the legislation and are senior members of the committee which handled the legislation. Conference committees are always bipartisan, with the majority party having a majority on each house's delegation. The number of conferees sent by each body is likely to vary, but the fact that the two bodies send delegations of unequal size is not of great importance since a conference report must be approved by a majority within *each* delegation. The Legislative Reorganization Act of 1946 specifies that conferees must have demonstrated support for the bill which has passed their respective bodies, but in practice this provision is often ignored.

The conferees meet, usually in the Senate wing of the Capitol, and discuss the differences in the two bills. Normally the conferees are free to compromise on any differences, but occasionally they are instructed by their respective bodies to insist on one or more of the provisions in the bill as it passed that body. The conferees, by the rules of both houses, are limited in their negotiations to differences between the two houses. They may not add new legislation, nor may they change provisions already agreed upon by both houses. Normally, however, they have wide leeway. The House, for example, may agree to Senate provisions in return for the Senate conferees agreeing to certain House provisions. That is, some provisions may be ironed out by simple logrolling. Or, the conferees may compromise their differences, choosing a position between the two sets of provisions.

Usually, the conference committee is able to settle the differences between the two bills and agree on identical language. If they cannot, they may report this fact to their respective bodies and either get instructions from them, recede in the outstanding differences, or try another conference. If they cannot agree, the bill fails.

Assuming that the differences are reconciled, each delegation reports back to its respective chamber. In each house, conference committee reports are privileged. In the House, for example, conference committee reports do not need a rule from the Committee on Rules. They may be brought to the floor as a matter of high privilege, even interrupting the pending business.

Occasionally, but only for special reasons, a conference report must go to the Committee on Rules for a rule. This can happen under two circumstances. A conference committee report must, like other reports of committees, lie over one day in the House (not so in the Senate). If the managers want to bring it up the same day it is reported then they must get a rule from the Rules Committee which, in effect, would suspend the rules. Second, occasionally a conference committee report will contain additional legislation. A point of order may then lie against it when the report is brought to the floor. A rule from the Rules Committee is then needed which will waive points of order against the conference report. This occurred, for example, on the foreign aid bill in December, 1963. Additional legislation was inserted in the bill which the floor managers discovered could rule the conference report out of order. A special rule from the Rules Committee was necessary to bring the conference report to the floor.

In the Senate a motion to consider is not even debatable as it is on other bills, although the conference committee report itself is debatable. The fact that conference committee reports are debatable in the Senate, and a two-thirds vote is necessary for cloture, has a number of consequences for a bill like a civil rights bill. For example, if the House sends a civil rights bill to the Senate and the Senate changes even a single word (which is quite possible), the House is, in a sense, forced to accept the Senate version. The alternative to accepting the Senate bill is to request a conference, the report from which would, in turn, require the approval of the Senate, thereby setting the stage for a possible second filibuster.

Conference committee reports, when they come to the floor, may not be amended. They are either accepted or rejected by each house. This, for obvious reasons, gives enormous power to the conferees. It is up to these relatively small groups to work out differences which may affect expenditures of millions of dollars, the initiation of new programs (such as medicare, for example), and the continuation of old programs. Conference committees, unfortunately for those interested in what is happening and why, are always held in executive session. Hence the kinds of bargaining which take place are not known precisely.

There is also a chance, even after the House and Senate have passed different versions of the same bill, that a conference committee may not be appointed.

> Both the House and Senate passed home rule legislation in 1965, but the measures were vastly different and, according to some observers, irreconcilable. After considering various alternatives, the Senate April 5, 1966, voted to send the bills to conference with the House. The House District Committee May 11, however, rejected a motion by Rep. Frank J. Horton (R N.Y.) asking that House conferees be appointed. The Horton motion was substituted for a motion by Rep. Basil L. Whitener (D N.C.) asking that conferees not be appointed this session. The rejection of the Horton motion dealt home rule another blow; but the Committee later could vote on another motion to appoint conferees. Observers believe the key to another vote is Committee Chairman John J. McMillan (D S.C.). Although McMillan, a staunch opponent of home rule, said he did not see "how we can get together on two absolutely different bills," he did not entirely rule out a conference, particularly if six other bills affecting the District, including anticrime legislation, can be cleared.
>
> Normally, sending differing versions of House and Senate bills to conference would be a routine procedure, but the political and parliamentary circumstances make each step in conferring on home rule a difficult one. Although the task is admittedly more difficult considering the House Committee's May 11 action, home rule could be enacted if it could make

its way through four steps. First, House conferees must be appointed. If the House is able to do this, it must then determine who the conferees will be. After this is done, the House and Senate conferees must reach a compromise on the measures. And finally, the compromise must be acceptable to both houses of Congress.

Traditionally, the chairman of the committee with jurisdiction over the matter (or some other designated committee member such as a subcommittee chairman) moves that conferees be appointed, and the House approves the motion by unanimous consent. As Speaker John W. McCormack (D Mass.) pointed out in January 1965, this works in "19 cases out of 20." If, however, someone objects to sending the bill to conference by unanimous consent, as appears likely or at least possible with home rule, the committee with jurisdiction over the subject can designate the chairman or any other member to move that conferees be appointed by a majority vote of the House. This rule was adopted at the beginning of the 89th Congress to facilitate sending bills over which there was some controversy to conference, but it has never been used. For this method to work in the case of home rule, the House District Committee would have to designate someone to make the move, the Speaker would have to recognize the designated person and the House would have to approve the move. Some question exists over whether or not the House District Committee would ever designate such a person, especially in view of the May 11 committee vote, and over whether or not a majority of the House would approve the action.

A bill also could be sent to conference by a special resolution from the House Rules Committee or under suspension of the rules. The Rules Committee, however, like the District Committee, was discharged from further consideration of the pending home rule legislation in 1965; thus, opposition exists there. And suspension of the rules requires a two-thirds vote of the House and is therefore seldom used.

If McMillan should move to send the issue to conference, the usual procedure calls for the Speaker of the House to appoint McMillan and other senior members of the District Committee, many of whom are opponents of home rule, as conferees rather than to name signers of the discharge petition who backed the Administration bill or proponents of Rep. B. F. Sisk's (D Calif.) substitute which passed the House. Actually, the House rules only say that the Speaker shall appoint conferees, but a list of recommended conferees is usually presented to the Speaker when the motion to appoint conferees is made and the Speaker generally follows the recommendation. As a matter of practice, the list normally contains the names of the senior members of the committee.

At one time there was discussion of the possibility of bypassing the District Committee in appointing conferees since the Committee had been discharged from further consideration of the pending home rule legislation in 1965. But such proposals apparently have been rejected as impractical, and McMillan has reportedly made it known that the District Committee intends to maintain jurisdiction over the matter for conference purposes.

Observers believe that any subsequent move similar to Horton's, to be successful, would have to be made with McMillan's help. With McMillan in the leading role, he and other senior committee members would again be placed in a position to be appointed conferees.

Home rule, then, if it reached the conference stage, could be caught between House opponents and Senate supporters. Therefore, if a conference were finally held, it could drag on until the end of the session without ever reaching agreement. Some observers, however, believe that if the bills are sent to conference, some decision will already have been made on what the grounds for discussion will be.

Finally, the conferees would have to seek a solution which not only would meet the approval of the conferees but also would be acceptable to both houses of Congress. Some observers doubt that such a solution can be reached. Most of those willing to compromise apparently believe a modified Sisk bill would have the best chance on enactment during 1966.

In the Senate there is a possibility that Sen. Wayne Morse (D Ore.) might filibuster a conference report recommending a charter board (as the Sisk bill does) on the grounds that it is not the best or quickest means of achieving home rule; that home rule opponents might join in such a filibuster to kill the bill; and that the Senate, which accepted the Administration bill by a 63–29 vote, might refuse to accept a modified Sisk bill as an unsuitable approach to home rule.

House observers generally agree that a proposed boycott of certain District merchants turned many "fence-sitters" against home rule and that the House in general has lost interest in

the issue. They say that home rule legislation will not pass
the House if it contains an automatic federal pay provision
as provided in the Senate bill (see below). These observers
also point out that the Sisk substitute passed the House under
a variety of circumstances and in an atmosphere that no
longer exists. The House is now divided among members committed to a number of positions, including opposition to
home rule and support of the Administration bill, the Sisk
substitute or an amended version of one of these measures.

The main reason for the attempts to work out a home rule
solution during the 89th Congress seems to be that the House
has passed home rule legislation for the first time in history.
Another reason is that the Democrats have a large majority
in the House — a number of whom are freshmen — and the
1966 election might modify the majority or the political atmosphere in the House, making enactment of any measure
in 1967 even more difficult than in 1966.

The Senate July 22, 1965, passed an amended Administration bill (S 1118) providing for election, on a partisan basis,
of a mayor, district council and a non-voting delegate to the
U.S. House of Representatives, and for election of a nonpartisan board of education. In what was probably its most controversial section, S 1118 authorized automatic annual appropriations of federal funds to the District on the basis of a flexible
formula reflecting the value of federal property in the District
and established a similar formula for determining the limit on
D.C. borrowing. Maximum limits on D.C. borrowing and
the federal payment were currently set by Congress and subject to annual Congressional appropriation. The bill, the
sixth D.C. home rule bill passed by the Senate, made its provisions contingent on approval by D.C. voters in a special
referendum.

The House Sept. 29, after the House District of Columbia
and Rules Committees had been discharged from further
consideration of S 1118's companion bill (HR 4644), passed
a completely new version of S 1118. The substitute was proposed by Rep. Sisk, a member of the House District and
Rules Committees.

Under the House version, if D.C. voters determined in a
referendum that they wanted home rule, a 15-member D.C.
Charter Board elected on a nonpartisan basis would be given
seven months to prepare a charter which would then be sub-

mitted to D.C. voters in another referendum. If accepted, it would go into effect in 90 days unless disapproved by either house of Congress. This was the first D.C. home rule legislation ever to pass the House.

No immediate attempts were made in 1965 to reconcile the two vastly different plans. A Congressional Quarterly survey of House offices and pressure groups concerned with the bill revealed that massive indifference doomed the Administration measure in the House in 1965.

With the Senate unwilling to accept the House-passed bill, three main means of breaking the impasse between the two versions were proposed between sessions of Congress. At the invitation of Sisk, Sen. Alan Bible (D Nev.), chairman of the Senate District Committee, flew to Fresno, Calif., where the two agreed that the best strategy would be for the Senate to amend the House bill and return the amended bill to the House for final approval. Joseph L. Rauh, Jr., chairman of the D.C. Democratic Central Committee and vice chairman of the Americans for Democratic Action, however, suggested attaching the Senate home rule measure as a rider to a high priority House-passed bill and sending it back to the House or going to conference with the House in hope of at least obtaining a modified version of the Senate bill. . . .

At this point it was generally conceded that a modified version of the Sisk substitute had the best chance of enactment during 1966. Bible Jan. 10 had rejected the idea of attaching home rule as a rider, saying that home rule "must stand or fall on its own." Going to conference presented the problems of appointing conferees and finding grounds on which to confer. Thus, it was speculated that the Senate would amend the Sisk bill in a manner acceptable to Sisk (some eight amendments were reportedly being considered) and return it to the House. Sisk was expected to seek a special resolutions from the Rules Committee to consider the amended version on the House floor. Such a move was opposed by certain home rule advocates who hoped that the House would accept the Senate version, if permitted to vote on it as a rider attached to priority legislation, and by home rule opponents who did not want the issue brought to the House floor again.

After the President's statements on home rule early this year, House Speaker McCormack reportedly told Bible that the next move was up to the Senate. The Senate District Committee Jan. 25 appointed Bible, Robert F. Kennedy (D N.Y.) and Winston L. Prouty (R Vt.) to confer with President Johnson and McCormack about the possibility of passing home rule legislation in 1966.

Sen. Morse, a staunch supporter of home rule and a member of the Senate District Committee, however, opposed the move, contending that the two measures were too different to try to combine and advising the home rule supporters "wait until 1967 and try again to clear a fresh mayor bill through both houses." Morse said he was "unalterably opposed" to any charter board home rule bill, a statement that was taken by by some observers to mean that he would filibuster such a proposal on the Senate floor. A Morse filibuster could be lengthened by a filibuster conducted by home rule opponents, who although differing politically with Morse on the issue saw the parliamentary situation to benefit their position. This could, of course, kill any amended Sisk bill which the Senate District Committee sent to the Senate floor.

Rauh Feb. 1 sent McCormack and certain home rule advocates in the Senate a memorandum proposing a plan to bring the House-passed bill, amended to provide for a mayor-council, back to the House floor for consideration. Because the House District Committee had been discharged from consideration of the home rule "until the bill is finally disposed of," Rauh said, "the House clearly intended that someone stand in the place of the . . . Committee" and that the signers of the discharge petition were the ones who should take the Committee's place. Any one of the signers, Rauh said, could move that the bill as amended in the Senate be taken up for House consideration, a move normally made by the chairman of the committee with jurisdiction over the bill—in this case the discharged committee. Rauh further states, "Mere absence of precedent for calling up a discharged bill that has subsequently been amended by the Senate is no reason that home rule legislation need be bottled up. Far more relevant here than the lack of precedent is the fact that there is no precedent to prevent the Speaker from permitting the House to act on the Senate's amendments." Observers generally considered Rauh's proposal impractical. . . .

The group appointed by the Senate District Committee met Feb. 24 with McCormack and Rep. Abraham J. Multer

(D N.Y.), who filed the discharge petition in 1965. After the meeting, Bible again expressed the belief that the best chance for passage of home rule legislation was in working within the provisions of the House-passed bill.

The Senate District Committee, however, reportedly influenced by warnings from certain Negro leaders that "deep unrest" existed in the District, March 29 voted 5 to 1 to send the problem to conference. The dissenting vote was cast by Morse, who, as he did earlier, contended that the move was useless. The action came after Bible reportedly conferred with Vice President Hubert H. Humphrey, who had supposedly discussed the issue with the President.

The Senate April 5 formally disagreed to House amendments to S 1118 and asked the House for a conference, appointing all seven members of the Senate District Committee as conferees.

Observers speculated that the Senate action resulted from the likelihood that Morse would filibuster any type of charter board bill brought to the floor and from the possibility that the D.C. community might misinterpret Senate rejection of an amended Sisk bill, especially if home rule opponents joined a Morse filibuster. Others felt that the Senate, believing home rule lost for the term, decided to send the problem back to the House where opposition to the proposal had been stongest and where many Senators were thought to feel that the blame for the failure in passage should lie.

Bible April 5 said he would appeal to McMillan to send the problem to conference, and McMillan said he would consider the request. McCormack April 21 said he would "do everything I can to get a conference. . . ."

The House District Committee May 11 by a 13-10 vote rejected a motion by Rep. Horton asking that conferees be appointed. The Horton motion had been substituted for a motion offered by Rep. Whitener asking that conferees not be appointed this session. The Committee later could, however, vote on another motion to appoint conferees. After the Committee May 11 vote, chairman McMillan said that the pending D.C. crime bill must be cleared for the President "before we'll act on home rule" and noted that he thought the Committee "should wait and see if the Senate agrees with us" on five other District bills which are ready for conference. He said that under the circumstances, "it is difficult for me to be hopeful" about home rule. . . .[3]

Even after the House and the Senate have acted separately, then, there is still much to be done and strategies to pursue. Which house asks for the conference, whether there will be a conference at all, and whether one house should recede in its demands are all important questions which have an effect on the course of public policy.

[3] This story is reprinted from the *Congressional Quarterly Weekly Report*, #20 (May 20, 1966), pp. 1017–1022. I wish to thank the *Congressional Quarterly* for its kind permission to reprint.

CHAPTER TEN

Congressional Organization
and Majority Rule

Before discussing questions of majority rule and congressional reform it might be useful to discuss, more abstractly, the functions of rules and procedures in organizations. Such a discussion may aid in our understanding of the role of rules in Congress more specifically and provide a basis for evaluating Congress in terms of proposed changes in its rules.

First, although Congress is not typical of organizations, especially in the sense that its members are elected, both the House and the Senate do share in the characteristics which are associated with institutionalized organizations. Organizations perform tasks and Congress, like other organizations, has a number of tasks to perform. Some of these tasks, like passing legislation, are explicit and recognized. Others, like legislative oversight of the executive branch, are less well known but still framed within the purpose of Congress. Still others, like conflict resolution and consensus building, are consequences of what Congress does.

Organizations also have a division of labor in performing tasks, and Congress, through the committee system, has a division of labor within its organization which is quite highly developed. Organizations have leaders and non-leaders and Congress, too, has such a dichotomy. And, most organizations have a relatively stable membership. In fact, this is one of the characteristics which distinguishes institutionalized organizations from less stable and lasting organizations. Congress also has a highly stable membership, especially at the leaderhip level, as well as among the rank and file. In any given election, for example, approximately 85 percent of the incumbents are returned to office. Table IX provides data on this point.

TABLE IX
MEMBERSHIP STABILITY
IN THE HOUSE AND SENATE

Percentage of Incumbents Re-elected

	1950	1952	1954	1956	1958	1960	1962
House	83.4	81.6	87.1	89.4	92.1	85.6	83.9
Senate	85.4	83.3	85.4	90.6	81.3	92.0	88.0

Finally, institutionalized organizations such as Congress have a highly developed system of rules, procedures, precedents, and customs. The functions of such rules, procedures, precedents, and customs include the following:

1. provide mechanisms whereby tasks can be performed,
2. determine the distribution of power within the organization,
3. determine how division of labor is to occur,
4. provide mechanisms for coordination,
5. settle and avoid disputes among members as to how things are to be done and,
6. legitimize the actions of the institution.

In some cases the rules are actually written down. In other cases they take the form of precedents not yet codified. In still other cases they are simply agreed upon customary ways of doing things (such as the seniority rule). But because some rules are written down does not make them any more binding. Precedents and customs can be equally constraining on members, and some written rules can be ignored or violated by mutual consent.

Rules and procedures, then, perform many functions in an organization. Perhaps most importantly they lend stability which allows an organization to carry out its tasks. But since most organizations have a number of functions for their members as well as functions for the organization as a whole, it is possible that consensus on the legitimacy of the rules will not be perfect. For example, individual members may have goals for themselves, such as doing well, gaining power, or getting the organization to adopt certain kinds of policies. Since rules and procedures, by and large, help to determine who among the members does well, gains power, and has a disproportionate voice in the setting of policy, we would expect there to be differential support for some rules by the membership. There is often controversy over the rules, and attempts to change them. And perhaps this is especially true of an organization like Congress where membership in the organization does not depend upon the leaders. Rather, members are, in the final analysis, responsible to their own constituencies. Thus, they are in a position to criticize the rules, and even the leaders, without fear of losing their jobs.

What we are suggesting, then, is that rules, procedures, precedents, and customs in all organizations affect different members differently. We would expect, for example, that in most organizations the younger members would be more dissatisfied with the rules than the older members. Often rules and customs reward those who serve for longer periods of time. Congress, in fact, has a built-in system of rewarding those who are repeatedly re-elected: the distribution of committee assignments and committee and subcommittee chairmanships is at least partially determined through seniority. We would expect, then, that those who have not been around long enough to participate in this distribution of rewards would be a greater source of dissatisfaction than those who have been in the institution for some time.

We will often also find in organizations that the distribution of rewards favors those with certain kinds of opinions and policies over others with different opinions and policies. It can probably be said of any organization that those who propose changes, and especially far-reaching changes, will be less successful than those who either propose small changes or no changes at all. Members, then, who are dissatisfied with current public policy and wish change will, in an organization such as Congress, come into conflict with those who prefer the *status quo*.

When it happens that these two sets of people coincide, that is, when the younger members also are those who are dissatisfied with the *status quo*, then there is, in a sense, a double reason why they will be dissatisfied. If the institution also professes to be one which operates on the principle of majority rule, violations of the majority rule principle which are built into any organization will come under the most severe criticism. The Congress of the United States does profess to be a majority rule institution, and it is to the question of how much majority rule we ought to expect, given the fact that Congress is an institution, that we now turn.

One of the questions which has been central to the concerns of political scientists and others is the extent to which majority rule is actually practiced in institutions which proclaim to make decisions by majority rule. The major question has been: given an organization with its characteristics of division of labor, leadership structure, and distribution of power, can such organizations be "democratic" in the sense of allowing the majority to rule? Robert Michels answered the question in the negative, and referred to the "iron law of oligarchy" which he felt to be characteristic of all organizations.[1] Lipset, Trow, and Coleman, many years later, suggested that organizations might approximate democratic decision-making under certain conditions.[2] More recently Senator Joseph Clark and others have characterized the Senate as being run by less than a majority of their number which he calls the "Senate Establishment."[3]

Apparently there is a relatively great likelihood that under most conditions organizational decision-making will tend toward oligarchy. Let us carefully inspect what this means in relation to the United States Congress.

Perfect democracy would mean that on *any* decision each member would have equal weight in the decision. It would mean that no decision of any kind could be made without the approval of 50 percent plus one of the members, participating equally. All decisions and all actions would be the product of a majority of all the members.

Now we can see from even a cursory glance that organizations, by *definition*, violate the rules of perfect democracy. First, all organizations have a division of labor. This means that some decisions are being made on some matters by something less than 50 percent plus one of the total membership. The concept of "division of labor" includes the delegation of decision-making over certain problems to a sub-group within the total institution. It is possible, of course, to provide for ratification of such decisions by the plenary body, but under most circumstances, it is very difficult to change such decisions. And,

---

[1] Robert Michels, *Political Parties* (New York: Free Press, 1949). This book was first published in 1917.

[2] Seymour M. Lipset, Martin Trow, and James Coleman, *Union Democracy* (New York: Free Press, 1956).

[3] Joseph S. Clark, *The Senate Establishment* (New York: Hill and Wang, 1963).

more importantly, it is possible that the sub-group will refuse to make a decision which might have been made by the total membership. Under such circumstances mechanisms are necessary whereby the total membership may take from the sub-group control over such issues. For many reasons, however, actions which discharge sub-groups of control are difficult to carry off. In effect what is being done is by-passing the normal organization structure, action which will be resisted by those who have some reason to want to preserve the structure.

Second, all organizations have a leadership. This, again almost by definition, gives to some members more power over decisions than others. Leaders, for example, may be able to determine the agenda of what is to be considered by the full membership. Again, it is possible to have mechanisms whereby the decisions of the leaders are reviewed and may be overturned. But to overturn the decisions of the leaders is an action which comes close to overthrowing the leadership itself, at least on that issue. Such overthrows may have serious consequences for the stability of the organization.

Since all organizations have a division of labor and provide for a leadership structure they all violate the principle of "perfect democracy" defined as all members participating equally in all decisions, with the majority winning. If this is true, then all organizations are to some extent non-democratic under this rather strict definition. To make distinctions among organizations, then, it is necessary to relax the criteria for democratic decision-making. The two distinctions which are most important are the two already mentioned: (1) are the leaders elected? and (2) is it possible for a majority to overturn decisions it does not like and to make decisions which are not being made by a sub-group within the institution?

Even using these criteria, most organizations are not democratic. Business organizations, many labor unions, many local and state political parties, and many other organizations are not democratic by either criterion. Leaders are often chosen by a small group of sub-leaders (such as at many party conventions) who may or may not be elected by a majority of the party members, and rarely if ever does a majority have the opportunity to substitute its decision for that of either the leaders or a particular sub-group within the institution. Having said this, it would be especially interesting if the United States Congress were in fact more democratic than most organizations and, in a sense, more democratic than we really have a right to expect of an organization. Let us briefly, then, explore Congress as an organization with these two criteria of democracy as our standard.

The first question to be answered is, are leaders in Congress elected? The answer to this question is rather complex because there are several different kinds of leaders in both houses of Congress. These would include party leaders (positions of leadership within the party), and formal leaders (e.g., committee and subcommittee chairmen). Each of these will be considered separately.

PARTY LEADERS IN THE HOUSE AND SENATE

With respect to party leaders, in the House of Representatives we would include the Speaker, majority leader, majority whip, minority leader, and the minority whip, the respective party Committees on Committees, and the Rules Committee. For the Senate we would include the majority and minority leaders and whips, and members of the Policy and Committees on Committees. There are also, in each house and in each party, other party positions which will not be considered here (such as chairman and secretary of the party caucus or conference and members of the campaign committees). They are being left out primarily because they are less important offices.

How these positions are filled varies between the House and the Senate and within the Republican and Democratic parties. In the House, the Speaker and majority leader of the majority party are chosen by the majority party caucus every two years (or when there is a vacancy). The Speaker, but not the majority leader, is then chosen officially by the entire House of Representatives by a straight party vote, the minority party running its party leader against the majority party's candidate. Competition for the offices does occur from time to time. For example in 1962 when Speaker Rayburn died John McCormack, then majority leader, was elevated to the Speakership by the party caucus without opposition, but Carl Albert, the party whip, was opposed for the position of majority leader by Richard Bolling.[4]

Competition for the highest party offices also occurs among the Re-

---

[4] See Nelson W. Polsby, "Two Strategies of Influence: Choosing a Majority Leader, 1962," in Robert L. Peabody and Nelson W. Polsby, eds., *New Perspectives on the House of Representatives* (Chicago: Rand McNally, 1963), Chap. 9.

publicans. Charles Halleck ousted Joe Martin from his position as minority leader by a close caucus vote of 74–70 in 1959. Then, in 1965, as though to illustrate the proposition that turnabout is fair play, Gerald Ford defeated Charles Halleck for the Republican leadership by a vote of 73–67.

The Democratic whip in the House is appointed by the majority leader and Speaker (or minority leader when the Democrats are the minority party). Prior to 1965 the Republican whip was ratified by the Republican Conference after appointment by the Committee on Committees.[5] Since the beginning of the Eighty-ninth Congress (1965–66) the Republican whip has been elected directly by the Conference. The Democratic whip, then, represents the party leaders' choice and is not necessarily powerful independently of the leaders, whose base of support rests in the caucus. The Republican whip, on the other hand, is elected by the party caucus and hence may be in a position of independence from the party leader. For example, after Gerald Ford defeated Charles Halleck for the minority leadership in the House, Ford, as *ex-officio* Chairman of the Republican Committee on Committees, got the Committee to nominate Peter Frelinghuysen as whip. Les Arends, who had been the party's whip since 1944 and had served in that capacity under both Martin and Halleck, decided to fight Ford and Frelinghuysen for the whip position. In another closely fought caucus battle, Arends defeated Frelinghuysen by a vote of 70–59.

Also to be included in the party leadership in the House are the Democratic and Republican Committees on Committees. These bodies make committee assignments within their respective parties. Since the substantive committees play such an important role in Congress, who gets assigned to which committees can be a major factor affecting the course of legislation. Thus, who is on the Committees on Committees is also of great importance.

The two parties fill vacancies on their respective Committees on Committees quite differently. The members of the Democratic Committee on Committees are the Democratic members of the Ways and Means Committee, and are officially elected to the Committee by the Democratic Caucus. The Committee is sub-divided into geographical zones consisting of anywhere from 1 to 8 state

[5] For a discussion of the Whip system in the House see Randall B. Ripley, "The Party Whip Organization in the United States House of Representatives," *American Political Science Review*, vol. 58 (September, 1964), pp. 561–576.

party delegations. Normally when there is a vacancy on the Committee on Committees the zone from which the vacancy occurs will make a recommendation to the party caucus. Occasionally, however, there is disagreement. In 1962, for example, the Speaker supported Phil Landrum of Georgia when a vacancy on the committee occurred. The Democratic Caucus, however, rejected the Speaker's choice in favor of Pat Jennings of Virginia.

The Republican Committee on Committees consists of one Republican member from each state which sends at least one Republican to Congress. The state delegations choose their representative on the Committee on Committees. Each representative, however, has as many votes on the Committee on Committees as there are Republicans in the state delegation. A subcommittee of the Committee on Committees, consisting of the representatives of the largest Republican state delegations plus several smaller delegations, is then appointed by the party leader. It is this subcommittee which, in effect, makes committee assignments.[6]

The House Committee on Rules is also a leadership group, but of a very peculiar sort. The Committee on Rules determines which legislation on the House and Union Calendars (and almost all controversial legislation, when reported from legislative committees, is placed on either the House or Union Calendar) will be considered on the floor of the House.

Normally, there is relatively close cooperation between the Speaker, the majority leader, and the Rules Committee in the scheduling of legislation for floor debate. But occasionally, and usually on dramatic occasions, the Committee will refuse to grant a rule, or the Chairman will refuse to call a meeting of the Committee to consider a rule.

What makes the Committee on Rules a peculiar leadership group is the fact that its membership is bipartisan. The ratio of members between the majority party and minority party is always kept at 2 to 1 regardless of the ratio in the House. Before 1961, when the committee size was 12, the ratio was 8 to 4. Since the enlargement in 1961 the ratio is 10 to 5.

This would obviously be a quite adequate majority for the major-

---

[6] For a more detailed account of the House Committees on Committees see Nicholas A. Masters, "House Committee Assignments," *American Political Science Review*, vol. 55 (June, 1961), pp. 345–357. Also reprinted in Peabody and Polsby, *op. cit.*, pp. 33–58.

ity party if the parties were highly cohesive organizations. But, as we have suggested, they are coalitions of diverse interests in which party loyalty is but one of the many influences upon party members. The Democratic members of the Committee on Rules (as is true of other committees) reflect this diversity.

Party leadership in the Senate is a similar mixture of elective and appointive offices. For the Senate Democrats, for example, the party leader and whip are elected by the party conference. The Democratic leader is also the Chairman of the Party Conference, Policy Committee and Steering Committee (the Committee on Committees). As Chairman of these party organs and leader of his party in the Senate he appoints the members of the Policy and Steering Committees. Since 1961 members of the Steering Committee are then ratified by the Party Conference, but the Conference does not vote on the appointments to committees which the Steering Committee makes.

There is, occasionally, competition for these offices. For example, when Hubert Humphrey resigned his Senate seat to become Vice President of the United States he left vacant the office of assistant floor leader, or whip. Three candidates emerged for the vacancy, John Pastore of Rhode Island, Mike Monroney of Oklahoma, and Russell Long of Louisiana. In a close vote requiring two ballots Russell Long was elected to the office.

The Republicans have an equally mixed system, although it is different from the Democrats. The party leader, whip, Chairman of the Conference, and Chairman of the Policy Committee are each elected by the Party Conference. Unlike the Democrats, they are all different people. The Chairman and members of the Committee on Committees are appointed by the Chairman of the Party Conference. Again unlike the Democrats, assignments to committees made by the Committee on Committees are then ratified by the Party Conference. Seven members of the Policy Committee serve *ex-officio,* the remaining six are appointed by the Chairman of the Policy Committee.

The most severe criticism of organizational procedure in the Senate has been of the Senate Democratic Steering Committee. It is the Steering Committee which makes the all-important committee assignments to freshman members as well as determines changes in committee assignments. We will discuss the Senate Democratic Steering Committee more fully in the next chapter.

COMMITTEES

The second major source of leadership in the Congress is the committee system, and especially the formal position of leadership on the committees, the committee chairmen. Formally, committee members and committee chairmen are elected by the whole House and Senate respectively. But before this formal stage of election committee members are appointed by the respective party Committee on Committees in consultation with the leaders and other interested parties.[7] The seniority rule has much to do with the appointment of members to committees and has everything to do with the designation of the committee chairmen. The ranking majority party member of each committee, ranked in terms of seniority on the committee, is the committee chairman. This system of *de facto* seniority appointment to committee chairmanships has the following sequences in the distribution of power[8]

1. Committee chairmen are older members,
2. Over 50 percent of the Democratic chairmen are from the South,
3. Over 50 percent of the Republican chairmen are from the Midwest,
4. Urban areas are under-represented among the chairmen.

For example, in the Eighty-eighth Congress (1963–64) although Southern Democrats represented only about 40 percent of the total number of Democrats in the House and the Senate, over 60 percent of the committee chairmen in each house were from the South.

Very few people are against the seniority system entirely. The major advantage of the seniority system is that it distributes power within the party and within the House and the Senate automatically. This is perceived, by most people, as being very advantageous. It avoids the inevitable fights which would occur if the seniority system were not part of the procedure. What people are against, however, is the inflexibility of the seniority system. Generally, committee chair-

---

[7] See Masters, *op. cit.*, and Clark, *op. cit.*, for further discussions.
[8] See George Goodwin, Jr., "The Seniority System in Congress," *American Political Science Review*, vol. 53 (June, 1959), pp. 412–37. For further discussion see Raymond E. Wolfinger and Joan Heifitz, "Safe Seats, Seniority, and Power in Congress," *American Political Science Review*, vol. 59 (June, 1965), pp. 337–349.

men are relatively intelligent and fair men. They do have biases with respect to public policy, but so does everyone else. The kinds of problems which arise when a chairman of a committee holds up legislation can probably best be solved by the procedures which involve taking the committee away from the chairman on that particular issue rather than by deposing the chairman. Occasionally, however, a chairman is elevated to power who really should not be in that position either because of age, cantankerousness, laziness, or some other infirmity.

Seniority as a method of naming committee chairmen is of considerable importance because the system introduces the biases previously mentioned. This is not to say that any other method of appointment (such as by the party leader, or even committee or caucus election) would produce a set of chairmen who would be more representative of the membership. It is merely to suggest that the seniority system does have a particular kind of bias. This becomes important because of the power which committee chairmen have and the ways in which that power can be exercised to influence public policy.

Committee chairmen have a number of important powers which give them leverage in the policy-making process that other members do not have. For example, almost all bills are referred to committee. Whether a bill is considered, whether hearings are held, and whether the bill is reported, then, is up to each individual committee. To a large extent it also hinges on the actions or inactions of committee chairmen. Committee chairmen, among other things, set meeting times, determine the committee agenda, preside over meetings, decide whether there will be subcommittees, and who will be on the subcommittees, hire the staff, recommend conference committee members to the presiding officer, who in most cases routinely accepts the recommendation, and manage bills on the floor (or designate subcommittee chairmen or others to do so).

Committee chairmen vary, of course, in the extent and purposes to which they use these powers. On most bills most chairmen will not be arbitrary. But on some bills almost all chairmen will be arbitrary. It is possible, in the face of a stubborn chairman, for a majority of the committee to act without the chairman's approval, but the precedents, traditions, customs, and norms not to do so are very strong. Sometimes the threat of a committee revolt is sufficient to get the chairman to act, however. In the Eighty-eighth Congress (1963–64), such a threat occurred twice, for example, with Judge Smith and the

Rules Committee in the House of Representatives. The Judge was holding up both the Civil Rights Bill and the Anti-Poverty Program. A majority on the Rules Committee threatened to act without him. In each case, Judge Smith called a meeting and a vote took place. Such threats, however, are not part of the "normal" legislative process. Committee members are reluctant to invoke such procedures. The reasons for their reluctance are similar to the reasons why members find it difficult to oppose the leader in party caucus. The chairman is the leader of the committee, he has certain prerogatives of office which most everyone recognizes as necessary if he is to be chairman, and he has certain rewards and punishments to distribute as a consequence of his position. There is really no other feasible alternative to the committee system (at least no one suggests an alternative) in a body which considers thousands of bills each year, and a revolt against the chairman, if successful very often, means in effect that there is no chairman. Only on a very limited number of bills, then, in which an intense majority is involved, will a revolt against the chairman even be considered. And, since committees reflect the approximate party ratios in each House, very often Republicans and Southern Democrats (and others not sympathetic with the legislation or reluctant to oppose the chairman) can combine to form a majority of the committee.

The following account illustrates how the structure of the committee system militates against committee revolts. During the Eighty-eighth Congress (196 ... the Senate there were only three committees (Commerce, Interior, and Public Works) out of sixteen in which a coalition ... of Southern Democrats and Republicans did ... a majority or ... less than a majority, and each of these three committees was chaired by a Northern Democrat, who will not ... delay legislation anyway. In the House there was only one committee (Education and Labor), chaired by a Northern Democrat ... ... "conservative coalition" did not at least equal a majority. Most often, if the chairman is to be temporarily defeated, it requires Republican help (such as on the Civil Rights Bill in the Rules Committee in the House) or Southern Democratic support (as on the Anti-Poverty Program in the Rules Committee).

A more concrete example of the difficulties encountered by a liberal senator with a Southern Democratic chairman occurred in 1964 on the Senate Banking and Currency Committee. The chairman of the full committee, A. Willis Robertson from Virginia, was opposed to the Truth-in-Lending Bill sponsored by Senator Paul Douglas of Illinois. Senator Douglas, after several years of trying, got this bill reported from the subcommittee which he chairs by a 5 to 4 vote (5 Northern Democrats against 3 Republicans and 1 Southern Democrat [Robertson]). Until 1964 Robertson, as chairman of the full committee, was able to convince at least one Northern Democrat not to support Douglas.

After the bill was reported by the subcommittee, the chairman was reluctant to hold full committee hearings on the bill and only through the persistent efforts of Senator Douglas in holding up other Banking and Currency legislation as well as badgering the chairman was he able to get a vote on the bill in full committee. Senator Douglas thought he might get a favorable vote of 8 to 7 on the full committee (he was counting on himself, Clark, Proxmire, Williams [New Jersey], Muskie, Neuberger, and McIntyre, all Northern Democrats, and Javits of New York [a liberal Republican]). Expected to be against the bill were the four other Republicans (Tower, Bennett, Simpson, and Dominick), the latter three on Senator Douglas's subcommittee and voting against the bill, and three Democrats (Robertson, Sparkman, and Long [Missouri]). Instead of winning as expected, Senator Douglas lost, 8 to 6. Senator Williams, a member of Senator Douglas's subcommittee who voted for the bill, was nowhere to be found the morning of the vote. Senator McIntyre seemingly switched his support and cast a negative ballot. Although it is difficult to find out exactly why Williams and McIntyre did what they did, the point is that these two normal supporters of liberal causes in their actions supported the chairman and the conservative coalition. It is reasonable to suppose that the chairman, who vigorously opposed the bill, might have had something to do with the outcome.

One major consequence of the seniority rule, then, is to distribute committee chairmanships to members who may, and do on certain issues (but not all), reflect a minority position of the party caucus. Both the House and the Senate do have procedures whereby the chairman and even the committees can be by-passed. These procedures are used and used successfully on occasion. The basic requirement of their successful use is that there be an intense majority (and in some cases in the Senate an intense two-thirds) who are willing to go outside the normal legislative process. There are many costs to a member if he attempts to do this, and generally he will not be successful unless he is supported by the leadership. He will court the enmity of the committee chairman and of others sympathetic with the chairman. This may result in certain things happening to him or not happening to him, such as lack of cooperation and aid on private bills, minor public bills, campaign funds, committee assignments, subcommittee chairmanships, help from other members on bills important to him, ability to logroll with other members, and other actions. Few members are willing to pay these costs.

SUMMARY

Both the House and the Senate, then, have most of the properties of organizations. They have a leadership, but unlike many organizations at least some of the leaders are elected. They have a high degree of division of labor with procedures for staffing the positions of leadership on the committees which generally over-represent the conservative interests within the party. They have strong norms, customs, and traditions which reinforce the distribution of power and make it difficult to go outside the normal legislative channels.

This decentralized leadership structure is combined with a system of support for members which makes them somewhat independent from the internal system. The ultimate sanction, removal from Congress, is held in the hands of separate and diverse constituencies rather than in the organization itself. This has the consequence of making it difficult for the party itself to enforce decisions on its members, or even to make decisions. As a result the party finds it difficult to change its own rules, and personnel and proponents for change must often go outside of the party to the House or Senate itself in an attempt to get around the difficulties which their own internal organizations impose on those party members who favor change.

The question of majority rule, then, is one which could partially be solved within the parties themselves if the parties could solve certain problems with respect to personnel. The fact that they cannot increases the importance of the rules and procedures in the entire House and Senate in their effects on majority rule.

CHAPTER ELEVEN

Congressional Reform

As was stated at the beginning of this book, the United States Congress, unlike most legislatures, is quite influential in the making of public policy. Because this is so, it comes under severe criticism, especially by those who support the interests more clearly represented in the presidential coalition. Since the President's program of requests sets the stage for legislative action, Congress is often criticized because it does not give the President all that he requests, or it delays enactment of his programs, or both.

We must be careful, however, to distinguish between two types of criticism of Congress. Many critics simply do not like what Congress does to the President's requests. They are critical of Congress for substantive reasons. Reform proposals emanating from this group attempt to make it easier for liberals to win in Congress and easier for the President's program to be enacted.

This kind of criticism is different, at least analytically, from critics who are concerned with majority rule in Congress. Their criticism concentrates on the process of decision-making and especially those aspects of the system which allow something less than a majority to make decisions.

In practice, however, the two sets of criticisms are mixed together. Little criticism of Congress is heard from conservatives. It is the liberals who, upset with the substance of congressional decisions, also criticize the process by which those decisions are made. It is still important, however, to keep the distinction clear, because it is quite possible that it is not the rules and procedures which hold up the President's program, but rather the distribution of power within the parties between liberals and conservatives. If the latter is the case, changing the power structure within Congress would be an alternative to changing the rules.

This consideration leads us to a similar point. We must also be careful to distinguish between the process by which decisions are made and the people who make the decisions. Critics of Congress might not be so vocal if the key decision-making apparatus were in the hands of the liberals rather than the conservatives. This may be true of the House Rules Committee, for example. Whether or not one is critical of the Rules Committee in the House or the Steering Committee in the Senate depends upon who is in control of the committee as well as what its powers are.

It is clear from the analysis of the party organizations within each House of Congress, discussed in the last chapter, that some of the complaints about the House and the Senate may not be the fault of rules and procedures at all, but rather of the ways in which the parties distribute power within the party. Whether a majority can rule or not is certainly a question of rules and procedures, but it is also a question of the context in which those rules and procedures operate. The major leaders of both parties are elected, but after that there is an interesting mixture of election and appointment, with the party conference or caucus sometimes playing an important role, sometimes merely ratifying the decisions of the leaders in a perfunctory fashion, and sometimes playing no role at all.

The arguments which are given against democratizing the party caucus have most to do with the question of party stands on policy. There are many good reasons why it may not be feasible or even desirable to increase the role of the party conference in matters of policy. Each party is, after all, a coalition of relatively diverse interests. Party conferences which discuss policy may in fact reduce the amount of party cohesion rather than increase it. It is quite possible to agree on policy without necessarily agreeing on the goals of policy. To the extent that goals would be discussed at a party conference, party conferences might be divisive instruments. Coalitions are fastened together with many different kinds of adhesive, including bargains which have nothing to do with the policy. To require or expect a consensus to emerge from a party conference which contains so many disparate elements would not be very fruitful. Add to this the inability of the party to impose the majority views on the minority because of the independent base of support of each congressman and senator, and we have a picture of a party conference which may be unable to act on matters of policy.

But increasing the role of the party conference with respect to matters of personnel is quite a different matter. Here it is more difficult to argue that the party conference should not be allowed to ratify the decisions of the party leaders with respect to choices in personnel. Undoubtedly arguments would erupt if one faction had a person of its choice replaced by someone less friendly by the majority within the conference. And this might be especially serious if the majority consisted mainly of younger, newer members pitted against the choices of the senior members. But then the basic question is posed: is the majority going to win (or at least be allowed the opportunity to win and with it the opportunity to bargain) or is something less than a majority going to win?

An interesting aspect of this argument is that it is possible for a majority of the party caucus to change the party rules. For example, in 1963 Senator Morse of Oregon moved in the Democratic party caucus that appointments to committees by the Steering Committee be ratified by the party conference. This would have been a significant step in the direction of democratizing party procedures in matters of personnel. This proposal by Senator Morse was defeated. Apparently Senator Morse's motion did not have majority support, or if it did some supporters of the motion defected to the other side.

The problem, then, changes significantly. Assuming it is desirable for the party to allow majority decision concerning personnel, why does not, or cannot, the party change its internal rules of procedure? Later we will pose and attempt to answer an even more difficult question: Why does it appear easier to change the rules and procedures of Congress rather than to change the rules and procedures within the party?

To answer the question of internal party procedure, we need to investigate the leadership-followership relationship within the parties. The answer to our question is related to several factors. First, part of the definition of leadership is that the leader be allowed to make choices to his liking. Members of any group, in electing a leader, delegate power to him. If the non-leaders do not like the decisions of the leader they may depose him. A leader is delegated by the membership discretion in the use of the powers he has as leader. No leader can please everyone and there will normally be grumblings among the ranks in any action which the leader takes. But there is an informal rule operating: that the leader is, after all, the leader. To overturn the decisions of the leader comes close to overthrowing the leader himself. Even people who oppose the decisions of the leader will often support him in an action simply because he is the leader. In the example given above concerning the motion of Senator Morse to allow the conference to ratify Steering Committee appointments, Mike Mansfield, the leader, was opposed to the motion. Had he supported it, however, it undoubtedly would have carried.

Second, leaders have certain prerogatives and resources which they may distribute. These resources include appointments to positions of party leadership, as well as less important things such as the scheduling of bills, support on the floor or in committees for amendments, influence or at least access with the President, and other prerogatives of office. To oppose the leader is to court his disapproval. Most members find it more expedient, as do most members of most organizations, to be on the good side rather than the bad side of the leader.

Third, the leader is elected by a particular coalition. If the election is unanimous there are certainly some elements of the coalition who support the leader more strongly than others. Under the most unfavorable conditions it is possible that the leader was the first choice of no senator or congressman but rather a compromise choice. The point is, however, that the election of the leader does represent an agreement, at one point in time, within the party conference. Support for that particular leader may have come for many different reasons. But it is probable that the leader, unless his choice represented a revolution, has the support of most of the more powerful members of the party conference. A leader is naturally somewhat beholden to the coalition who elected him and he will not usually act in a fashion which radically departs from the *status quo*. In a sense this is not the function of the leader but rather of the more aggressive and dissatisfied members within the party. It is the function of the leader to hold the party together, not to split it apart.

The conditions under which the decisions of the leader will be overturned, then, or the leader himself deposed, will be very limited. The amount of slack any leader has, of course, is not infinite, but unless the leader's actions represent long-term arbitrariness, or a particularly flagrant short-term action violating the preferences of an intense majority, the leader will retain a great amount of discretion.

The slack or leeway which is allowed the leader means that although he must act within boundaries, the boundaries are rather broad and flexible.

One conclusion from this discussion is that even if the party caucus has the power to overturn the decisions of the leader (for example, in Steering Committee membership, or in committee assignments), they will probably not do so. The factors we have been discussing operate every bit as much in a situation where the party caucus may overturn the leader as in a situation where they must change the rules to do so. For this reason, it probably would not change the distribution of power very much if the leader supported a rules change which allowed for review of his decisions in the party caucus. Such a change would, of course, encourage dissidents to challenge some actions taken by the leader and the Steering Committee, but it is unlikely that the leader would lose many of these challenges. The informal processes just described would be strong enough to withstand most attacks. An attempt to democratize the party caucus, however, will be resisted by those who have a stake in the present distribution of power within the party and would undoubtedly cause some trouble for the party. Under present practice dissidents have little recourse other than to bring their discontent onto the Senate floor in the form of proposals for changes in the Senate rules. Given the existence of the filibuster rule and its probable use in changes in the rules which are designed to redistribute power, the Senate floor is very unfavorable ground for the dissidents in their attempts to change the distribution of power within the Senate.

Democratization of the internal party structure within the House and the Senate is, however, a necessary first step in making Congress more responsible to majority rule. We will argue later that changes in the party might very well obviate the need for most changes in the House and Senate rules themselves. It will be suggested that most problems which Congress currently faces are, in fact, problems of personnel rather than strictly rules and procedures within Congress. For a number of reasons such problems are best handled within the party conference rather than on the floor of the House and Senate. The difficulty comes, however, in the fact that it is easier to change the Senate and House rules than it is to change the distribution of power within the parties.

The changes which would be necessary within the party would not be large ones. The changes would simply involve the election of all leaders by the party conference (even if nominated in some other way, as by the party leader). Alternatives from the floor should be allowed, and voting should be by secret ballot. This procedure would allow for the exceptional case where the rank and file were so disgruntled with the leadership choice that voting against the leader would be preferable to accepting the leader's choice.

RULES CHANGES

It may now be appropriate, in this final chapter, to discuss some over-all effects of rules and procedures in Congress and the conditions under which changes in the rules can take place. This will help give us some idea of the possibilities of congressional reform and what is involved when attempts to change the rules are made.

First, few rules and procedures are neutral, politically, in their effects. That is, rules and procedures define the conditions under which the "game" will be played. When there is conflict among the players in the game, as there is in most important pieces of legislation in Congress, the rules and procedures lay out the conditions for the conflict and provide certain processes, sometimes alternative processes, under which proponents and opponents may "make moves" in the "game." But some rules and procedures will favor one side, some rules and procedures will favor the other side. Strategies and tactics will be built around the rules and procedures which will be most favorable to one side or the other.

For example, the cloture rule in the Senate obviously gives an enormous advantage to any intense minority. A filibuster can be used by conservatives, moderates, or liberals, but in each case it is a protection for those who are against change. Filibusters are used, for example, by Southern Democrats against those who wish to regulate race relations. It is also used by Northern Democrats against those who may wish to change certain decisions by the Supreme Court (in the field of state legislative apportionment, for example). Since it is the liberals who are most in favor of change and the conservatives who are least in favor of change, the filibuster rule, in balance, favors conservatives. But in any case it favors those who favor the legislative *status quo*.

The argument favoring retention of the present cloture rule is that although it is all right to have a system of majority rule, it must be tempered with some provision to protect minorities against the majority. Minority rights, in other words, as well as majority rule, must be preserved and protected. Requiring two-thirds to end debate simply means that nothing can be done to the minority unless an extraordinary majority can be formed.

The argument in favor of changing Rule XXII suggests that the majority, when it is ready to act, should be allowed to act. If the majority is not allowed to act, then, in effect, the minority wins. A justification that the minority should win over the majority, and that the filibuster rule allows such an event to happen, promotes a system of minority rule, not majority rule.

The two arguments, then, directly conflict. To help us around the conflict it would be useful to make a distinction between kinds of majorities and minorities. Robert Dahl suggests, for example, that when there is a conflict between an *intense* minority and an *apathetic* majority, it is probably a good idea to let the minority win.[1] If a majority is going to impose an extreme hardship on the minority, then the majority should at least be intense too. The alternative is to allow apathetic majorities to prevail over intense minorities, a practice which may lead to dissatisfaction and instability. The cloture rule does allow minorities to win cases where they are opposed by apathetic majorities.

But let us take the difficult case, an intense minority opposed by an equally intense majority. Who should win in this case? All other things being equal (and in this case intensity is assumed to be roughly equal), democratic principles would prescribe majority rule. To allow the alternative to occur would be to allow a minority to prevail with no other justification than that the minority is "right" and the majority "wrong." The cloture rule does allow intense minorities in opposition to apathetic or intense majorities. In each case where the intense majority is greater than two-thirds.

The cloture rule, then, does not distinguish between intense minorities in opposition to apathetic or intense majorities. In each case the minority can win. How, then, can one set up a rule which would allow intense minorities to win over apathetic majorities but not over intense majorities? Establishing a two-thirds rule is not the answer. A two-thirds rule clearly favors the minority in cases where each is equally intense. It would be extremely difficult and imprac-

---

[1] Robert A. Dahl, *A Preface to Democratic Theory* (Chicago: University of Chicago Press, 1956), Chap. 4.

tical to develop, independently, a measure of intensity which would distinguish between apathetic and intense majorities.

We are left, apparently, with the dilemma with which we began. It is probably a good idea for there to be some provision for intense minorities to win over apathetic majorities. But it is not a good idea for intense minorities to prevail over intense majorities. The cloture rule allows intense minorities to win in both cases, and no rule can be provided which, independently, could distinguish between intense and apathetic majorities.

The proponents of majority rule argue, however, that there are other safeguards against apathetic majorities winning over intense minorities. The entire congressional system is so complicated and involves so many steps that *status quo* proponents will always be favorably situated in at least one of these many steps. Then, too, the Senate is not the only legislative body, and Congress is not the only governmental institution. There are the federal courts, the President, administrative agencies, independent regulatory commissions, state and local governments, and special districts which also make public policy. That is, to argue that the Senate, any more than any other institution, needs a rule to prevent a majority from tyrannizing over a minority seems a little far-fetched. Also, in Congress the bargaining process probably favors intense minorities rather than apathetic majorities. It is only when the majority is intense that it might prevail over an intense minority.

It is probably the case, then, that intense minorities are quite adequately protected through other mechanisms. To add to these mechanisms Rule XXII is to increase the likelihood that intense minorities will also prevail over intense majorities. There are some factors which mitigate the effects of the two-thirds cloture rule, but these factors are hardly justification for such a system.

Similarly, rules in the House of Representatives are of significant advantage to those who want to maintain the *status quo*. The requirement of 218 signatures for a discharge petition gives considerable advantage to committees and committee chairmen who stall legislation proposing change. In some cases those who benefit from the *status quo* will be liberals, as, for example, with the so-called Quality Stabilization Bill which would allow national price-fixing by manufacturers whose goods travel in interstate commerce. More often than not, however, this rule works to the advantage of conservatives who are able to prevent liberal legislation from reaching the floor. Two hundred eighteen signatures are very difficult to get, not only because most issues do not have an already formed intense majority to support them, but also because the norm of reciprocity works against its use.

The fact that rules and procedures generally favor those who are resisting change has a number of important implications. One is that those congressmen and senators who wish to change the *status quo* are forced, by the rules, to do a considerable amount of bargaining, not only on the differences which occur among themselves but also with those who favor the *status quo*. The alternative to bargaining will often be defeat, since those who wish to protect the *status quo* are often numerous, intense, and in strategic positions. It is possible, under some conditions, to avoid bargaining with those who favor the *status quo* by invoking special rules and procedures which may by-pass the opposition, but often even some members of the coalition that favor change will desert the coalition on such procedural issues. Again, the factor of reciprocity looms as an important reason why this would be the case.

A second implication of the fact that rules and procedures, generally speaking, favor those who prefer the *status quo* over change, has to do with attempts to change the "rules of the game." Looking at rules and procedures as not being neutral in the congressional contest, proposals to change the rules, in many cases, are attempts to change the ability of certain members, and hence certain interests, to prevail in future contests. In other words, changes in the rules may change the advantage of one group of players over others. In this sense, some rules changes redistribute power. Because this is so, certain proposals to change the rules are the most bitterly fought contests in congressional politics.

Not all rules changes, however, can be considered to be redistributive. Some rules changes simply increase or decrease the alternatives of the players without redistributing power. These kinds of changes are not necessarily easy to pass, but they are easier than rules changes which redistribute power. Rules changes which are regulatory in their effects involve a considerable amount of bargaining, especially compromises among those who feel most directly affected by the new regulations. Such changes take place as a result of changes in the work loads or functions of the members over long periods of time.

Two such regulatory changes, already discussed, occurred in the

Senate in 1964. One rule change allowed Senate committees to meet during the morning hour. Previously, committees were not allowed to meet when the Senate was in session except by unanimous consent. Since no important business is usually conducted during the morning hour, and since committee work-loads are increasing, it was felt by a large group of senators that such a change would be desirable.

A second change concerned the question of germaneness of debate. Previously, debate in the Senate did not have to be germane to the pending business. A senator could talk on any topic at any time. Some members found this to be an inconvenience and proposed that debate be germane for four hours after the close of the morning hour. This figure was cut back to three hours and agreed to.

Although both changes in the Senate rules were fought by a significant minority they were not bitterly fought. This was primarily because a redistribution of power was not involved in either case. These changes were simply regulatory changes producing what some members felt was a more convenient schedule, given their enormous work-loads. It is significant to note, in fact, that the most intense debate took place over Senator Clark's amendments to these two changes in the rules which would have had redistributive consequences. Senator Clark wanted to allow a majority of the Senate, without debate, to allow committees to sit anytime during a Senate session, not just during the morning hour, and he wished to allow a majority of the Senate, again without debate, to be able to require that debate be germane for any period of time. Both of these proposed changes would have allowed majority decisions without debate. For this reason, each proposal would have had some effect on the ability of senators to filibuster, and hence were strongly opposed by Southern Democrats and Republicans, as well as many Northern Democrats. Part of the strategy of a filibuster is to force a halt to all work in the Senate, thereby holding up all bills. This, it is felt, might have the effect of increasing the pressure on those who want to turn to other things. If the strategy works, the bill is withdrawn or, at the minimum, significantly modified along the lines desired by the filibusterers. Allowing committees to meet at any time by a non-debatable majority vote would interfere with this strategy.

Similarly, Senator Clark's proposal to allow the Senate to determine, by a non-debatable majority vote, that all debate must be germane would also interfere with a filibuster, since filibusterers sometimes may want to speak non-germanely. Since both of Clark's proposals were viewed as affecting another very important rule which distributes power in a certain way, both were strongly opposed and both were defeated.

The House of Representatives, on the other hand, has had a number of recent successes in changing rules which significantly redistribute power in favor of the more liberal members. In 1961 the size of the Committee on Rules was changed from 12 to 15 members. In 1965 the House made three rules changes, previously discussed. One rule change provided for a 21-Day Rule, a second rule change allows a majority to send a bill to conference with the Senate rather than requiring a rule from the Committee on Rules, and the third change prevents the objection of a single member demanding an engrossed copy of a bill from delaying a vote on final passage of a bill. In each case the changes in the rules redistributed advantages from the conservatives to the liberals. It is clear, however, that such changes would not have been possible without the extraordinary Democratic majority after the 1964 election and without the help of a small, but crucial, group of Republicans. It is entirely possible, as happened in 1951 after the 1949 adoption of the 21-Day Rule, that a future Congress, not so heavily populated by Northern Democrats, will reverse one or more of these decisions. The rule most likely to be changed is the 21-Day Rule since this is the rule most seriously objected to by the more conservative members of Congress. [The 21-Day Rule was in fact repealed by the Ninetieth Congress.]

REPRESENTATION BY COMMITTEE

Arguments rage back and forth concerning the adequacy and fairness of the committee system. Almost all bills are referred to committees, members basically specialize in the legislation handled by their committees or subcommittees, and committee chairmen are extremely powerful individuals in the handling of legislation which is referred to their committees. The Speaker does have some discretion in the referral of bills to committees but this discretion is not very great. Committee chairmen have more discretion in what they do with a bill which is referred by the Speaker to their committee and it is possible, and occurs frequently enough to occasion comment, that committee chairmen and the elected party leaders, supporting the Administration, do not agree that a bill should be reported from committee.

Whether a bill gets out of committee, then, and in what form it emerges are two highly significant questions. Especially since, with few exceptions, only minor changes, if any, are usually made once a bill has been reported from a committee. The committee bill structures legislative debate on the floor, and amendments, especially strengthening amendments, will be accepted only under unusual circumstances.

The arguments in support of the committee system are many. In a body as large as Congress it is impractical for all members to be concerned with all bills and resolutions. Not only are members of Congress busy with other things (such as constituency matters), but the sheer amount of legislation which Congress handles each year, and the variety of topics which are considered, would make it impossible for congressmen to become sufficiently knowledgeable on any one bill to be of any value in the legislative process. Abolishing committees would, in effect, be abdicating significant control over legislation to the executive branch. It is only because relatively few congressmen are concerned with relatively few bills that the legislative branch can exercise control over the policy-making process. Members can become experts on a few bills and need not become experts on all bills. For these and other reasons division of labor and specialization become necessary.

It is also the case that the committee system allows bargaining and negotiation to go on within as well as between parties. This is important because congressmen and senators represent widely diverse interests in a large and heterogeneous society. Political parties are, in effect, umbrellas under which a wide variety of interests are sheltered. National parties have few controls over their members. To attempt to bind the members to a caucus decision on policy which represents the majority of the majority party is unworkable. Members in a loose party system cannot be so bound. In fact their re-election may require that they oppose the majority decision. And, if the majority party is to remain the majority party, some flexibility of its members needs to be maintained.

What results is a political system within Congress which requires careful accommodation of a wide variety of interests. It is also useful to include in the decision-making process a wide representation of the many diverse interests. It is important, for example, that congressional committees attempt to represent, if only approximately, the entire House. If the necessary bargains cannot be made within the party caucus of the majority party, then to insure a majority some mechanism must be present to allow the necessary coalition-building to take place. Hence, the argument can be made that committees should include minority party members as well as majority party members, and a sampling of the diversity of interests within each party. It may be necessary, after all, to bargain with members of the opposition party if a winning coalition cannot be built within the majority party. The Civil Rights Act of 1964 provides an excellent example of the need for mechanisms which allow members of the majority party to bargain with members of the minority party.

Congressional committees as approximate cross-sections of the entire membership facilitate bargaining, compromising, and logrolling, three political processes necessary to building a majority coalition through accommodation. To bring a bill onto the floor which has not had an opportunity to go through this process is to court defeat for a number of different reasons. Members will want to know how they should vote, and they can more readily pick up voting cues if members who come from similar constituencies have had an opportunity to study the bill and to offer their suggestions as to the content of the bill. Cross-sectional committees, then, provide a decentralized cue-giving mechanism whereby other congressmen busy on other matters are able to make decisions on complicated questions which they themselves have not had an opportunity to study.

The argument is, then, that decentralized, cross-sectional committees help rather than hinder the passage of bills on the floor. They provide a mechanism whereby the many diverse interests within and sometimes between parties can attempt to settle their differences outside of strong public scrutiny and can "mark up" a bill with many of the divisive features already accommodated before the bill comes onto the floor. If a bill can pass a committee, it has a pretty good chance of passing the floor. To bring out a bill without committee consideration is to act prematurely. A committee, with a relatively small number of people outside the glare of public opinion, is a much easier place to bargain, compromise, and logroll than the floor of the House with many more people involved and much more public attention focused upon it.

Most opponents of the way in which Congress conducts its business probably would not quarrel much with what has been said here. What they would like, however, is a committee system which *in fact* does represent *fairly* the constellation of interests within Congress. Some do argue, however, that the majority opinion of the majority party should be allowed to prevail. It is being suggested here that this proposal would be unworkable. It would require the ability to bind the members of the majority party to a majority caucus decision, a circumstance which, unfortunately or not, is not feasible given the nature of our two-party system.

Assuming that one agrees that some kind of committee system is necessary, and that a committee system which allows a cross-section of the respective house to be represented on the committee is desirable, several inequities may still develop within such a system. First, committees may be skewed or packed to favor certain interests over others. Thus, they may not, in fact, represent a cross-section of the whole House or Senate. Bargaining, therefore, may favor some interests over others. To rectify the bias at a later stage in the legislative process, such as on the floor, is a more difficult task than to start out "fairly" in the first place. Furthermore, the bias which may be introduced is especially serious if it is an anti-majority bias, that is, if the committees hold up or block legislation which would in fact be acceptable to the majority of the whole House if they had a chance to vote on it. It is simpler for a majority to reject something they do not like than to get a bill to the floor that they do like if it is being held up in committee.

A second inequity which may develop, even if committees are "fairly" apportioned, is that the members, once on a committee, may develop interests which would not reflect the interests of the membership at large. That is, it is possible for the members to start out with one set of interests, and change those interests over time in a way different from the entire House. This is also related to the possibility that the interests of the entire membership may change (such as through an election in which a larger number of liberals are elected), but the membership on the committees may lag behind this change.

To get some idea of the extent to which committees are representative of a cross-section of the membership (although an imperfect measure), Table X compares presidential support by Democrats and Republicans on committees with the average presidential support for all Democrats and Republicans. The measure used is the *Congressional Quarterly*'s Kennedy Support Score for Domestic Policy, a statistic which gives the percentage support by each member on 92 roll-call votes which President Kennedy personally favored in the House of Representatives for the Eighty-seventh Congress

(1961–62).[2] The average score of the Democratic members on each committee was compared with the average score for all House Democrats, and the average score for committee Republicans was compared with all House Republicans. From this measure we can get an idea of the extent to which Democrats and Republicans on committees represent all Democrats and Republicans.

TABLE X
PRESIDENTIAL SUPPORT SCORES BY COMMITTEE
AND PARTY — HOUSE OF REPRESENTATIVES

Democrats	%	*Republicans*	%
District of Columbia	(59.7)	Un-American Activities	(20.8)
Un-American Activities	(65.2)	Ways & Means	(30.0)
Agriculture	(66.7)	Rules	(31.4)
Veterans Affairs	(68.0)	Agriculture	(32.2)
House Administration	(68.9)	Education & Labor	(32.3)
Appropriations	(70.3)	Appropriations	(33.6)
Interstate & Foreign Commerce	(70.6)	House Administration	(35.9)
Post Office & Civil Service	(70.6)	Judiciary	(36.8)
Public Works	(70.7)	Public Works	(36.8)
Merchant Marine & Fisheries	(71.3)		
Armed Services	(71.4)	*Average for all Republicans*	(37.2)
Judiciary	(71.9)	Interior & Insular Affairs	(37.6)
Average for all Democrats	(73.0)	Post Office & Civil Service	(37.7)
		Merchant Marine & Fisheries	(38.2)
Science & Astronautics	(75.0)	Banking & Currency	(38.3)
Interior & Insular Affairs	(75.9)	Science & Astronautics	(39.1)
Rules	(76.0)	Interstate & Foreign Commerce	(39.5)
Foreign Affairs	(76.5)	Government Operations	(41.1)
Ways & Means	(76.8)	Foreign Affairs	(41.7)
Education & Labor	(78.5)	Armed Services	(41.9)
Government Operations	(80.5)	District of Columbia	(43.6)
Banking & Currency	(81.1)	Veterans Affairs	(44.1)

The average Democratic support for the President on these 92 roll-call votes is 73 percent. Twelve of the 20 committees have Democratic averages below this figure, 8 above it. The average support among House Republicans is 37.2 percent. Eleven committees have Republican averages above this figure, 9 below it.

It is difficult to draw any definite, general conclusions from this data but we can say that the degree to which committees represent

[2] *Congressional Quarterly Almanac* (Washington: Congressional Quarterly Service, 1962), vol. 18, pp. 705–717.

a cross-section of the entire membership varies tremendously from committee to committee. Using presidential support as a measure, there are inequities on all committees, some in a "liberal" direction, some in a "conservative" direction. Some of the inequities appear to be very large, others not very large at all. We can also probably conclude that this distribution of committee scores may result in a different pattern of legislation than some other distribution, and especially from a distribution which more equitably clusters around the party averages.

But even Table X hides sources of potential conflict on some bills because of skewed representation. Democrats on the Rules Committee, for example, are not selected to represent only the majority opinion of the Democratic Caucus, but also a cross-section of the party. In the Eighty-eighth Congress (1963–64) there were 95 Democrats from the former 11 Confederate States. The total number of Democratic members was 257. Southern Democrats, then, represented approximately 37 percent of the total number of Democrats. The Rules Committee, however, has 5 Southern Democratic members, or 50 percent of the Democratic membership on the Rules Committee. In the Eighty-ninth Congress (1965–66), Southern Democrats constituted only 90 of 295, or 30 percent of all Democrats. Membership in the Rules Committee is now 2 more than the Southern Democrats are entitled to if the Rules Committee membership were made by sectional proportional representation. We may conclude, therefore, that the Rules Committee not only does not reflect the majority opinion within the majority party on some issues (although it does so on the average), but it also tends to over-represent the interests of Southern Democrats.

In 1965 Northern Democrats had an opportunity to reduce Southern Democratic membership on the Rules Committee from 5 to 4 members, thereby more nearly reflecting Southern Democratic strength in the whole House. Carl Elliot from Alabama, the southern member appointed to the Committee when it was enlarged in 1961, was defeated for re-election to the House in a primary in 1964. A vacancy, therefore, occurred at the beginning of the Eighty-ninth Congress (1965–66) on the Committee on Rules. The Speaker, however, supported Claude Pepper of Florida for the vacancy and he was appointed to the seat by the Committee on Committees without opposition. The reason why he was not opposed had to do with a number of factors, including the fact that Pepper, a former senator, is a strong Administration supporter and a liberal Democrat. Unlike most Southern Democrats, Pepper has an almost perfect record of support for liberal legislation, including the Civil Rights Bill of 1964. It would be difficult for Northern Democrats to oppose Pepper on ideological or policy grounds.

The appointment of Pepper, however, did preserve the 50 percent Southern Democratic representation among Democrats on the Rules Committee. Very few Southern Democrats are as liberal as Pepper. When Pepper leaves the Committee it is unlikely that the Northern Democrats will be in as good a position as they were in 1965, given their huge Democratic majority in the Eighty-ninth Congress, to reduce the number of Southern Democratic seats on the Rules Committee. This was a good example of how the Southern Democrats lost a battle (that they could not have won anyway) by not opposing Pepper, but probably won the war. The principle of 50 percent Southern Democratic membership on the Rules Committee remains intact, although in fact Pepper does not vote like a "typical" southerner. If the Northern Democrats wanted to reduce the Southern Democratic representation on the Committee this was the time they should have done it. Faced with Pepper as the candidate, however, they were unable to make a battle out of it. Given another Southern Democratic vacancy on the Committee, and another Congress, it is less probable that the Southern Democratic over-representation on the Rules Committee can be reduced, or that as liberal a southerner as Pepper will be appointed to the Committee.

The over-representation of Southern Democrats on the Rules Committee makes it quite possible, then, that one or more of the Democratic members will, on a controversial piece of legislation, oppose the stand taken by a majority of their party. If the Republicans are also in opposition it may spell defeat. The Democrats can "afford" to lose 2 members to the 5 Republicans and still have a majority of 8 to 7. If they lose more than 2, and do not pick up Republican votes, the predominant opinion within the Democratic party will lose.

James Robinson, in his book on the House Rules Committee,[3] states that the Rules Committee denies hearings to about 20 bills per Congress. Some of these bills are brought up on the floor either through unanimous consent or suspension of the rules. In addition, the Rules Committee denies, on the average, a rule to about 12 re-

---

[3] James A. Robinson, *The House Rules Committee* (Indianapolis: Bobbs-Merrill, 1963), pp. 23–30.

quests per Congress after a hearing has been held. These bills vary in importance but generally, if the rule is denied, the bill is not debated on the floor. Some of these bills eventually become law (such as Alaskan and Hawaiian statehood). Most, however, do not. Again, we do not know whether the bills which were denied hearings and rules would have been passed on the floor.

It may also be useful to inquire whether the Rules Committee as so constituted performs some useful functions which a differently constituted Committee or a different manner of scheduling legislation would not perform. We have already suggested that the House (as well as the Senate) is a body in which bargaining, compromise, and logrolling are the paramount tools of the trade. Behind every piece of legislation lies the same question: How does one create a coalition which is larger than 50 percent of the membership? Because Congress, like all organizations, has a division of labor, this question must be asked several times. How does one create a majority on the subcommittee? How does one create a majority on the full committee? How does one create a majority on the Rules Committee? How does one create a majority on the floor?

It is possible that these coalitions are cumulative. That is, if one builds a winning coalition in subcommittee it will be easier to build a winning coalition at the next stage. The reason this may be true is related to a principle we have already discussed: The division of labor within Congress is based on a cross-section (albeit sometimes a less than fully representative cross-section) of the entire membership. At each stage one runs into some of the diversity that one will encounter at the next stage.

For example, all subcommittees and committees, like the Rules Committee, are composed of Democrats and Republicans, and usually at each stage there are Southern Democrats as well as Northern Democrats, rural as well as urban congressmen, representatives of districts with large ethnic, racial, and religious minorities as well as those from essentially white, Protestant districts. To the extent that the sub-groups do not represent this diversity, or to the extent that some interests were not a part of the winning coalition, the bill will face increasing difficulty at the next stage. This is because as one goes from subcommittees to full committees, to the Rules Committee, to the floor, one will encounter these interests somewhere along the line. If the bargains and compromises have not already been struck, opposition to the bill will involve larger numbers of people, and more intensely opposed people, simply because the stage reached is closer to the last stage before passage when more people will be involved and where fewer future chances to defeat the legislation are available.

One could also argue that it is important to have this diversity at each stage in the legislative process to develop the kind of coalition and support which is necessary at the next stage. Division of labor often means, among other things, that members not on a committee or subcommittee will defer to the expertise of those who are on the particular sub-group which is handling the legislation. If someone similar to them is represented, it will be possible to defer to that person's judgment as to whether they themselves should support or oppose the bill, and how intensely they should support or oppose it. If a relatively large group does not feel itself represented at a particular stage, it may not support the legislation at the next stage.

This system of "miniature legislatures" provides a mechanism which makes compromises early. This helps to avoid several problems:

1. The cross-section principle allows all of the basic interests some weight in the development of the policy or bill. By not excluding anyone *a priori,* firm opposition is less likely to result. Those opposed are able to have some say in what the legislation will be like.
2. The cross-section principle can also avoid a large number of losses by the leadership. To the extent that the above analysis is true, if legislation were brought to the floor without this kind of consideration, it is possible that the leadership would suffer many more defeats than it does.
3. The cross-section principle helps to prevent ideological disputes. Because so many diverse interests are represented at every stage in the decision-making process, and because concessions, bargains, compromises, and logrolls will probably be necessary to build a winning coalition, bills brought to the next stage probably will not have a high ideological content. Rather, bills are usually written to include the interests of many people and to exclude the exclusive interests of some people.
4. The cross-section principle also helps to gain support for the legislation outside of the Congress. To the extent that legislators represent interests within their states and districts, and to the extent that it is helpful to gain support in the general population for legislation, support for legisla-

tion is promoted in the general population by a system
which allows for diverse interests to have a say in the development of policy.

One further point is also worth discussing. No system will be
perfect. In any system in which division of labor is the rule, there
will undoubtedly be some inequities in the cross-sections. It would
be very difficult to make each sub-group within the system a "perfect"
replica of the total group. Inequities in the cross-sections might occur
for a number of reasons. For example, it is possible that there will
be a time lag. Certain groups may be entitled, according to past
membership, to a certain proportion of the seats available. After a
period of time the total membership may change but the sub-groups
reflect the earlier proportions. There was a time, for example, when
the Southern Democrats represented approximately 50 percent of the
total number of Democrats. In the Eighty-ninth Congress (1965–66)
Southern Democratic representation was approximately 30 percent.
The Rules Committee currently continues to provide for 50 percent
Southern Democratic membership, still reflecting the earlier proportions.

Inequities also occur because of certain distributions of power
within the total membership. Southern Democratic members have
been able to take better advantage of the seniority rule which gives
power to those who stay in Congress for long periods of time. Since
Southern Democratic members have more power than their numbers
would give them without the seniority rule, other distributions will
reflect this power.

Deviations from cross-sections are also possible because of interest
specialization. For example, members from rural areas are apt to have
a special interest in being on the Agriculture Committee whereas
urban members would probably prefer Education and Labor or some
other Committee which is more concerned with urban-area problems.

When we judge the Rules Committee, therefore, and the committee system in general, we can place it in one of several categories,
depending upon our judgments about how the system ought to work.
Either the Rules Committee is (1) the best possible system, (2) a
system as good as most, (3) a system worse than most, or (4) the
worst possible system. In which category we place the Rules Committee depends upon a number of factors. First, since the Rules Committee generally has a conservative bias in several important areas of

legislation, whether we favor or oppose its actions depends upon whether we are conservatives or liberals. Second, it could be argued that the Rules Committee does perform an important function in the coalition-building process. Since there is a conservative bias on the Committee, if a bill can win majority support on the Committee it is likely to pass the floor. If it cannot win majority support, there will be intense opposition on the floor which might kill the bill. Third, there are several ways in which objections to the Rules Committee could be settled. Perhaps it is important to have a Rules Committee but the personnel might be changed to reflect more accurately the majority within the Democratic party. Alternatively, the Rules Committee itself might be abolished and the function of scheduling legislation placed in the hands of the leadership (Speaker and majority leader). Whether this would prove more satisfactory would itself depend upon a number of factors. In any event, the number of factors which need to be considered in such a discussion are large, and the problem of changes in the rules is quite complex.

A similar analysis may be made of Senate Committees. We will take, as we did with the House, the Kennedy Support Score on Domestic Policy for the Eighty-seventh Congress (1961–62).[4] The average Kennedy Support Score for Senate Democrats on 184 issues was 62.7 percent. The average for Republicans was 35.8 percent. Table XI shows the average support for Democrats and Republicans by committee. Although this information must be treated cautiously, it does give us some indication of how committees may be skewed in favor or against general presidential leadership.

From the Table we see, for Senate Democrats, that 8 committees are above the mean and 8 at or below the mean. But looking more closely at which committees are above and which committees are below the mean we find a very interesting pattern. Both Donald R. Matthews and George Goodwin have ranked Senate committees in terms of their relative desirability.[5] Although each author used different criteria, the 7 top committees in terms of desirability were the same, although the rank orders were somewhat different. The important point for us, however, is that each of these 7 committees

---

[4] *Congressional Quarterly Almanac, loc. cit.*

[5] Donald R. Matthews, *U. S. Senators and Their World* (New York: Vintage, 1960), p. 153, and George Goodwin, "The Seniority System in Congress," *American Political Science Review*, vol. 53 (June, 1959), p. 433. Both rankings are reprinted in Nelson W. Polsby, *Congress and the Presidency* (Englewood Cliffs: Prentice-Hall, 1964), p. 40.

Table XI
Presidential Support Scores
by Committee and Party — Senate

Democrats	%	Republicans	%
Finance	(55.9)	Finance	(27.5)
Judiciary	(56.7)	Foreign Relations	(32.0)
Aeronautical & Space	(57.6)	Rules & Administration	(33.7)
Armed Services	(57.9)	Banking & Currency	(34.2)
Agriculture & Forestry	(59.1)	Labor & Public Welfare	(34.6)
Appropriations	(60.2)	Armed Services	(35.0)
Foreign Relations	(61.8)	Interior & Insular Affairs	(35.2)
Commerce	(62.7)	Average for all Republicans	(35.8)
Average for all Democrats	(62.7)	District of Columbia	(37.0)
Government Operations	(63.7)	Appropriations	(38.1)
Rules & Administration	(66.5)	Agriculture & Forestry	(40.5)
Interior & Insular Affairs	(67.5)	Commerce	(40.7)
Banking & Currency	(67.9)	Aeronautics & Space	(41.0)
Post Office & Civil Service	(68.2)	Judiciary	(41.7)
District of Columbia	(71.0)	Post Office & Civil Service	(42.7)
Labor & Public Welfare	(72.7)	Government Operations	(42.7)
Public Works	(73.4)	Public Works	(44.2)

which were ranked, in two different ways, as being the top 7 committees in the Senate are among our 8 committees in Table XI which rank below the mean for presidential support (Finance, Judiciary, Armed Services, Agriculture, Appropriations, Foreign Relations, and Commerce). The eighth committee, Aeronautical and Space Sciences, was not part of either Goodwin's or Matthews' rankings because of its recent origin (1958). In other words, the data suggest that the 7 most important committees in the Senate are all skewed against the Administration. The committees which are considered less important are skewed in favor of the Administration.

The Senate Republicans, however, do not show the same pattern. Three of the top 7 are below the mean for Republicans (Finance, Foreign Relations, and Armed Services), the other 4 are above the mean. This seems to bear out Senator Clark's contention (to be discussed more fully in the next section) that Senate Republicans are less prone than Democrats to use committee assignments to load the dice in favor of conservatives.

As we mentioned when we discussed House committees, one of the problems with a division of labor is that the smaller units may not be representative of the larger group from which they are drawn.

The under-representation of liberal Democrats on important committees in the Senate and the over-representation of conservatives seems to be clear. It is interesting to point out that a situation in which conservatives are over-represented probably results in a quite different outcome from a situation in which liberals are over-represented. That is, conservative over-representation would result in bills not reaching the floor which might have passed on the floor. Liberal over-representation, on the other hand, could result in bills reaching the floor which might not pass on the floor. In the former, a minority is able to prevent an entire body from taking action. In the latter the entire body simply rejects the action taken by its sub-units.

Why do committee assignments of Democrats reflect this pattern? To answer such a question requires that we investigate the Democratic Steering Committee, the committee which makes Democratic assignments.

The Steering Committee. Since political power is so widely dispersed in the Senate, and since much of the power resides in committees, who gets on what committee and what the committee ratios are between Democrats and Republicans is a very important question. Seldom is legislation brought to the floor without first having gone to a committee. The Senate, like the House, jealously guards its committee system and reciprocity is no less a part of its way of doing things than it is in the House of Representatives.

The body which is responsible for the appointment of new members to committees, the transfer of members from one committee to another, and the party ratios on committees for the Democrats is the Democratic Steering Committee. Since 1965 its membership has been 17; prior to that time membership was 15. Four are members by virtue of their leadership positions (majority leader, majority whip, secretary of the conference, President Pro-Tempore). The chairman of the Steering Committee is the Democratic leader. He then appoints the remaining members (previously 11, now 13) on the committee who, since 1961, are then ratified by the party conference. Once on the Steering Committee a member remains on the committee until resignation, defeat, or death.[6] It should also be pointed out that the committee assignments made by the Steering Committee are not subject to conference ratification. The choices

6 Joseph S. Clark, *Congress: The Sapless Branch* (New York: Harper & Row, 1964), pp. 121–172.

of the Steering Committee for committee assignments go to the floor for full Senate approval, normally a formality since Democrats and Republicans have already worked out the party ratios and who gets on what committee is understood to be primarily a party matter.

As Senator Clark has pointed out,[7] the conservatives within the Democratic Party clearly dominate the Steering Committee. For example, in the Eighty-eighth Congress (1963–64), although southern senators represented only 31 percent (21 of 67) of the Democrats in the Senate, they represented 47 percent (7 of 15) of the Steering Committee. Similarly in the Eighty-ninth Congress (1965–66), Southern Democrats represented only about 30 percent (21 of 68) of all Democrats but again their representation on the Steering Committee, even with an enlarged Committee, was still 47 percent (8 of 17). These eight, coupled with just one more make a majority of the committee.

The Steering Committee has essentially two functions to perform: determining the ratio of Democrats to Republicans on each committee, and giving committee assignments to new members as well as to members who wish to switch committees. Each of these functions will be discussed separately.

After the election of 1962, and hence for the Eighty-eighth Congress (1963–64), there were 67 Democrats and 33 Republicans, a slightly more than two to one majority in favor of the Democrats. This would mean, since committee ratios between the parties generally reflect the ratio in the Senate as a whole, that each committee should have at least twice as many Democrats as Republicans. During the Eighty-eighth Congress, however, four committees had less than a two to one Democratic-Republican ratio (Finance, 11–6, Agriculture, 11–6, Interior & Insular Affairs, 11–6, and District of Columbia, 4–3). Eight other committees had exactly a two to one ratio, and only four committees (Commerce, Foreign Relations, Public Works, and Armed Services) had a ratio as large or larger than the ratio to which the Democrats were entitled. Since Republicans are, by and large, more conservative than Democrats, to the extent that the committee ratios do not reflect the larger than two to one majority among Democrats, Republicans, and therefore conservatives, are over-represented. This is especially serious, of course, on such a committee as Finance.

[7] Clark, *op. cit.*, and Joseph S. Clark, *The Senate Establishment* (New York: Hill & Wang, 1963).

In 1965, when the Democratic membership increased in the Senate by one (68–32), the committee ratios were changed. The only committee which still had less than a two to one majority was the Finance Committee, but 5 committees had exactly a two to one majority (still an under-representation) while 10 committees had larger than two to one majorities, reflecting the Democratic majority in the whole Senate.

The second way in which the Steering Committee can use its influence is in making committee assignments. Here Senator Clark, a member of the Steering Committee, reveals a fascinating story.[8] At the beginning of 1963, as has been true of the opening of the last several Congresses, there was a fight to change Rule XXII, the cloture rule. Those who wished reform proposed that the number necessary to invoke cloture be reduced from two-thirds of those present and voting to three-fifths. On a vote to invoke cloture against the debate which ensued, the proponents of a change were able, for the first time, to muster a majority, but not a sufficient number to reach the necessary two-thirds. But while the filibuster against the proposed change in Rule XXII was going on, the Southern Democrats refused to allow the Steering Committee to meet to consider committee assignments.

After the filibuster fight was over the Steering Committee met. There were 22 non-freshman Democratic senators (i.e., Democratic senators elected before 1962) who wanted to change their committee assignments. Of these 22, 8 had voted against cloture (and, by inference, for the maintenance of Rule XXII), and 14 had voted for cloture (and, by extension, for changing Rule XXII). Of the 8 who voted against cloture, 7 got new committee assignments, and 6 received their first choice. Only Strom Thurmond, a conservative senator beloved neither by the conservatives nor the liberals (and now a Republican since the nomination of Goldwater by the Republicans in 1964), was not given a new assignment. Of the 14 who voted for cloture, 5 received new assignments, but only one, Mike Mansfield, the majority leader, received his first choice.

Although Clark himself is hesitant, for obvious reasons, to draw explicitly any conclusions from this data, the figures certainly suggest that the conservative majority of the Steering Committee punished 13 of the 14 senators who wished to reduce the necessary

[8] Clark, *op. cit.*, *The Senate Establishment*, pp. 100–101.

majority needed to bring debate to a close. Those who voted against change (except for one) faired a good deal better.

This is but one example of the ways in which party procedures can affect the distribution of power within the Senate. Since committee assignments made by the Steering Committee are not submitted to the party conference for ratification or rejection, whoever controls the Steering Committee controls the appointments to committees and thus helps to control the passage of legislation through the committee system.

This analysis of the distribution of power on the committees and the role of the Steering Committee in determining committee size and committee appointments illustrates a point made earlier concerning the "conservative bias" in the Senate (as well as in the House). Much of the conservative bias could be changed without any change in the rules and procedures of Congress. Much the same effect as a change in the rules, and perhaps a more lasting and workable change, would be a change in the internal politics within the Democratic party in the Senate or the House. If, for example, the Rules Committee in the House was so constituted as to reflect the majority of the majority party, bills which sometimes get blocked there would not be blocked. Similarly, if the Steering Committee in the Senate were so constituted as to reflect a majority of the majority party, committee assignments would be more fairly distributed and committee size and committee ratios would more nearly reflect the views of the liberal majority of the Democratic party.

What would be required is an increase in the power of the party caucus. At present the Democratic Conference cannot even ratify committee appointments made by the Steering Committee. The move by Wayne Morse of Oregon in 1963 to change the conference rules to allow such ratification was opposed by the leadership (on the advice of Bobby Baker, then majority secretary, that there were not sufficient votes to pass it), and it was defeated.

Because conference ratification of these important appointments is not possible, Senator Clark took to the floor to try to overturn the decisions of the Steering Committee in several crucial instances. Under the rules of the Senate, the Senate itself elects committee memberships (after the Committee on Committees of both parties has acted). His attempts did not get very far, however. The question of committee assignments is a very delicate matter and it is not very realistic to try to undo actions by the party Committee on Committees on the Senate floor.

What is being suggested here, then, is similar to a point which was stressed in our discussion of the House of Representatives. For a number of reasons it is apparently easier to change the rules of the Senate (or the House) than it is to change the rules and procedures within the party conference or caucus.

There are many reasons why this is the case. First, of the 16 standing committees, 10, or 62.5 percent, are chaired by Southern Democrats (defined as those from the 11 former Confederate States), even though Southern Democrats constitute only about 30 percent of the total number of Democrats in the Senate. An eleventh committee, Appropriations, is chaired by Carl Hayden, a member who is sympathetic to the desires of the conservative wing of the party, especially with respect to rule changes. These committees include all of the top 7 committees (except Commerce). Committee chairmen have enormous power over the affairs of their committees and the legislation which is referred to them. They are in control of a large amount of what we have called "side-payments." That is, they have control over a number of resources which are important to other members; these resources include private bills, non-controversial public bills, access to other committee chairmen and to executive agencies, and to the Steering Committee which makes committee assignments. When fights do occur they are often able to manipulate the outcome through the distribution of these side-payments. Senator Douglas's attempts to get his Truth-in-Lending Bill through the Banking Currency Committee cited earlier is but one example of what may happen to a liberal senator on a committee which is not even particularly stacked against liberals. Conservative Democrats have more resources at their disposal than do the liberal Democrats, even though the liberals outnumber the conservatives. In the Senate Democratic Conference, as in other political situations, numbers are· simply one resource among many.

To change the rules of the caucus, then, requires the cooperation of those members of the caucus (or at least some of them) who have the most resources. By and large, these resources are concentrated in the hands of those who are against change in caucus rules. Hence if change is to occur, widening the scope of the conflict to the Senate floor is an alternative move. On the Senate floor it is much easier to bring public pressure to bear, as well as the possibility of picking up dissatisfied Republicans. As we saw in 1963 such a strategy picked up a majority to change Rule XXII, but in that case more than a majority was required.

A parallel can also be made with the House of Representatives. In 1961 when it was decided to "do something" about the Rules Committee, the decision was made to make a floor fight, which would include both Republicans and Democrats, to change the rules of the House increasing the size of the Rules Committee, rather than an internal fight within the Democratic party itself to purge Representative Colmer, the Mississippi Democrat who opposed Senator Kennedy's bid in 1960 to become President of the United States and who also opposed most liberal legislation which came before the Rules Committee. It was felt that it would be more difficult to disturb the informal rules within the party as to seniority and committee membership than to change a rule of the House.

It is being argued here that this is one of the reasons why liberals propose rules changes. The alternative to change in the rules is a change in the distribution of power within the party through the party caucus. The former is considered easier to accomplish than the latter.

Although Republicans less often use their Committee on Committees to reward and punish conservatives and liberals, committee assignments are not free from interesting negotiations and manipulations. A most interesting example of this occurred in 1965 at the beginning of the Eighty-ninth Congress (1965–66).

Strom Thurmond of South Carolina had decided, after the Democratic Convention's support of civil rights, that he could no longer stay within the Democratic Party. He decided, instead, to become a Republican. At the beginning of the Eighty-ninth Congress the question arose as to his committee assignments. During the previous Congress he had been seventh ranking Democrat (out of 12) on the Armed Services Committee and fourth ranking Democrat (out of 12) on the Commerce Committee. He wanted, in his defection to the Republican Party, to be treated differently from freshman senators who would be just recently elected in 1964. Conservative Republicans, led by Bourke Hickenlooper of Iowa and Carl Curtis of Nebraska, attempted to give Thurmond special treatment. Liberal Republicans, led by Jacob Javits of New York and Hugh Scott of Pennsylvania, objected to special treatment.

Thurmond preferred to remain on both Armed Services and Commerce as a Republican, and also wanted to keep his seniority which he had already built up as a Democrat. Although the negotiations are quite complex, the decisions of the Committee on Committees were quite favorable to Thurmond.

Clifford Case of New Jersey was awarded a seat on the Foreign Relations Committee. To do so he had to give up his seat on Armed Services (following a new "Javits Rule" to the effect that no Republican senator may sit on more than one of the four major committees until all Republican senators have had an opportunity to sit on one). Case's resignation from Armed Services left a vacancy for Thurmond. Bourke Hickenlooper of Iowa resigned from the Agriculture Committee to allow Jack Miller from the same state a seat, and Miller and John Tower of Texas both waived seniority to Thurmond on Armed Services. Thurmond, then, became third ranking Republican on Armed Services.

Thurmond did not find his second appointment as easily, however. He was blocked from staying on Commerce, and Jacob Javits prevented him from getting appointed to Judiciary by himself claiming the seat. Javits resigned his seat on Banking and Currency, to which Thurmond was appointed. To top it off, Hickenlooper, who had just been appointed to Banking and Currency after having resigned from Agriculture for Jack Miller, waived seniority to Thurmond and Thurmond, as a consequence, became third ranking on Banking and Currency.

It is very tempting, of course, to attribute cause and effect to these machinations, and to some extent it would be correct to do so. One must be very careful in their interpretation, however. For example, it is unlikely that Bourke Hickenlooper would resign from the Agriculture Committee and get himself appointed to the Banking and Currency Committee simply to allow Miller to be appointed to Agriculture and waive seniority on Armed Services to Thurmond, and to allow Hickenlooper himself to waive seniority to Thurmond on Banking and Currency. Hickenlooper's main reason, probably, was to give Jack Miller, his colleague from Iowa, a good committee position from which to run for re-election in Iowa in 1966. But committee switching was useful for this other purpose as well. It is very helpful if one can accomplish many things with a single act. This Hickenlooper was able to do. How would Jack Miller be able to turn down a request by Hickenlooper to waive seniority on Armed Services to Thurmond after Hickenlooper had just resigned from a seat coveted by most mid-western senators to make room for Miller? Such an action would have been ungracious at best.

This story is illustrative, also, of the notion that political activities, especially activities in a highly institutionalized body such as the Senate in which the stakes are relatively high, often have very special meanings. Sometimes the meaning is very clear and the activities very straightforward. Sometimes however, as in the "Thurmond Story," the meanings get very complicated and the activities something less than straightforward.

MAJORITY RULE IN CONGRESS

We now come to the last of the questions which will be raised, and that is, how do the rules and procedures of Congress relate to the question of majority rule? We are now, however, better equipped to answer that question than we were at the beginning of this book.

The question of majority rule is indeed a very complex one. One of the reasons this is so, as we have already suggested, is that the concept of a "majority" itself is very complex. Given the multiple points at which crucial decisions can be made in Congress one has to carefully distinguish between subcommittee majorities, committee majorities, Rules Committee majorities (in the House), and floor majorities. One also has to consider, at the same time that numerical majorities are being discussed, the question of intensity of feeling among those on one side or the other. Given a decentralized Congress, and the fact that most bills generate intense feelings among only some of the members, the classic majority rule model is not of much help. Rather, it is much more useful to talk about Congress in terms of the kinds of bargaining which might take place, the conditions under which certain kinds of bargains are usually made, and the relationship between those who favor change, the numerical size of the proponents of change, how intense they are, how strategically they are located in leadership positions, and the strategies and tactics which are available to them, given the rules and procedures which define the "plays" of the game. When we consider majority rule in this context, the answer to the question indeed becomes much more complex. In fact, majorities, in the usual sense of that word, rarely rule. This is primarily because majorities, again in the usual sense of that word, rarely exist. The contest, rather, is played among a large group of members, representing diverse interests, more or less intense, more or less strategically located, and with more or less resources at their disposal, with varying opportunities to employ strategies and tactics which revolve around the invocation of rules and procedures.

We must distinguish, I think, between several different kinds of majorities before we can accurately begin to even think about the question and provide tentative answers. The major difficulty is that we have no way of knowing what the majority of the American people would like if they were faced with the same decision as are congressmen and senators. Public opinion polls help in determining sentiment concerning isolated views, but it is well known that if you phrase a question in different ways different answers will probably occur. A congressman's choice is more complex than a citizen's choice in a poll because of the complexity of the issue when specific, alternative courses of action are brought into the discussion. In most cases, then, whether a particular bill reflects the majority wishes of the general population is irrelevant to our major question. The relationship between the outputs of Congress and the satisfaction of certain interests in the United States is not irrelevant, however.

A second reason why majority rule is a difficult concept to talk about abstractly is the problem of the intensity of opinions held by the majority and minority. In most cases, a majority simply means anything larger than 50 percent, a numerical majority. But it is possible that if 51 percent of any group prefers X, but is lukewarm in its preference, and 49 percent prefers Y, and is very intense in its preference, that, depending upon the issue, it may be desirable that the minority prevail over the majority. It is also quite possible that the minority will prevail in this case because of the ability of intense minorities to sacrifice other values and the willingness of the majority members to give up their preferences for something else. That is, some majority members, not being very intense, would be willing to join the minority (thereby making it the majority) if given something that they value intensely in return. Also, of course, intense minorities have advantages which intensity alone can provide, such as eagerness to win, stamina, disposition of resources, and, not least, a set of rules which they may be able to use to good advantage.

There is also another meaning of majority rule which complicates this discussion. Does majority mean the majority of Congress or the majority of the majority party? In a sense this is a moot question because as we have already pointed out there is no way in which the majority of the majority party can bind the other members of their party to make a majority of Congress. But it is important when majorities are thought of in terms of programs and party platforms.

We are left, then, with inadequate ways of even expressing the question, let alone answering it. Majority rule may not even be the central problem which needs asking and answering. There is after all, in a formal sense, majority rule in the House of Representatives. The discharge procedure allows a majority to act when a minority is holding up legislation. But this is really a mechanism which can only be used successfully by intense majorities. The requirement of two-thirds to end debate in the Senate means that majority rule is not possible on certain kinds of legislation.

The "real" question being asked is not whether majorities can rule, but whether the rules and procedures favor certain groups of members and certain interests over others. This does not make the question any easier to answer, but it does put the problem in a slightly different perspective.

The question cast in this way leads to a discussion of the question of how the rules and procedures favor certain groups over others. Fortunately, then, we have already answered much of this question by our discussion of the specific rules and procedures and how they affect outcomes and strategies and tactics. In an over-all sense, however, I think it is clear that the decentralization of power within Congress, the distribution of power within this decentralized structure, the many steps which bills must pass through, and the complexity of the rules and procedures which protect, quite closely, the rights of minorities, add up to a decision-making body which generally favors conservative interests and the *status quo*. In other words, it takes a lot of hard work to pass liberal legislation. Whether you are in favor of this or not depends upon whether you are a liberal or conservative. Whether you will be in favor of certain relatively minor rules changes will also depend upon whose interests you wish to expedite.

If one persists, however, in an answer to the question, "Can majorities rule in the House and Senate?" using the classic model of majority rule as the context in which the question is to be answered, then we can say that there is only one rule which clearly violates the principle of majority rule, and that is the cloture rule in the Senate. For change to occur against the determined efforts of a minority in the Senate, two-thirds, rather than one-half plus one, is numerically necessary. If one believes strongly in majority rule, it is clear that the cloture rule should be changed. The other rules in the Senate and the House are not as clearly anti-majoritarian. In the House especially, if a majority, in the classic sense of that word, exists the majority can act. The fact that this answer is less than satisfactory, and hardly descriptive of what actually occurs in the majority-building process, is an indication of the weakness of the classical model of majority rule to even ask interesting or useful questions.

As we have repeated numerous times, Congress is a highly decentralized institution which gives disproportionate power to small groups, including committees and subcommittees, committee and subcommittee chairmen, the elected party leadership, the Committee on Rules in the House, committees on committees, and policy committees. This would not be terribly serious if the majority party were united and if the majority of the majority party, in the party caucus, could bind its members in support of the majority's programs. But the facts of the situation are contrary to this. I cannot, for example, think of a rule in the House which would need to be changed if changes were made in the distribution of power within the majority party. For example, the Rules Committee is a powerful and influential committee. Controlled by conservatives it can hold up and even prevent legislation from reaching the floor. Controlled by liberals it could expedite legislation, even to the extent of reporting legislation being detained in committees or reporting legislation which has not been introduced. The question here is clearly who is in control of the rules, not the rules themselves.

Barring, then, a majority party caucus which is able to act as a majority in the classic sense, it now becomes clearer as to why it is easier to change rules and procedures of the House or Senate rather than to change the distribution of power within the majority party. The answer lies, of course, in the nature of the party system in Congress. Leaders have very few sanctions over non-leaders. The party is simply a loose federation of members representing many diverse interests. If disputes arise within the party they can seriously threaten the whole coalition and the ability of the majority party to control and organize the House.

This point needs to be emphasized a little more precisely. If we divide, for purposes of simplification, the members of the House of Representatives into Northern Democratic, Southern Democratic, and Republican, we find that none of the three separate groups has a majority in Congress. In the last twenty-five years, except for two Congresses (the 86th Congress, 1959–1960, and the 89th Congress, 1965–1966) the Republicans have been the largest single group. In the 88th Congress (1963–64), for example, Republicans numbered 178, Northern Democrats numbered 162, and Southern Democrats accounted for the remaining 95. Assuming that the major conflict within the Democratic Party is a Northern Democratic vs. Southern Democratic one, it is clear that neither wing of the party would benefit by "going it alone." The alternative to living together within one party is to form a coalition with the Republicans, a condition which Northern Democrats would not desire (since they have more in common with Southern Democrats than with Republicans) and a condition which Northern Democrats would not like to see happen between Southern Democrats and Republicans. The alternative, then, to a Northern Democratic, Southern Democratic coalition is a Southern Democratic-Republican coalition. Such a coalition could then organize Congress, gain control of the committees and committee chairmanships, gain control of the leadership positions in Congress, and be in a position to block, even more so than now, the proposals of liberal Northern Democrats. This is, of course, an oversimplification for purposes of illustration. There are actually a good many more "splits" within both parties besides the Northern-Southern split.

For these reasons, a number of traditions have grown up to avoid intra-party conflict. The informal rule which looms largest among these traditions is the seniority rule. Through this mechanism committee assignments are at least partially determined, and committee chairmanships are entirely determined. The seniority rule is an automatic device which settles a number of conflicts before they can get started. Herein lies both its strength and weakness. For example, one effect of the seniority rule, in addition to committee assignments and committee chairmanships, is to settle the question of committee membership when the control of Congress changes party hands. When a Congress changes from control by one party to control by the other party, the committee ratios change. Some members of the majority party will have to leave the committee (unless the committee is greatly enlarged). Who will leave? The question is now automatically solved—those with the least seniority on the committee leave. This, quite obviously, nicely avoids a number of potential conflicts within the party.

The seniority rule, then, is a useful device whereby a party with many factions can avoid the inevitable fights over at least some leadership positions. To tamper with the seniority rule by purging members could produce party conflicts which might be irreparable. The preferred method of redistribution of power, therefore, if redistribution of power is to take place at all, is through changes in the rules. This method allows the strongest faction within the majority party to go outside of the party to the whole body, majority and minority alike. But changes in the rules would not be necessary if the majority party would be able to gain control of the present rules through changes in the distribution of power within the party. And so the problem remains. Changes in the rules are necessary to reflect changes in the distribution of strength within the party precisely because it is not possible to make the changes within the party. Were it possible to make changes within the party (by the addition of more liberals, for example), changes in the rules would not be necessary.

Index